INFORMATION STATUS AND NONCANONICAL WORD ORDER IN ENGLISH

STUDIES IN LANGUAGE COMPANION SERIES (SLCS)

The SLCS series has been established as a companion series to STUDIES IN LANGUAGE, International Journal, sponsored by the Foundation "Foundations of language".

Volume 40

Betty J. Birner and Gregory Ward

Information Status and Noncanonical Word Order in English

INFORMATION STATUS AND NONCANONICAL WORD ORDER IN ENGLISH

BETTY J. BIRNER
University of Pennsylvania

GREGORY WARD
Northwestern University

JOHN BENJAMINS PUBLISHING COMPANY
AMSTERDAM/PHILADELPHIA

The paper used in this publication meets the minimum requirements of American National Standard for Information Sciences — Permanence of Paper for Printed Library Materials, ANSI Z39.48-1984.

Library of Congress Cataloging-in-Publication Data

Birner, Betty J.
Information status and noncanonical word order in English / Betty J. Birner, Gregory Ward.
p. cm. -- (Studies in language companion series, ISSN 0165-7763 ; v. 40)
Includes bibliographical references (p.) and index.
1. English language--Word order. 2. English language--Discourse analysis. I. Ward, Gregory L. II. Title. III. Series.
PE1390.B575 1998
401'.41--dc21 98-6210
ISBN 90 272 3043 9 (EUR) / 1 55619 926 0 (US) (alk. paper) CIP

John Benjamins Publishing Co. · P.O.Box 75577 · 1070 AN AMSTERDAM · The Netherlands
John Benjamins North America · P.O.Box 27519 · Philadelphia PA 19118-0519 · USA

Contents

List of Tables

Acknowledgments

For their endless patience, support and encouragement during the writing of this book, we thank our families: Andrew Birner, Suzanne Birner, and William Lachman. For insightful discussions of the issues raised in this work, we thank Barbara Abbott, Caroline Heycock, Julia Hirschberg, Larry Horn, Andy Kehler, Bill Ladusaw, Knud Lambrecht, Beth Levin, Bob Levine, Shahrzad Mahootian, Louise McNally, Philip Miller, Janet Pierrehumbert, Ellen Prince, Beatrice Santorini, M. James Scott, Yael Ziv, and the students in Gregory Ward's Advanced Pragmatics seminar in the spring of 1997. For their help in providing native speaker judgments on Italian, we thank Salvatore Attardo, John Bartlett, Manuela Pinto, Massimo Poesio, and Raffaella Zanuttini. For supplying us with some of the naturally-occurring data used in this study, we thank Georgia Green, Judith Levi, Beth Levin, Lori Levin, Shahrzad Mahootian, Kathy McCoy, Richard Sproat, Claude Steinberg, and David Yarowsky. We are especially grateful to Julia Hirschberg for providing us with access to the Challenger Commission corpus. This research was supported in part by NSF Science and Technology Center Grant SBR93-47355 A03 (Birner) and NIDCD grant R01-DC01240 (Ward).

Portions of this book first appeared, in different form, as articles, book chapters, or conference proceedings. We gratefully acknowledge the publishers for permitting us to include in the present work revised versions of the following publications:

> Pragmatic constraints on the verb in English inversion, by Betty J. Birner, reprinted in part from *Lingua* 97 (1995), pp. 233-56, with kind permission from Elsevier Science - NL, Sara Burgerhartstraat 25, 1055 KV Amsterdam, The Netherlands.

On the topicalization of indefinite NPs, by Gregory Ward and Ellen F. Prince, reprinted in part from *Journal of Pragmatics* 16 (1991), pp. 167-77, with kind permission from Elsevier Science - NL, Sara Burgerhartstraat 25, 1055 KV Amsterdam, The Netherlands.

Functional constraints on inversion in English and Farsi, by Betty J. Birner and Shahrzad Mahootian, reprinted in part from *Language Sciences* 18 (1996), pp. 127-38, with kind permission from Elsevier Science - NL, Sara Burgerhartstraat 25, 1055 KV Amsterdam, The Netherlands.

Definites and the English existential, by Gregory Ward and Betty J. Birner, reprinted in part from *Language* 71 (1995), pp. 722-42, with kind permission from the Linguistic Society of America.

The discourse functions of VP Preposing, by Gregory Ward, reprinted in part from *Language* 66 (1990), pp. 742-63, with kind permission from the Linguistic Society of America.

Information status and word order: An analysis of English inversion, by Betty J. Birner, reprinted in part from *Language* 70 (1994), pp. 233-59, with kind permission from the Linguistic Society of America.

Form and function in English *by*-phrase passives, by Betty J. Birner, reprinted in part from Lise M. Dobrin, et al. (eds.), *Papers from the 32nd Regional Meeting of the Chicago Linguistic Society, Volume 1: The Main Session* (in press), with kind permission from the Chicago Linguistic Society.

A crosslinguistic study of postposing in discourse, by Betty J. Birner and Gregory Ward, reprinted in part from *Language and Speech: Special Issue on Discourse, Syntax, and Information* 39 (1996), 111-40, with kind permission from Kingston Press Services Ltd.

For Suzanne
— *B.J.B.*

In memory of Louis Elmer Ward
— *G.W.*

Chapter 1

Introduction

An important aspect of a native speaker's pragmatic competence is his or her implicit ability to assess the appropriateness of a grammatical sentence in a particular context. This knowledge has been shown not to be derivable from other cognitive or social abilities, and is therefore quintessentially linguistic (Prince 1988a, Lambrecht 1994, inter alia). It is well known that every proposition can be expressed in a number of (truth-conditionally equivalent) ways; however, speakers do not choose randomly from among these options. The central premise of studies on the relationship between syntax and discourse function has been that speakers exploit their structural options to specific pragmatic ends. Over the past several decades, a vast literature has emerged investigating this relationship; it is the purpose of such studies to examine the non-random alternation in the use of various syntactic forms. Chafe (1976) uses the term 'packaging' to refer to this use of syntactic structuring to serve pragmatic functions, noting that by choosing to package information using one structure rather than another, a speaker accommodates his or her speech to various "states of the addressee's mind." Vallduví (1992) similarly argues that the purpose of information packaging is to "optimize the entry of data into the hearer's knowledge-store."

Recent work in discourse has uncovered a variety of specific discourse functions served by individual syntactic constructions.[1] Notions such as given/new,

[1]We use the term 'construction' in the conventional sense, to refer to each of the various grammatical configurations of constituents within a particular language. See Fillmore 1988,

topic/comment, theme/rheme, focus/ground, and others have been invoked to account for a speaker's use of some marked, or noncanonical, syntactic construction in a particular context. However, much less attention has been devoted to the question of generalizations that may apply across constructions — in particular, how a given functional principle may be variously realized in similar but distinct constructions. That is, current theory has not yet adequately addressed the question of how or whether a syntactic commonality between distinct constructions may correspond to discourse-functional commonalities in the uses of these constructions.

Our purpose in this book is to address this issue by providing a comprehensive account of three classes of noncanonical constituent placement in English and showing how their interaction is accounted for in a principled and predictive way. In doing so, we will detail the variety of ways in which information can be 'given' or 'new' and show how a more complete understanding of this variety can allow us to account for the functional distributions of these constructions. Moreover, although each individual construction is sensitive to distinct discourse factors, we will show that there nonetheless exist broad and empirically verifiable functional correspondences within classes of syntactically similar constructions, while the formal differences between these classes of constructions correspond, predictably, to functional differences. In developing broad generalizations concerning the functional behavior of large classes of English constructions, we hope to make a significant contribution to the growing literature on the ways in which word order is used to structure information in discourse.

Preposing and Postposing Constructions

The constructions we will consider in this work involve either 'preposing', 'postposing', or both ('argument reversal'). We take preposing constructions in English to be those in which some argument of the verb appears to the left of its canonical position, typically but not always sentence-initially, leaving its

---

Prince 1994, and Goldberg 1995, inter alia, for alternative theories of what constitutes a linguistic construction.

canonical position empty. Similarly, we take postposing constructions to be those in which some argument of the verb appears to the right of its canonical position, typically but not always sentence-finally, leaving its canonical position either empty or else occupied by an expletive element.[2] Finally, we take argument-reversing constructions to be those in which the logical subject appears in postverbal position while some canonically postverbal argument of the verb appears in preverbal position.

For convenience, we will use the terms 'preposed' and 'postposed' in referring to these noncanonically positioned constituents, although we wish to remain neutral with respect to their syntactic analysis.[3] The syntax of the constructions we will be dealing with remains controversial, and we will not attempt to assess the relative merits of various syntactic treatments.

It should also be noted that, although the constructions to be investigated will be defined in syntactic terms, we do not intend to argue that a one-to-one correspondence holds between syntactic form and discourse function. On the contrary, we have found that interesting and complex relations hold between sentence-type and function-type, as will become evident in the chapters to follow. We will begin by defining in more detail the sentence-types to be covered in this book.

Preposing

As we will use the term, a 'preposing' is a sentence in which a lexically governed phrasal constituent (NP, AP, PP, VP) appears to the left of its canonical position, typically sentence-initially (Ward 1988). Again, while the syntax of preposing remains an open question, nothing in the theory being presented rests on the resolution of these syntactic issues. Suffice it to say that under any theory of grammar, the 'preposed' constituent must be interpreted at some level of

[2]While English does not permit a null argument in canonical position in the case of postposing, other languages, e.g. Italian, do; see Chapter 6 for discussion.

[3]Similarly, we will use the standard names for constructions, such as 'inversion' and '*there*-insertion', because of their widespread use in the literature; nevertheless, we remain neutral with respect to the appropriateness of the movement metaphors associated with these terms.

grammatical analysis as corresponding to an empty argument position.

Note that, under this definition, preposing is not restricted to any particular phrasal category, as illustrated by the following examples of a preposed NP, PP, VP, and AP in (1a) through (1d), respectively:

(1) a. **NP**
I work on the 6th floor of a building. I know some of the elevator riders well. *Others I have only that nodding acquaintance with and some are total strangers.*
[*Philadelphia Inquirer*, 9/5/83]

b. **PP**
Consume they did–not only 15 kegs of beer, which they guzzled like soda pop, but also the free Coors posters which they seized as works of art to adorn their dorm walls. *For their heads, they were given free Coors hats* and for their cars free Coors bumper stickers.
[*Philadelphia Inquirer*, 10/7/83]

c. **VP**
And there's a new breed of television viewers in Cable America who not only tend to be younger and better educated, with higher household income, but also have developed dramatically different viewing patterns. These Cable Americans are no longer chained to the networks; faced with a cornucopia of programming choice, *choose they do!*
[*New York Times*, 11/14/83]

d. **AP**
"In the early days, our productions were cheap and cheerful," says producer John Weaver of London-based Keefco. "We'd go into a seven-light studio, shoot the band in one afternoon and edit as we went along. The client would walk out with a tape that day."

Today's tapes may still be cheerful, *but cheap they are not.* The cost of an average video hovers between $35,000 and $45,000

but several performers have splurged lavishly.
[*Newsweek*, 4/18/83]

This definition of preposing excludes left-dislocation, illustrated in (2), in which a pronoun that is coreferential with the marked constituent appears in that constituent's canonical position:

(2) a. The machine dictates. *This crummy little machine with buttons on it you've got to be there to answer it.*
[Terkel 1974:59]

b. I bet she had a nervous breakdown. That's not a good thing. *Gallstones, you have them out and they're out.* But a nervous breakdown, it's very bad.
[Roth 1969:162]

Left-dislocation is not only syntactically distinct from preposing, but is functionally distinct as well, as we will show in Chapter 2.

Postposing

As defined here, the term 'postposing' denotes any construction in which a lexically governed phrasal constituent appears to the right of its canonical position, typically but not exclusively in sentence-final position, leaving its canonical position either empty or else occupied by an expletive (Birner & Ward 1996). The postposing constructions we will concentrate on are those in which the logical subject is postposed and the expletive *there* appears in the canonical subject position — i.e., what have traditionally been known as existential and presentational *there*-sentences, as in (3a) and (3b), respectively:

(3) a. *"There's a warm relationship, a great respect and trust"* between [United Air Lines]'s chairman, Stephen M. Wolf, and Sir Colin Marshall, British Air's chief executive officer, according to a person familiar with both sides.
[*Wall Street Journal*, 8/23/89]

b. *Not far from Avenue de Villiers there lived a foreign doctor, a specialist, I understood, in midwifery and gynecology.* He was a coarse and cynical fellow who had called me in consultation a couple of times, not so much to be enlightened by my superior knowledge as to shift some of his responsibility on my shoulders. [Munthe 1929:143]

Existential *there*-sentences, as in (3a), contain *be* as their main verb, whereas presentational *there*-sentences, as in (3b), contain some other main verb. As we will demonstrate in Chapter 3, this lexical difference corresponds to a functional difference as well.

Notice also that this definition of postposing excludes right-dislocation, in which the canonical position left vacant by the marked constituent is filled by a pronoun which is coreferential with that constituent:

(4) a. Below the waterfall (and this was the most astonishing sight of all), a whole mass of enormous glass pipes were dangling down into the river from somewhere high up in the ceiling! *They really were* ENORMOUS, *those pipes.* There must have been a dozen of them at least, and they were sucking up the brownish muddy water from the river and carrying it away to goodness knows where. [Dahl 1964:74-75]

b. Can't write much, as I've been away from here for a week and have to keep up appearances, but did Diana mention the desk drama? Dad took your old desk over to her house to have it sent out, but he didn't check to see what was in it, and forgot that I had been keeping all my vital documents in there — like my tax returns and paystubs and bank statements. Luckily Diana thought "that stuff looked important" so she took it out before giving the desk over to the movers. Phew! *She's a smart cookie, that Diana.* [personal letter]

And, as with left-dislocation and preposing, we will show in Chapter 3 that the syntactic difference between right-dislocation and postposing corresponds to a functional difference between them.

Argument reversal

While preposing involves the noncanonical leftward placement of a constituent, and postposing involves the noncanonical rightward placement of a constituent, argument reversal incorporates both. The English argument-reversing constructions we will consider in this book are *by*-phrase passives and inversion. The data indicate that both constructions are subject to the same discourse constraint.

By-phrase passives are passive sentences with a *by*-phrase containing the logical subject, as exemplified in (5):

(5) Connaught said it was advised that the Ciba-Geigy/Chiron offer would be increased to $26.51 a share from $25.23 a share if the company adopted a shareholder-rights plan that facilitated the Swiss and U.S. firms' offer. *That offer was rejected by Connaught, which cited its existing pact with Institut Merieux.*
[*Wall Street Journal*, 9/12/89]

We will refer to the preverbal NP in a *by*-phrase passive (e.g., *that offer* in (5)) as the syntactic subject, and to the postverbal NP (e.g., *Connaught* in (5)) as the *by*-phrase NP (Birner 1996a).

Inversion, on the other hand, denotes any clause in which the logical subject appears in postverbal position while some other, canonically postverbal, constituent appears in preverbal position (see Birner 1994), excluding cases where expletive *there* occupies syntactic subject position (which will be shown to be distinct on both formal and functional grounds). We will refer to the noncanonically positioned constituents as the 'preposed' and 'postposed' constituents for convenience, although again we wish to remain neutral with respect to the correct syntactic analysis of the construction.

The examples in (6) show that, as with preposing, any phrasal constituent can be preposed via inversion:

(6) a. **PP**

George, can you do me a favor? *Up in my room, on the nightstand, is a pinkish-reddish envelope that has to go out immediately.*
[T.L., 7/24/89, on the telephone]

b. **AP**

Immediately recognizable here is the basic, profoundly false tenet of Movie Philosophy 101, as it has been handed down from "Auntie Mame" and "Harold and Maude": Nonconformism, the more radical the better, is the only sure route to human happiness and self-fulfillment.
[*Chicago Tribune*, 1989]

c. **NP**

She's a nice woman, isn't she? *Also a nice woman is our next guest...*[4]
[David Letterman, 5/31/90]

d. **VP**

Arrested were Nathan Thomas, 23, of New York, and his brother, WO Victor Thomas, 32, a 13-year Army veteran.
[*Chicago Tribune*, 11/12/89]

As defined here, inversion is to be distinguished from PP preposing with concomitant *there*-insertion, as illustrated in (7):

(7) a. There are two O-rings around the seal, and on about five, perhaps half a dozen STS flights, *on each flight there are six seal areas, three segments, three breaks in each of two solids.*
[Challenger Commission transcripts]

b. The Government of Canada has declared a world heritage site and this particular administration has put the finishing touch on a

[4] Although the linear word order in this example (NP-*be*-NP) is the same as that of a canonical-word-order sentence, it is nonetheless an inversion, given that the postverbal NP (*our next guest*) represents the logical subject, of which the information represented by the preverbal NP (*a nice woman*) is being predicated. See Birner 1996c for discussion.

national park at that location. *In this land that received the first settlers to the new world, today, centuries later, there exists small communities of people who are close to the land and sea.*
[token provided by D. Yarowsky, AT&T Bell Laboratories]

As noted above, we will show in Chapter 4 that such examples are both formally and functionally distinct from inversion.

Theoretical Framework

It is often observed that many languages show a tendency to order 'given' information before 'new' information in an utterance, and indeed Prince (1981a:247) posits a "conspiracy of syntactic constructions" preventing NPs representing relatively unfamiliar information from occupying subject position (see also Kuno 1971, inter alia). In a similar vein, Horn (1986) argues that leftward movement in general serves to prepose 'thematic' or familiar information, whereas rightward movement serves to postpose nonthematic or unfamiliar information. Dichotomies such as theme/rheme, topic/comment, and focus/ground have all been proposed by researchers attempting to account for the intuition that given information tends to precede new information; however, none has succeeded in accounting for a wide range of naturally occurring linguistic data in a rigorous and predictive way. In the chapters to follow, we will present an approach that synthesizes and expands on a number of previous theoretic insights, no one of which can on its own account for the data, but which, when brought together into a new and unified account, can be shown to have predictive power and in fact account for a wide range of naturally occurring data.

What previous approaches have in common is a general approach based on the degree to which information is assumed to be available to the hearer prior to its evocation in the current utterance. One aspect in which they differ is the source of this availability — the prior discourse, for example, or the hearer's knowledge store. Related to but distinct from this issue is that of the relations that may hold between given information and the source of its givenness. As we will see, both questions are relevant for noncanonical word order — not only the issue of what constitutes familiar vs. unfamiliar information within an utterance, but also the relationship between familiar information and the source of its familiarity.

Chafe (1976) defines given information as "that knowledge which the speaker assumes to be in the consciousness of the addressee at the time of the utterance," while new information is defined as "what the speaker assumes he is introducing into the addressee's consciousness by what he says" (1976:30). However, 'consciousness' is a slippery notion. It is defined by Chafe (1980) as "the activation of some available information in the service of the self"; however, it is not clear how the term 'consciousness' is rendered any clearer by being defined in terms of 'activation'.

Other notions of given information have allowed for a looser relationship between the given information and the discourse model, relying on such notions as predictability and shared knowledge (see the discussion in Prince 1981a). Prince (1981a, 1992) rejects these terms in favor of 'assumed familiarity', reflecting the fact that only an omniscient observer can truly know what information is in fact shared between interlocutors, while actual language users must operate on the basis of what they assume to be familiar to their interlocutors.[5] In reviewing the previous literature on givenness in discourse, Prince (1992) finds that three basic approaches may be distinguished, which she terms focus/presupposition, hearer-old/hearer-new, and discourse-old/discourse-new.[6]

[5]Notice that this is a much more restricted sense of 'familiarity' than that presented by Siewierska (1988), who, following Ertel (1977), takes familiarity to be "a relative notion dependent on variables internal to the speaker", including "topicality, givenness, definiteness, referentiality, and perhaps temporal priority, but also purely idiosyncratic factors such as personal preference, emotive involvement, expertise in a given field, etc." (1988:61).

[6]Along similar lines, Lambrecht (1994) identifies three categories of 'information structure' (Halliday 1967): presupposition and assertion (the structuring of propositional information into given and new); identifiability and activation (the information status of discourse referents); and topic and focus (the relative predictability of relations among propositions).

Focus/presupposition

Chomsky (1971) uses the concepts of focus and presupposition to argue that certain aspects of semantic interpretation are determined by surface structure. In his account, focus is a syntactic notion; the focused constituent contains and is determined by the 'intonation center', and the presupposition is obtained by replacing the focus with a variable. The focus-related intonation directly affects what constitutes a well-formed question/answer pair:

(8) a. is it JOHN who writes poetry?

b. it isn't JOHN who writes poetry.

c. no, it is BILL who writes poetry.

[=Chomsky 1971, exx. 38, 39]

Chomsky notes that "[u]nder normal intonation the capitalized word receives main stress and serves as the point of maximal inflection of the pitch contour" (1971:199). The semantic representation of (8a) and (8b), he argues, must show *John* to be the focus of the sentence, and *someone writes poetry* to be the presupposition. In (8c), a natural response to (8a) or (8b), the presupposition remains the same, while the focus changes to 'Bill'.

Chomsky further observes that a given utterance with a given intonation center may nonetheless be ambiguous as to its focus, since the intonation center may be embedded within increasingly large constituents, any one of which could be the focus (cf. Wilson & Sperber 1979, Ward 1988, inter alia). Consider (9):

(9) (was he (warned to (look out for (an ex-convict (with (a red (SHIRT))))))) [Chomsky 1971, ex. 53]

Here, any one of the phrases given in parentheses, up to and including the entire sentence (so-called 'broad focus'), may be interpreted as the focus, with corresponding appropriate responses, including those in (10):

(10) a. no, he was warned to expect a visit from the FBI

b. no, he was simply told to be more cautious

c. no, nothing was said to anyone.

[=Chomsky 1971, ex. 54]

An appropriate response, then, is one sharing the presupposition of the question.

Jackendoff (1972) agrees that "intuitively, it makes sense to speak of a discourse as 'natural' if successive sentences share presuppositions" (1972:230). He defines the focus of a sentence as "the information in the sentence that is assumed by the speaker not to be shared by him and the hearer," and the presupposition, then, as "the information in the sentence that is assumed by the speaker to be shared by him and the hearer" (1972:16). He also agrees with Chomsky that the division into presupposition and focus is part of the semantic representation of the sentence, reflected in its syntactic structure. This reflection, in Jackendoff's account, consists of a syntactic marker F which is associated with a node in the surface structure to indicate focus. Focus is realized as stress, such that "if a phrase P is chosen as the focus of a sentence S, the highest stress in S will be on the syllable of P that is assigned highest stress by the regular stress rules" (Jackendoff 1972:6.58). This formulation, while consistent with Chomsky's, is somewhat more specific in that it determines where within the focus the intonation center will appear.[7]

Drawing on this tradition, Prince (1986) defines a class of syntactic constructions which serve to mark an 'open proposition' (OP) as shared knowledge in the discourse, where the OP corresponds to Chomsky's and Jackendoff's 'presupposition'. An open proposition is a proposition containing one or more variables, and represents what is assumed by the speaker to be salient (or, we will argue, inferrable) in the discourse at the time of utterance. The OP is obtained

[7]Lumsden (1988) argues that a presupposition of the sort defined by Chomsky and Jackendoff need not always be present:

(i) I think I'd better stop talking now because JOHN is at the door.
[=Lumsden 1988, ex. 70]

In (i), focus on *John* does not require that 'someone is at the door' be presupposed, Lumsden claims; that is, "elements in a sentence may be neither focused nor presupposed" (1988:234). However, the possibility remains that some larger constituent (e.g., *John is at the door*) is actually the focus in this case. This is not to say that Jackendoff's formulation is unproblematic; see Ward 1988 for a critical discussion.

by replacing the 'tonically stressed constituent' of the utterance with a variable whose instantiation corresponds to the new information, or focus, of the utterance (see also Rochemont 1978, Wilson & Sperber 1979, Prince 1981b, Ward 1988, Välimaa-Blum 1988, Vallduví 1992, and Lambrecht 1994).[8] Prince classifies a variety of preposing types, including what we will call 'PP inversion', as marking an OP as salient in the discourse, and it will be shown in Chapters 2 and 5 that the notion of an OP is indeed crucial to the analysis of some, but not all, types of preposing and inversion.

A typical preposing, for example, consists of two parts: the open proposition and the focus. The OP contains an unbound variable whose instantiation within the preposing represents a member of some salient or inferrable set; this instantiation is the focus of the utterance. The focus constitutes the 'new information' of the utterance, and is realized prosodically with an accented syllable. Consider, for example, the preposing in (11):

(11) I think she was Japanese. No — *Korean she was.*
OP: She was X, where X is a member of the set {nationalities}.

Here, the open proposition may be paraphrased informally as 'she was some nationality'. This OP is clearly salient in the discourse, given the previous utterance *she was Japanese*. The focus, 'Korean', has not been evoked in the prior discourse and is therefore not part of the open proposition; however, it is in a salient set relationship with the previously evoked 'Japanese'. The nature of the relationships that may hold between the various elements in the OP and the prior context will be discussed at length below.

'New to the discourse' vs. 'new to the hearer'

The other two approaches to given and new information that Prince (1992) distinguishes are, first, the distinction between what is new to the discourse and what has previously been evoked within the discourse, and second, the distinction between what the speaker believes is new to the hearer and what the

[8] Rooth (1992) presents a somewhat different account of focus (within the framework of alternative semantics) which nonetheless shares certain features of an open-proposition analysis.

speaker believes is familiar to the hearer. Like OPs, these notions will prove crucial to the analysis of the constructions to be discussed in the chapters to follow.

Noting that a two-way division of information into given and new is inadequate, Prince (1992) offers a pair of crosscutting dichotomies which classify information as, on the one hand, either 'discourse-old' or 'discourse-new' and, on the other hand, either 'hearer-old' or 'hearer-new'.[9] Discourse-old information is that which has been evoked in the prior discourse, while discourse-new information is that which has not; likewise, hearer-old information is that which the speaker believes to be present within the hearer's knowledge store, while hearer-new information is that which is not assumed to be present within the hearer's knowledge store.[10] Familiarity of information within the discourse is thus distinct from its (assumed) familiarity to the hearer. This distinction captures the fact that what is new to the discourse needn't be new to the hearer (cf. Firbas 1966, Chafe 1976, Lambrecht 1994); that is, an entity may be familiar to the hearer yet new to the discourse. However, presumably information that is discourse-old will, by virtue of having been evoked in the prior discourse, be assumed to be hearer-old as well.[11]

---

[9]While Prince (1992) uses discourse-old/discourse-new and hearer-old/hearer-new exclusively for entities (i.e., referents evoked by NPs), we will be using it somewhat more broadly to cover a wide variety of constituent and information types, including states, events, attributes, etc.

[10]It should be noted that what is relevant here is the presence of the information in question within the hearer's knowledge store, not the hearer's beliefs regarding its truth (in the case of a proposition), existence (in the case of an entity), attributes, etc. That is, what matters for hearer-status is the hearer's (assumed) knowledge *of*, rather than *about*, the information in question.

[11]The discourse-old/discourse-new distinction is clearly related to, though not isomorphic with, the theme/rheme distinction discussed by Firbas 1966, inter alia, where the theme is said to convey "facts that are known or can be gathered from the preceding sentence" (Firbas 1966). The theme/rheme distinction is situated within the theory of 'communicative dynamism'; thematic material exhibits a lower degree of communicative dynamism than does rhematic material, where communicative dynamism is defined as "the extent to which the sentence element contributes to the development of the communication, to which it 'pushes the communication forward'" (Firbas 1966:270). The 'basic distribution' of communicative dynamism is that theme precedes rheme. Although the same intuitions motivating the theory of communicative dynamism motivate the

The distinction between discourse-familiarity and hearer-familiarity thus defines a four-celled matrix of possible information statuses, of which only three occur regularly in naturally occurring discourse:

> Hearer-old, discourse-old — Information which has previously been evoked in the current discourse, and which the speaker therefore believes is known to the hearer.
>
> Hearer-old, discourse-new — Information which has not been evoked in the current discourse, but which the speaker nonetheless believes is known to the hearer.
>
> Hearer-new, discourse-new — Information which has not been evoked in the current discourse, and which the speaker does not believe to be known to the hearer.
>
> Hearer-new, discourse-old — Theoretically, information which has been evoked in the current discourse, but which the speaker nonetheless believes is not known to the hearer. Prince notes that this type of information typically does not occur in natural discourse.

Thus, consider a simple discourse-initial utterance such as (12):

(12) Last night the moon was so pretty that I called a friend on the phone and told him to go outside and look.

Here, *the moon* represents information that is discourse-new but hearer-old, denoting an entity that has not been evoked in the prior discourse but which can be assumed to be known to the hearer; *a friend* represents information that is both discourse-new and hearer-new, having not been previously evoked and also being (presumably, given the indefinite) unknown to the hearer; and *him* represents information that is discourse-old and (therefore necessarily) hearer-old, having been explicitly evoked in the previous clause (as *a friend*). The status of what Prince calls 'inferrable' information (e.g., *the phone* in (12), on

---

discourse-old/discourse-new distinction, we believe that the latter provides a more concrete way of describing the data. A theme/rheme-based account of inversion is offered by Hartvigson & Jakobsen (1974); it is discussed in Chapter 4.

the assumption that people are typically assumed to have telephones) is left unresolved in Prince 1992 and will be discussed at length in Chapters 4 and 5.

Constructions vary not only with respect to whether they are sensitive to discourse-familiarity or hearer-familiarity, but also with respect to whether they are sensitive to 'absolute' or 'relative' familiarity. That is, the felicitous use of one construction may require that a certain constituent represent discourse-old information (an absolute constraint), while the felicitous use of another may require only that a certain constituent represent *less* familiar information within the discourse than does another constituent (a relative constraint). Thus, there exist three interacting dimensions along which constructions can vary with respect to the pragmatic constraints to which they are sensitive: old vs. new information, discourse- vs. hearer-familiarity, and relative vs. absolute familiarity. We will argue that, while constructions may be grouped on the basis of whether they require new or old information, they differ within each group with respect to the other two dimensions. Specifically, we will show that constructions involving a preposed constituent require that constituent to represent information that is old in some sense (either to the hearer or to the discourse, and either relatively or absolutely), while constructions involving a postposed constituent require that constituent to represent information that is new in some sense (again, either to the hearer or to the discourse, and either relatively or absolutely). Moreover, we will show that in both preposing and inversion, the preposed constituent represents a discourse-old 'link' (Reinhart 1981, Davison 1984, Fraurud 1990, Vallduví 1992, Ward & Birner 1994a, inter alia) standing in a specific type of relation to information evoked in the prior context.[12] The range of relations that support this linking will be discussed next.

[12]Although strictly speaking it is the information itself that possesses some information status (and not the constituent representing that information), where no confusion will result we will continue to speak of constituents as being discourse-old, discourse-new, evoked, etc. for convenience.

Linking relations

It is commonly accepted that the coherence of a discourse may depend on its component propositions being related to each other in certain ways (Halliday & Hasan 1976); on a more basic level, coherence is likewise dependent on relationships among the smaller informational units of which these propositions are comprised, such as discourse entities, attributes, and actions. That is, in a coherent discourse, the information presented in the current utterance typically draws on and builds on the information that is already present in the discourse model. Given this fact, we may ask about the nature of the relationship that holds between the information presented in the current utterance and that which has already been evoked in the discourse.

Posets

We will argue that the discourse-old link in a given utterance is related to previously evoked information via a partially ordered set relationship.[13] A partially ordered set, or 'poset', is any set defined by a transitive partial ordering relation R such that R is either reflexive and antisymmetric, or irreflexive and asymmetric (Hirschberg 1991). An example of a poset relation which is reflexive and antisymmetric is 'is-as-tall-as-or-taller-than', as in (13a), while an example of one which is irreflexive and asymmetric is 'is-taller-than', as in (13b):

(13) a. **is-as-tall-as-or-taller-than**
reflexive: X is as tall as or taller than X.
antisymmetric: If X is as tall as or taller than Y, and Y is as tall as or taller than X, then X=Y.

b. **is-taller-than**
irreflexive: X is not taller than X.
asymmetric: If X is taller than Y, then Y is not taller than X.

[13]Thus, the 'discourse-old' link need not itself have been explicitly evoked within the prior discourse; as long as it stands in an appropriate relationship with previously evoked information, it is treated by speakers as discourse-old. See Chapter 4 for discussion.

A reflexive relation is one that always holds between an element and itself, as in (13a), whereas an irreflexive relation is one that never holds between an element and itself, as in (13b). An antisymmetric relation is one that cannot hold bidirectionally between two distinct elements (thus, if it holds between X and Y, they must be the same element), whereas an asymmetric relation is one that cannot hold bidirectionally between X and Y, regardless of whether they are distinct. Thus, the difference between the two types of poset relation is that in one case the relation may (and indeed must) hold between an element and itself, as in (13a), and in the other it may hold only between one element and another. Neither type of relation is symmetric; that is, in neither case may it hold bidirectionally between distinct elements. Finally, in both cases the relation is transitive — that is, if it holds between A and B, and between B and C, then it holds between A and C. Note that one can always start with an irreflexive relation and produce a reflexive relation by by adding an equality disjunct to the relation, as with the 'is-as-tall-as-or-taller-than' relation.

Two elements A and B that cooccur in a poset can be related to each other in one of three possible ways, in terms of their relative rank in the poset: A can represent a lower value than does B, A can represent a higher value than does B, or the two can be of equal rank, or 'alternate values' sharing a common higher or lower value but not ordered with respect to each other, as illustrated by the preposed constituents in (14a)-(14c), respectively.

(14) a. **Lower Value**
G: Do you like this album?
M: Yeah, *this song I really like.*
[M. Rendell to G. Ward in conversation]

b. **Higher Value**
C: Have you filled out the Summary Sheet?
T: Yeah. *Both the Summary Sheet and the Recording Sheet I've done.*
[T. Culp to C. Wessell in conversation]

c. **Alternate Values**
G: Did you get any more [answers to the crossword puzzle]?

S: No. *The cryptogram I can do like that.* The crossword puzzle is hard.
[S. Makais to G. Ward in conversation]

In (14a), the relation 'is-a-part-of' orders the poset {album parts}, within which the referent of the preposed constituent *this song* represents a lower value than does the referent of *this album*, evoked in the prior utterance; that is, 'this song' is a part of 'this album'. In (14b), the *the Summary Sheet and the Recording Sheet* represents a higher value than does *the Summary Sheet* within the poset {forms}, ordered by 'is-a-member-of' relation; that is, 'the Summary Sheet and the Recording Sheet' is a superset of 'the Summary Sheet'.[14] Finally, in (14c), *the crossword puzzle* and *the cryptogram* represent alternate, equally-ranked values within the poset {newspaper puzzles}, ordered by the relation 'is-a-type-of'.

An element in a poset may be associated with an entity, attribute, event, activity, time, or place, or with a set of such items (Ward & Hirschberg 1985, Ward 1988, Hirschberg 1991, and Ward & Prince 1991). Examples of poset relations include not only scales defined by entailment (Horn 1972), but also a much broader range of relations, such as part/whole, entity/attribute, type/subtype, set/subset, and equality relations. Different types of elements can be ordered in different ways; for example, an event might be ranked with other events according to a temporally-prior-to relation, whereas an attribute might be ranked with respect to the entity which possesses it via an attribute-of relation, and so on.

Links

Up to this point, we have been using the term 'link' rather informally to denote the discourse-old information within a marked syntactic construction.[15] A more

[14]Higher-value preposings are actually quite rare, and are usually explicitly designated as such, as with the quantifier *both* in (14b).

[15]The metaphorical use of the terms 'link' and 'anchor' to describe the relationship between elements of the current sentence and the prior context is relatively widespread in the literature. Consider for example the following quote from Garrod and Sanford 1994:

> This brief discussion of what constitutes a text gives some clues about the kind of processes required in sentence resolution. The key processes will be those that anchor the interpretation of the sentence or its fragments to the prior discourse

explicit definition is provided below. (See also Reinhart 1981, Davison 1984, Fraurud 1990, Vallduví 1992, and Ward & Birner 1994a, inter alia.)

> The **link** within an utterance is the linguistic material representing information which stands in a contextually licensed poset relation with information evoked in or inferrable from the prior context, and serves as a point of connection between the information presented in the current utterance and the prior context.

By a 'contextually licensed' poset relation we mean a relation involving a posetthat the hearer is (believed to be) able either to construct or retrieve from his or her knowledge store based on the information evoked in the current discourse. This constraint is designed to restrict these posets to those that are salient or inferrable in context, since in principle any random set of items could constitute a poset, yet most such combinations will not license linking relations between utterances and their contexts:

(15) a. I walked into the kitchen. *On a/the counter was a large book.*

b. I walked into the kitchen. *#On a/the jacket was a large book.*

In (15a), the inversion is licensed by the fact that the hearer may readily retrieve a culturally available posetcontaining both 'kitchen' and 'counter' — specifically, the poset{elements of a house}, ordered by the relation part-of, with 'counter' representing a lower value than does 'kitchen' (since a counter is part of a kitchen). In (15b), on the other hand, there exists no salient or inferrable posetrelating 'kitchen' and 'jacket'; hence, this posetis not contextually licensed.

> representation. Some of this anchoring will involve establishing referential links, some will involve establishing temporal links, while other anchoring processes will depend on the logical and psychological links between the events and states portrayed (i.e., in terms of their coherence). (1994:677)

Although the various studies utilizing these terms have by and large used them in very similar ways, these previous studies have failed to draw the (in our view) crucial distinction between the linguistic items being related, the poset relation connecting the information represented by these items, and the poset itself. See below for discussion.

We will refer to the posetrelating the link and the prior context (in (15), {elements of a house}) as the 'anchoring set', or more concisely, the 'anchor'.[16] The relation between the link and the anchor, which we will refer to as the 'linking relation' (cf. Strand 1996a), is always a poset relation.[17] The relation between the anchor and the prior context, however, is not always a poset relation. Consider (16):

(16) a. I promised my father — *on Christmas Eve it was* — to kill a Frenchman at the first opportunity I had.
["The Young Lions"]

b. She got married recently and *at the wedding was the mother, the stepmother and Debbie.*
[E.B. in conversation]

In (16a), the link is *on Christmas Eve*. The prior context (*I promised my father*) renders inferrable the notion that this promise was made at some time, which in turn contextually licenses the anchor {times}. This anchor stands in a poset relation with set member *Christmas Eve*. However, the anchoring poset {times} does not stand in a poset relation to the prior context; that is, *I promised my father* itself does not stand a poset relation with the set {times}. Thus, the anchor here is inferrable from, but does not stand in a poset relation to, information in the prior discourse. Similarly, in (16b), mention of someone getting married renders inferrable the anchor {the wedding}. Notice that here the linking relation that

[16]Fraurud (1990) uses the term 'anchor' in a similar but not identical way to denote "entities or elements in relation to which first-mention definites may be interpreted" (1990:415). That is, the anchor for Fraurud is the previously mentioned or inferrable entity that licenses the use of a first-mention definite (as in *a restaurant ... the waitress*). This use of the term 'anchor' corresponds roughly to Hawkins' (1978) 'trigger'. We will use these two terms for distinct notions, however; in particular, we will argue that we must have a notion of a contextually licensed poset(i.e., the anchor) distinct from the linguistic material that gives rise to the inference to this poset (i.e., the trigger). See below.

[17]Strand (1996a, 1996b) also uses the term 'linking relation', albeit slightly differently, in discussing the relations that may obtain between a felicitous definite NP and an element in the prior context; however, the set of linking relations presented by Strand is somewhat distinct from those developed here.

holds between the link and the anchor is one of identity, which is also a poset relation. That is, the link *the wedding* stands in the identity relation with the anchor {the wedding}.

That linguistic or situational material which licenses the inference to the anchor we will call the 'trigger(s)' (Hawkins 1978). As we have seen, this inference may be based on a poset relation (as in (15a)), but it need not be (as in (16)). The inference may be triggered by one or more items, one of which may be the link itself. Thus, in (15a), mention of *the kitchen* alone does not give rise to the poset{elements of a house}, since, if it did, every utterance of an NP would give rise to a cognitive explosion of instantaneously constructed part/whole relations in which the referent participates (Fraurud 1990). Rather, it isn't until the speaker utters *on the counter* that mention of the kitchen and the counter combine to evoke the posetthat relates the two. Thus, in this case both *the kitchen* and the link *the counter* are triggers for the inference to the anchor {elements of a house}. In general, however, in using the term 'trigger' we will be referring specifically to the trigger(s) occurring in the prior linguistic or situational context.

Notice, finally, that it is entirely possible for the trigger, anchor, and link to all represent the same information, as in (17):

(17) On one of September's last blast-furnace days, Emil Peterson parked his car along a quiet street in the tiny Delaware County burg of Eddystone and pulled a yellow plastic bucket from the back seat. *In it he had expertly wedged an assortment of brushes and cans of cleanser, a hollyberry room deodorizer, knives, scissors, a couple of no-slip no-crease pants hangers and a box containing a boulder-sized zircon ring.* A toilet-bowl swab protruded from the pail like a fluffy white pompom flouncing as he set off determinedly down the sidewalk.
[*Philadelphia Inquirer*, 10/2/83]

Here, the trigger *a yellow plastic bucket* trivially evokes the singleton set of which that bucket is the sole member. This set is the anchor, which in turn is trivially related to the link *it* via a linking relation of identity.[18] Thus, even cases where the machinery of posets and linking relations may not seem necessary are nonetheless consistent with this account, allowing the development of a unified theory.

To summarize, we have suggested that a complete functional account of English preposing, postposing, and argument-reversing constructions will require reference to open propositions, discourse- and hearer-familiarity, and linking relations. In the remainder of this book we will show that these constraints are not randomly assigned to the various construction types, but rather that broad generalizations can be made regarding the correlation of syntax and discourse function. Specifically, we will argue that:

- preposing constructions require that the preposed constituent represent information that is old in some sense, while postposing constructions require that the postposed constituent represent information that is new in some sense;
- the constraints placed by 'pure' preposing and postposing constructions on their marked constituents are absolute, while those placed on argument reversal are relative;
- the preposed discourse-old constituent in both preposing and inversion contains a link representing information that stands in a contextually licensed poset relation with information evoked in or inferrable from the prior context;
- a certain well-defined subclass of both preposings and inversions additionally require an open proposition to be salient or inferrable in the discourse; and
- the functional constraints observed for the classes of preposing and postposing constructions do not hold for superficially similar constructions in

[18]Note that in this example the preposition *in* does not constitute part of the link, unlike the preposition in (16a). The difference between the two types of links will be discussed in Chapter 5.

which the marked constituent's canonical position is filled by a referential pronoun (i.e., right- and left-dislocation).

Finally, in Chapter 6 we will consider additional data from constructions in Farsi, Italian and Yiddish to suggest that broader, crosslinguistic, generalizations can be made. First, we will show that there is no simple one-to-one mapping between constructions and functions, in that formally equivalent constructions in different languages may be subject to distinct functional constraints, while formally distinct constructions in different languages may be subject to the same constraint. Nor, however, is the form/function mapping arbitrary; using the crosslinguistic data discussed in Chapter 6, we will show that by considering preposed vs. postposed position and the number of noncanonically positioned arguments in a construction, we can identify a simple matrix that correctly predicts for English constructions — and more tentatively for the other languages discussed — what the range of possible discourse constraints will be for a particular noncanonical construction. This in turn suggests that the discourse function that may be served by a particular construction in a particular language may itself be partially constrained by the construction's form.

Weight

It has long been assumed that at least some uses of noncanonical word order have their basis in the grammatical 'weight' of the constituent or constituents in question, the most obvious example being what is traditionally known as 'heavy NP shift'. Indeed, Hawkins (1994) argues that "the major determinant of word-order variation, and indeed of all word order, is syntactic weight" (1994:111); moreover, he claims that "pragmatics appears to play no role whatsoever" in linear ordering and that in fact "pragmatic principles are epiphenomenal" (1994:240-1).[19]

[19]Hawkins notes that there is a single exception to this rule; in languages (such as, e.g., Hungarian) that have a 'discourse-configurational' node (i.e., a topic or focus node) in their syntactic representation, that node may indeed have a pragmatic function. But even in this case, he argues, the grammatically fixed position of the node itself is determined by weight considerations.

Using a node-counting algorithm for determination of weight, Hawkins claims that "words and constituents occur in the orders they do so that syntactic groupings and their immediate constituents (ICs) can be recognized (and produced) as rapidly and efficiently as possible" (1994:57). This recognition, in turn, is facilitated by organizing constituents so as to minimize the number of nodes that must be processed in order to recognize the overall constituent structure of the sentence.[20] This, in a right-branching language like English, essentially means placing a heavy constituent toward the end of the sentence so that the hearer needn't process it in its entirety before reaching the first node of the next constituent.

Although Hawkins amasses a considerable range of empirical evidence for his hypothesis, his claim cannot be maintained for the types of word-order alternations we examine in this work.[21] Consider, for example, the inversion in (18):

(18) Yes, this is no ordinary general election.

'Evans is a Democrat; Daley is a Democrat. Different Democrats have different points of view about the city of Chicago and its politics,' Jackson noted. 'The war between forces within the party continues, and within our coalition.'

Standing in the middle of it all is Jesse Jackson.

[*Chicago Tribune*, 3/6/89]

Here, it seems clear that under virtually any conceivable algorithm for determining weight, *standing in the middle of it all* must be heavier than *Jesse Jackson*; more specifically, Hawkins' own algorithm predicts that the canonical-word-

[20]Wasow (1997) argues that weight effects cannot be fully explained in terms of facilitation of parsing, but rather that the primary role of weight considerations is to facilitate utterance planning and production — that is, for Wasow, weight factors are speaker- rather than hearer-based.

[21]Although our study does not include the constructions upon which Hawkins bases his claim (e.g., heavy NP shift, extraposition, the dative alternation, and particle movement), Arnold et al. (1997), using a corpus of naturally occurring data, found that for both the dative alternation and heavy NP shift "both givenness and [syntactic] complexity were significantly correlated with constituent ordering."

order variant would result in greater parsing efficiency by permitting earlier recognition of the constituent structure of the sentence.

On the contrary, what determines the felicity of inversion will be shown to be the relative information status of the preposed and postposed constituents. Consider (19):

(19) a. Each of the characters is the centerpiece of a book, doll and clothing collection. The story of each character is told in a series of six slim books, each $12.95 hardcover and $5.95 in paperback, and in bookstores and libraries across the country. More than 1 million copies have been sold; and in late 1989 a series of activity kits was introduced for retail sale. *Complementing the relatively affordable books are the dolls, one for each fictional heroine and each with a comparably pricey historically accurate wardrobe and accessories...*
[*Chicago Tribune*, 1/4/90]

b. Each of the characters is the centerpiece of a book, doll and clothing collection. The dolls are hand-painted in exquisite detail using organic dyes, and feature real hair and eyelashes. More than 1 million of the dolls have been sold; and in late 1989 a series of activity kits was introduced for retail sale. *#Complementing the relatively affordable books are the dolls, one for each fictional heroine and each with a comparably pricey historically accurate wardrobe and accessories...*

Here, by altering the relative information status of the dolls and the books in the context prior to the inversion in (19b), we render it infelicitous. If weight alone accounted for word order, we would expect no such dependence on contextual factors. Contra Hawkins, what renders the inversions in both (18) and (19a) felicitous in context is the fact that the information represented in the preposed constituent is more familiar (here, in the sense of having been more recently mentioned) than that represented in the postposed constituent. (See Chapter 4 for discussion.) Although we do not dispute that weight plays an important role in certain word-order phenomena, it will be a major thesis of this book that context and information status are crucial to the felicity of the noncanonical-word-order constructions we are considering.

Data

One of the unresolved problems in linguistics is how to access linguistic knowledge in the absence of direct evidence. One way of tapping this knowledge is to elicit native-speaker intuitions. Intuitions, however, are still only indirect evidence, as they reflect a variety of memory and processing constraints, as well as subjects' efforts to conform — consciously or not — to prescriptive grammar. For these and other reasons, intuitions are frequently unreliable or inconsistent, and these effects may be magnified when it comes to the marginal sentences or discourses which are often all that distinguishes one theory from another (cf. Labov 1972). Another method for tapping into linguistic knowledge is to consider naturally occurring linguistic data as evidence in deciding between competing analyses. One practical reason to rely on such data is the crucial role that context plays in constraining the use of noncanonical word order. The drawback to usage data is that they, too, when available, are affected by a wide range of factors involving the sentence processing apparatus which must implement the grammar (cf. Kroch 1981). Thus, both judgment data and usage data are subject to limitations, and relying on one type exclusively can be problematic. Nonetheless, both are valuable, and in using one to complement the other, we may hope to obtain a more accurate reflection of a speaker's linguistic knowledge. That is, if a form (or form-type) is repeatedly attested within the corpus and is moreover judged by native speakers to be acceptable, we may assume that the form accurately reflects the linguistic knowledge of native speakers. Therefore, both kinds of data are taken into account in this work, with intuitions serving as a check on the felicity and significance of naturally occurring data.

The corpora used for the research reported in this book consist of several thousand naturally occurring tokens collected over a period of approximately ten years. The data can be described as more or less standard American English,[22] and were drawn from a wide range of sources. Whenever possible, the prior and subsequent context was noted for each token. Data were collected from both speech and writing; the written sources include newspapers, magazines, novels, nonfiction books, academic prose, and portions of the Brown Corpus (Kucera and Francis 1967). Spoken data were drawn from personal conversations, films, interviews from Terkel 1974, transcripts of the 1986 Challenger Commission meetings,[23] and a variety of television and radio programs. We were careful to collect data from formal and informal registers, and from planned and unplanned speech.[24] As some authors (e.g., Green 1982, Quakenbush 1992) have noted, certain constructions are more typical of one register, genre, or modality than another (for example, some constructions are considered more colloquial than others); however, we will not in general note these differences, since it is our goal to provide a comprehensive analysis that will be applicable to the entire range of linguistic styles.

It should be noted that the tokens were not collected randomly (indeed, it is unclear to us what would constitute a truly random sample of the English language); the corpora, therefore, do not constitute a representative sample of English in the statistical sense. For this reason, it would be inappropriate to draw conclusions regarding natural-language proportions of various constructions based on their proportions in the corpora. However, conclusions can be drawn concerning what occurs (and, more tentatively, does not occur) in English based on these data. In addition, although data were collected from a variety of sources, no attempt was made to collect them in proportion to their overall distribution in the various sources. Thus there exists the possibility that the sample

[22]One exception is Yiddish-Movement, which is dialectally restricted and distinguishable from other types of preposing on syntactic and pragmatic grounds.

[23]This corpus consists of over 1.3 million words of transcribed oral data drawn from the official transcripts of The Presidential Commission on the Space Shuttle Challenger Accident (1986). We are grateful to Julia Hirschberg for making an on-line version of these transcripts available to us.

[24]Rubin (1978) observes that the oral-written distinction is oversimplistic and argues instead for a multidimensional approach to the issue of stylistic differences. See also Ochs 1979; Kroch 1982; Tannen 1982; Biber 1986, 1988; Chafe & Tannen 1987; Fox 1987; Chafe 1994; inter alia.

is skewed in this respect; that is, if some construction were strongly favored in some speech style, a corpus of data such as this one would not reveal this (see Green 1982 and Birner & Ward 1992 for discussions of possible correlations between sentence-types and speech styles).

Although from a purely syntactic point of view it is irrelevant whether some construction occurs, for example, primarily in literary contexts, from a functional or historical perspective much can be gained by considering the distribution of that construction throughout a speech community. The sociolinguistic status of these constructions is an interesting question that merits investigation; however, it lies outside the scope of this book. Thus, although we have found that certain noncanonical constructions occur with lesser or greater frequency in one or another genre, we shall nonetheless assume that our findings apply to the language as a whole. Put another way, our framework is designed to capture what certain classes of constructions have in common, while leaving open the possibility of additional genre- or modality-specific constraints.

Notational Conventions

The following conventions are employed throughout the book:

- Naturally occurring examples appear with their source/attribution. Examples appearing without a source are constructed. (See the Appendix for bibliographic details of source materials.)

- In each example consisting of more than one sentence, the sentence illustrating the marked construction under consideration appears in italics.

- Names of posets are surrounded by curly brackets, as in {elements of a house}.

- Following standard practice, the symbol '#' is used to designate pragmatic ill-formedness, or infelicity, while an asterisk is used to designate syntactic ill-formedness, or ungrammaticality. Very few of the examples in this book, however, are starred as ungrammatical, given that the focus of this work is not grammaticality, but rather contextual factors affecting the felicitous use of grammatical sentences.

Chapter 2

Preposing

As described in Chapter 1, preposing constructions are those sentence-types in which a canonically postverbal phrasal constituent appears in preverbal position. Moreover, following Ward 1988, we will restrict our analysis of preposing to those phrasal constituents that are lexically governed by the matrix verb. Thus, subcategorized NPs, APs, VPs and PPs are included, while various adverbials and adjuncts are not. To see that the preposing of lexically governed constituents is more constrained than that of constituents that are not lexically governed, consider (20):

(20) a. #In a basket, I put your clothes.

b. I put your clothes in a basket.

(21) a. In New York, there's always something to do.

b. There's always something to do in New York.

The preposing in (20a), in which the preposed locative PP is lexically governed by the verb *put*, is infelicitous as a discourse-initial utterance. Note that the corresponding sentence in which the PP is not preposed (20b) is fully acceptable in the same context. Where the PP is not lexically governed, as in (21b), both orderings are possible. Constituents that are not lexically governed are also less constrained with respect to word order in other contexts, as in the case of verbs of direct discourse, whose complements freely appear in preposed position — e.g.,

"This type of preposing is less constrained," John said. Moreover, certain non-lexically-governed preposed locative and temporal prepositional phrases serve to establish the spatiotemporal context of some event (Kuno's (1975) 'thematic scene-setting' adverbials), a function not served by lexically governed preposing. We conclude, then, that the conditions under which non-lexically-governed preposing is acceptable are distinct from those under which lexically governed preposing is acceptable. Non-lexically-governed preposing will therefore not be considered in the present study, and we will henceforth use the term 'preposing' to refer to lexically governed preposing.

Extending the theory of preposing presented in Ward 1988, we claim that the various preposing constructions of English form a natural class on pragmatic grounds, in that they are subject to the following discourse constraint:

> Felicitous preposing requires that the referent or denotation of the preposed constituent be anaphorically linked to the preceding discourse (see Reinhart 1981, Vallduví 1992).[1]

The information conveyed by the preposed constituent can be related to the preceding discourse in a number of ways, including such relations as: type/subtype, entity/attribute, part/whole, identity, etc. These relations can all be defined as 'partial orderings', and in Ward 1988 it is argued that the range of relations that can support preposing are all partially ordered set (poset) relations. Below we will see how discourse entities can be ranked as values within such posets.[2]

Reinhart (1981) identifies a number of distinct ways in which one (canonical-word-order) sentence can be referentially linked to an adjacent one, including: when the two sentences contain a mention of the same referent; when a referent in one sentence stands in a set relation with a referent in the other; and

[1]In Ward 1988, the anaphoric relation was cast in terms of Centering Theory (Grosz et al. 1983); here, our account of the anaphoric relations that hold for noncanonical word order is more inclusive than this earlier formulation.

[2]Givón 1993 argues for the following 'pre-posed order principle': More important information is more likely to be placed earlier in the clause. However, Givón also equates 'importance' with 'topicality' and, as we shall see, topicality is neither necessary nor sufficient for felicitous preposing.

when a referent mentioned in the second sentence belongs to a 'frame of reference' established in the first. However, our notion of a linking relationship, as defined in Chapter 1, provides a unified account of Reinhart's referential links. The notion of a partially ordered set subsumes Reinhart's links while providing an explicit and general device that characterizes the class of relations that can hold between a sentence's preposed link and its anchor. Although there need be no referential link in a canonical-word-order utterance, preposing necessarily marks the constituent in noncanonical, preverbal position as a link to the prior discourse.

This notion of a poset subsumes both coreferential links, where the linking relation between link and posetis one of identity, and non-coreferential links. To illustrate the difference with respect to preposing, consider the example in (22):

(22) Customer: Can I get a bagel?
Waitress: No, sorry. We're out of bagels. *A bran muffin I can give you.*
[service encounter]

Here, the link (*a bran muffin*) and trigger (*bagels*) stand in a poset relation as alternate members of the inferred anchor set {breakfast baked goods}. However, note that the link could also have been explicitly mentioned in the prior discourse, as in (23):

(23) A: Can I get a bagel?
B: Sorry — all out.
A: How about a bran muffin?
B: *A bran muffin I can give you.*

Here, although the link *a bran muffin* is coreferential with the trigger explicitly evoked in A's second query, the salient linking relation is not identity. Rather, the link is related via a type/subtype relation to the anchoring set {breakfast baked goods}, of which both bagels and bran muffins are members.

Thus, both (22) and (23) are instances of anchors that represent posets with multiple members. However, some types of preposing also permit links to anchors with a single member. Consider the topicalization in (24):

(24) Facts about the world thus come in twice on the road from meaning to truth: once to determine the interpretation, given the meaning, and then again to determine the truth value, given the interpretation. *This insight we owe to David Kaplan's important work on indexicals and demonstratives, and we believe it is absolutely crucial to semantics.*
[Barwise & Perry 1983:11]

Here, the link stands in a relation of identity to the anchoring poset, consisting of a singleton member. By virtue of this poset relation, the link serves as the point of connection to the prior discourse.[3]

Another case of a link to an anchor with a single member is a type of preposing called 'proposition affirmation', illustrated in (25):

(25) The other half of the double bill is "Sister Mary Ignatius". Whereas Lohrmann has to overcome a poor script to be bright, Durang has handed Ginny Brown Graham, via Sister Mary Ignatius, a fantastic script, and all she has to do is shine. *And shine she does.*
[*Au Courant*, 4/1/85]

Here, the link *shine* is evoked in the immediately preceding sentence. Thus, as in (24), the anchor consists of a singleton member, evoked by the trigger and repeated in the link. However, unlike the preposing in (24), the link of proposition affirmation is sensitive to the linguistic form of the trigger. Consider the infelicitous proposition affirmation in (26), where the trigger and link are semantically identical but lexically distinct:

(26) The other half of the double bill is "Sister Mary Ignatius". Whereas Lohrmann has to overcome a poor script to be bright, Durang has handed Ginny Brown Graham, via Sister Mary Ignatius, a fantastic script, and all she has to do is glow. *#And shine she does.*

Here, although *shine* and *glow* could be seen as standing in a relation of *semantic* identity, infelicity results because the salient relation between the link and trigger is not one of *morphological* identity. Thus, the relation between the link and

[3] Additional discourse constraints on singleton posets will be discussed in Chapter 5.

trigger in a proposition affirmation is more constrained than in other types of preposing.

In addition, Ward 1988 shows that certain types of preposing constructions require a salient or inferrable 'open proposition' in the discourse. Recall from Chapter 1 that an open proposition is a sentence that contains one or more variables; in a felicitous preposing, this OP represents what is assumed by the speaker to be salient or inferrable at the time of the utterance. The variable in the OP is instantiated with the focus, which constitutes the 'new information' of the utterance, and is constrained to be a member of a contextually licensed poset. Prosodically, the focus is realized with a nuclear pitch accent. This packaging of information into an open proposition and a focus corresponds closely to the 'focus/presupposition' distinction of Jackendoff 1972 and Rochemont 1978, inter alia (see also Lambrecht 1994, Vallduví 1992).

An examination of naturally occurring data reveals that preposings can be classified into two major types based on their intonation and information structure: 'focus preposing' and 'topicalization' (see Prince 1981b, Ward 1988). The preposed constituent of focus preposing contains the focus of the utterance, and bears nuclear accent; the rest of the clause is typically deaccented.[4] Topicalization, on the other hand, involves a preposed constituent *other than the focus* and bears multiple pitch accents: at least one on the preposed constituent and at least one on the (non-preposed) focus.[5] Nonetheless, both types of preposing require a salient or inferrable OP at the time of utterance for felicity.[6]

Consider first the focus preposing in (27), where the focus is contained within the preposed constituent:

---

[4]By 'accent', we mean 'intonational prominence' in the sense of Terken & Hirschberg 1994: "a conspicuous pitch change in or near the lexically stressed syllable of the word" (1994:126); see also Pierrehumbert 1980.

[5]Of course for both topicalization and focus preposing, other constituents may bear pitch accents. Intonationally speaking, the difference between focus preposing and topicalization is that only the former requires that the nuclear accent be on the preposed constituent.

[6]There is one preposing construction — 'locative preposing' — that does not require a salient OP but does require a locative element in preposed position. See Chapter 5 for discussion.

(27) A: Where can I get the reading packet?
B: In Steinberg. [Gives directions] *Six dollars it costs.*
[two students in conversation]

The preposed constituent in this example, *six dollars*, contains the nuclear accent, which identifies it as the focus of the utterance.

To construct the relevant OP, the preposed constituent containing the focus is first placed in its canonical argument position. The focus is then replaced with a variable, which is restricted to be a member of some contextually licensed poset, as represented informally in (28a). A gloss of the OP is provided in (28b). The focus, provided in (28c), instantiates the variable in the OP and represents a member of the poset.

(28) a. OP = It costs X, where X is a member of the poset {prices}.
b. It costs some amount of money.
c. Focus = six dollars

Here, *six dollars* serves as the link to the preceding discourse. Its referent is a member of the poset{prices}, which is part of the inferrable OP in (28a). In this example, the OP can be inferred on the basis of the prior context; from mention of a reading packet, one is licensed to infer that the packet costs some amount of money. While the anchoring poset {prices} is discourse-old, the preposed constituent itself represents information that has not been explicitly evoked in the prior discourse. In the case of focus preposing, then, since the anchoring poset must be discourse-old yet the link is the focus (and therefore new), it follows that the posetmust contain at least one other member in addition to the link.

The focus in a topicalization, on the other hand, is not contained in the preposed constituent but occurs elsewhere in the utterance. Intonationally, preposings of this type contain multiple accented syllables: (at least) one occurs within the constituent that contains the focus and (at least) one occurs within the preposed constituent, which typically occurs in a separate 'intonational phrase' (Pierrehumbert 1980). Consider (29):

(29) G: Do you watch football?
E: Yeah. *Baseball I like a lot better.*
[G. McKenna to E. Perkins in conversation]

Here, the preposed constituent is not the focus; *better* is. The preposed constituent *baseball* serves as the link to the inferred poset{sports}. This posetconstitutes the anchor, and can be inferred on the basis of the link (*baseball*) and the trigger *football*, explicitly evoked by G in the prior utterance. Note that *baseball* is accented in (29) not because it is the focus but because it occurs in a separate intonational phrase in sentence-initial position. While all foci are accented, not all accented items are foci; typically a single utterance contains a variety of pitch accents, each making a distinct contribution to utterance interpretation (see Ladd 1980, Pierrehumbert & Hirschberg 1990, Zacharski 1993, inter alia).

The OP is formed in much the same way as in the case of focus preposing, except that the posetmember represented by the preposed constituent is replaced in the OP by the anchoring poset, as in (30):[7]

(30) a. OP = I like-to-X-degree {sports}, where X is a member of the poset{amounts}.[8]

b. I like sports to some degree.

c. Focus = better

In (30a), the OP includes the variable corresponding to the focus, but note that the link *baseball* has been replaced by its anchoring set {sports}, i.e. the posetthat includes both the trigger and the link. In other words, the OP that is salient in (29) is not that the speaker likes baseball per se, but rather that he likes sports to some degree, as indicated in (30b). This OP is salient given the prior context in which E is asked if he watches football, from which it can be inferred that G is asking about E's interest in and evaluation of the sport in question.

[7] While the link typically represents a subset of the anchoring poset, we shall for notational convenience use the set itself in the representation of the OP, e.g. '{sports}' as opposed to 'y such that y stands in a poset relation to {sports}'.

[8] As with focus preposing, we present the OP in canonical word order for ease of exposition.

Thus, the focus of a preposing may appear either in preposed or canonical position. However, in both cases the preposed constituent — be it focus or not — serves as the link to the preceding discourse via a salient linking relation. In what follows, the two general types of preposing outlined above are described in more detail.

Topicalization

Previous functional studies of topicalization have by and large limited the scope of investigation to preposed NPs (Halliday 1967, Gundel 1974, Langacker 1974, Rodman 1974, Chafe 1976, Clark & Clark 1977, Creider 1979, Prince 1981b, Reinhart 1981, Davison 1984).[9] However, such a restriction is quite arbitrary in that the same discourse functional principles that apply to NP topicalization will be shown to apply to the topicalization of other major phrasal categories as well.

Many of these same studies have argued that the primary function of the construction is to mark the preposed constituent as the sentence topic (Halliday 1967, Gundel 1974, Langacker 1974, Reinhart 1981, Davison 1984).[10] For example, with regard to the preposing in (29), repeated below as (31), these authors would claim that the preposed element, *baseball*, is identified as the current topic of the sentence.

(31) G: Do you watch football?
E: Yeah. *Baseball I like a lot better.* [=(29)]

However, it could be argued that the topic of the preposing in (31) is not baseball, but rather the more inclusive category sports. In fact, the intuitive topic of many

---

[9]Despite our position that topicalization bears little relation to the notion of 'topic' (as currently understood in the literature), we shall nonetheless retain the term in the interests of lexical parsimony. Moreover, while the term 'topicalization' has come to be used to refer both to NP preposing in general and to a pragmatically defined type of preposing in particular, we shall follow the latter usage.

[10]Implicit in these studies is the assumption that the same constituent/entity if not preposed would be less perceived or less perceptible as the topic, an assumption for which insufficient evidence is provided.

topicalizations corresponds not to the preposed constituent per se, but rather to the posetof which the link is a member. Nearly 25% (227/915) of the preposed constituents in a corpus of naturally occurring data were found not to represent the topic of the sentence, where 'topic' was taken to be intuitively what the sentence is 'about'.

Some authors claim that preposing marks only *new* sentence topics. Under this view, the preposing in (31) would serve to shift the topic from 'football' in the preceding utterance to the new topic 'baseball'. Both approaches, however, explicitly confine their analysis of topic to the level of the sentence. Only those constituents (or discourse entities, depending on the study) that actually appear (or are referred to) in a given sentence are possible topics. We maintain that it is this overly restrictive view of sentence topic which is the basis for the failure of the topic-based studies to account satisfactorily for the function of preposing.[11]

In contrast to the topic-based studies of topicalization, which by and large analyze (constructed) examples in isolation, a few studies have gone beyond the level of the sentence in examining the phenomenon. These studies have analyzed topicalization as marking some kind of *relationship* between the referent of the preposed constituent and other entities in the discourse.

Chafe (1976) argues that preposing in English is necessarily 'contrastive', with the preposed constituent marking the 'focus of contrast'.[12] For Chafe, contrast involves an assertion on the part of a speaker that one of 'a limited number of candidates' is 'correct'. Consider one of the examples of contrast provided by Chafe (1976:34):

---

[11]One problem is that studies differ as to whether 'topic' is a *linguistic* phenomenon, i.e. a property of sentences, or a *psychological* one, i.e. a property of speakers. (See Reinhart 1981 for discussion.) Another problem is the well-known difficulty in defining sentence topic, despite the fact that the notion is used extensively in the literature. In fact, several attempts have been made to develop an independent — i.e. non-circular — test to identify sentence topics in English. These tests and their relation to topicalization are discussed in detail in Ward 1988.

[12]See also Givón 1993, which argues that preposing, or in Givón's terms, 'contrastive topicalization', involves the "breaking" of "speaker-generated expectations", i.e. those "most typically created by listing various members of a group (type, genus), whose members are expected to display similar behavior or receive similar treatment" (1993:181). However, as will be argued below, preposing requires neither contrast nor multiple members of a group for felicity.

(32) Ronald made the hamburgers.

Chafe glosses this sentence as an assertion on the part of the speaker that 'I believe that you believe that someone made the hamburgers, that you have a limited set of candidates (perhaps one) in mind as that someone, and I am telling you that the someone is Ronald, rather than one of those others' (1976:35). Chafe calls this asserted alternative the 'focus of contrast'. As a diagnostic for contrast, Chafe proposes the following rule of thumb: Can the phrase *rather than* ... (or *instead of* ..., or *not* ...) be felicitously inserted after the focus? This diagnostic, applied to (32), produces: 'Ronald, rather than Susan, made the hamburgers.'

Chafe also notes (1976:35) that a sentence may contain more than one focus of contrast, as illustrated by his example in (33):

(33) Perhaps Sally made the salad, but Ronald made the hamburgers.

In (33), what is being asserted by the speaker is the pairing of 'candidates' with 'roles': "That is, if we are to take possible pairings of agents with patients of *make* in this particular situation, one of the correct pairings (the speaker asserts) is *Ronald* with *the hamburgers*" (1976:35).

Chafe claims that it is this pairing of contrast foci that is involved in Gundel's (1974) 'topic topicalization'. According to Chafe, then, (33) could have just as felicitously incorporated a preposing, as in (34):

(34) Perhaps Sally made the salad, *but the hamburgers Ronald made.*

Here, Chafe would say that the speaker is pairing cooks with food items. The preposed constituent, *the hamburgers*, "is evidently a given item from a list which is being run through (either explicitly or implicitly)", whereas *Ronald* "is being brought in as new information to be paired with it" (1976:49).[13]

While Chafe's notion of contrast does, in fact, account for much of the preposing data, over half of the tokens in the corpus (469/915, or 51%) fail to satisfy the diagnostic Chafe provides for determining contrast. For example, consider (35), where it seems very unlikely that the speaker is asserting that one

[13]Chafe distinguishes between preposings with two foci of contrast, as in (34), and those with a single focus, which are termed 'focus preposings' in the present study.

little nuance in particular is the 'correct selection' from some set of little nuances, or that nuances are being 'paired' with anything:

(35) The only time the guy isn't considered a failure is when he resigns and announces his new job. That's the tipoff, "John Smith resigned, future plans unknown" means he was fired. "John Smith resigned to accept the position of president of X company" — then you know he resigned. *This little nuance you recognize immediately when you're in corporate life.*
[Terkel 1974:537]

Nonetheless, considering that almost half of all preposings satisfy Chafe's diagnostic, we see that contrast is relevant to topicalization, since it is doubtful that 50% of canonical-word-order sentences are contrastive in this way. However, an alternative, or at least an additional, explanation is necessary to account for the full range of data.

Clark & Clark (1977) analyze topicalization in terms of 'frame' and 'insert':

> When speakers place a particular phrase at the beginning of a sentence, they are deliberately trying to orient their listeners toward a particular area of knowledge — to give them a point of departure for the sentence. Speakers then use the rest of the sentence progressively to narrow down what they are trying to say. For this reason, the first phrase can be called a *frame*, and the remainder of the sentence an *insert* for that frame. (1977:34)

Clark & Clark claim that this distinction corresponds often, but not always, to both the subject-predicate distinction and that of given-new information. As an illustration of a case in which it does not, they offer the following example of (Gundel's) 'focus topicalization':

(36) Mr. Fields she met.
[=Clark & Clark 1977, ex. 52]

Clark & Clark observe that the predicate 'met Mr. Fields' in (36) is part given information ('met someone') and part new information ('Mr. Fields'). Moreover, the preposed constituent in (36) does not represent given information as does the subject NP. Thus, to distinguish sentences like (36) from canonical-word-order cases that do correspond to the given-new distinction, Clark & Clark designate the preposed element 'Mr. Fields' as the frame and the remainder of the sentence 'she met someone' as the insert.

However, they provide no indication as to how the preposed constituent *Mr. Fields* serves the frame function of 'orienting the hearer toward a particular area of knowledge'. Furthermore, it is not clear how the non-preposed version of (36), *She met Mr. Fields*, does not also orient the hearer toward the same area of knowledge. Moreover, when other data are considered, it is difficult to see how Clark & Clark's analysis can be maintained. Consider the topicalization in (37):

(37) But opinions about the reliability or accuracy of information can differ. Automobile companies, for instance, often resist attempts by consumer groups and governmental bodies to get them to recall vehicles for safety reasons. In general, they tend to disagree with the contention that the vehicles are unsafe. Yet, "*the vast majority of the recalls — about 90% — we do voluntarily*," said David Hudgens, a spokesman for General Motors Corp. *The other 10%, the companies sometimes do reluctantly.* [*Philadelphia Inquirer*, 7/26/84]

In this example, while it could conceivably be argued that the preposed constituent of the first preposing serves to direct the reader to the area of knowledge involving automobile recalls, it is not clear how the rest of the sentence — *we do voluntarily* — constitutes the 'insert'. In fact, it would seem that, if anything, it is the frame, and not the insert, that is performing Clark & Clark's 'narrowing down' function. Given the set of automobile recalls, the speaker is taking a subset of that set (90%) and predicating of that subset the proposition 'we do them voluntarily' while predicating of the remainder of that set (10%) that 'the companies do them reluctantly'.

Another non-topic based analysis of topicalization, and one that is closer in spirit to the approach taken in the current study, is Prince 1981b. Prince's analysis represents a marked departure from previous topic-based analyses in demonstrating that preposing is significantly more constrained in discourse than had previously been believed. First, Prince argues that the discourse entity represented by the preposed constituent must be related to other entities in the discourse in one of a limited number of ways. Second, Prince's analysis is the first in which a constraint is proposed involving the discourse-status of the entire proposition associated with the preposing — not just the preposed element.[14]

What Prince (and we) call 'topicalization' corresponds to Gundel's (1974) 'topic topicalization', and Chafe's (1976) 'multiple foci of contrast'. Prince argues that topicalization performs two simultaneous discourse functions. First, as noted above, Prince argues that topicalization marks an open proposition as salient in the discourse. Second, Prince claims that topicalization marks the entity represented by the preposed NP as being either already evoked in the discourse or else in a salient set relation with another discourse entity, the latter being itself evoked or inferrable from the discourse.[15]

This analysis of topicalization involving set relations is not unlike Chafe's analysis of preposing as some sort of pairing of items on a list for purposes of contrast, where Prince's 'set' corresponds to Chafe's 'list'. However, as Prince (1984) points out, contrast is not a *necessary* effect of topicalization, but "obtains just in case first, a list understanding is induced, and, second, a salient opposition is inferred in the new information of the [open proposition]" (1984:220). It does not follow from the salience of a set of entities that members of that set are being contrasted. Moreover, the entity represented by the preposed constituent in a topicalization is sometimes a singleton member of a posetand thus need not be interpreted with respect to other discourse entities.

While we draw heavily on Prince's condition regarding open propositions, we have identified a number of drawbacks to Prince's original formulation of the constraints on the preposed constituent. First, the disjunctive nature of her condition shows a lack of generalization: Why should evoked entities pattern like entities related by a set-relation inference? Second, her notion of 'set relation'

[14]Clark & Clark's (1977) 'frame-insert' distinction discussed above may also be viewed as involving the entire proposition, but no constraints are imposed on either the frame or the insert.

[15]Prince restricts her analysis of topicalization to preposed NPs.

was rather loosely construed to accommodate examples like those in (38):

(38) a. A: You know this album?
B: *This song I know.*
[conversation]

b. Fraternity president Jim Stewart said that Feher was having financial problems but that the problems had not seemed serious. "He was good at putting up a facade" that nothing was wrong, Stewart said, and added, "He couldn't deal with pressure. *Just the slightest pressure he found difficult to handle...*"
[*Philadelphia Inquirer*, 11/13/84]

c. R: If there're fewer than five students [waiting in line] then I guess we can start. How many are there?
T: Five.
R: *Five students we don't have to wait for. More than that we would.*
[R. Stockwell to T. Stowell in conversation]

In (38a), an album is not quite a set of songs; rather, it is a unitary object which has songs as parts. Similarly, to characterize the preposed superlative in (38b) — *just the slightest pressure* — as simply an unordered member of some set of pressures seems to underspecify the particular relationship that holds in this context. Finally, the relation between the two preposed links of (38c) — *five students* and *more than that* — does not seem one of simple set inclusion.

In the next section, a new analysis of topicalization is presented that can accommodate not only Prince's set-member relations but also a broad range of additional relations which will be shown to be possible between the discourse entity evoked by the preposed constituent and other salient entities in the discourse model. However, in the interest of not contributing to terminological proliferation, we shall retain the term 'topicalization' to refer to those preposings with non-preposed foci, irrespective of the type of linking relation that holds between the link and the anchoring poset.

General constraints

Topicalization (like preposing in general) requires that the link of the preposed constituent be related to the anchor by means of a contextually licensed linking relation. As initial evidence, consider first the constructed examples in (39), in which there exists no apparent link.

(39) a. Someone broke into the garage last night. *#My father I need to talk to.*

b. I'm really tired tonight. *#Maybe a movie I'll rent.*

In these examples, there is no plausible linking relation between the preposed constituent and the prior context. For instance, in the absence of additional information, there is no obvious poset relation between the speaker's father in (39a) and the garage. Indeed, an examination of 747 naturally occurring tokens of topicalization reveals that in all cases there is a salient linking relation that holds between the preposed constituent and the prior discourse. We have found five such linking relations to occur most frequently in discourse: set/subset, part/whole, type/subtype, greater-than/less-than, and identity. In Chapter 5, these relations will be examined in more detail.

As we have defined it, neither preposing in general, nor topicalization in particular, is limited to any particular phrasal category. Consider the examples of topicalization involving each of the four major lexical categories in (40):

(40) a. **NP**

Colonel Bykov had delivered to Chambers in Washington six Bokhara rugs which he directed Chambers to present as gifts from him and the Soviet Government to the members of the ring who had been most co-operative. *One of these rugs Chambers delivered to Harry Dexter White.* Another he gave to Hiss — but not as a routine "payment on rent." In the classic tradition of espionage operations, Hiss had parked his car on a street corner, and Chambers had driven to a point nearby.
[Nixon 1962:58]

b. **PP**

To back up Wattenberg's contention that American women are getting what they wanted — with or without the ERA, there are statistics offered, statistics about how many married women are now in the labor force, statistics about the number of women in "good" jobs. "With better jobs and more education," he writes, "women are also moving forward on the dollar front." *For that last bold assertion there are no statistics.* That's because they wouldn't back up the argument, not even a little.
[*Philadelphia Inquirer*, 6/1/83]

c. **VP**

And the end of the term I took my first schools; it was necessary to pass, if I was to stay at Oxford, *and pass I did*, after a week in which I forbade Sebastian my rooms and sat up to a late hour, with iced black coffee and charcoal biscuits, cramming myself with the neglected texts. I remember no syllable of them now, but the other, more ancient, lore which I acquired that term will be with me in one shape or another to my last hour.
[Waugh 1945:45]

d. **AP**

The plan is to purchase the quaint fishing village of Ferness and replace it with a giant new refinery. The villagers — who've been farming, fishing, raising families and pub crawling in splendid isolation for generations — offer amazingly little resistance. *Humble they may be. But daft they ain't.* If the Americans are all that eager to turn a few industrious Scotsmen into instant millionaires, they should not be denied the privilege.
[*Philadelphia Inquirer*]

In each of the above examples, a salient linking relation holds between the link of the preposed constituent and the anchoring poset. In (40a), for example, the linking relation is set/subset; the link *one of these rugs* is a member of the set of rugs evoked by the trigger (*six Bokhara rugs*) in the preceding utterance. In this example, the focused element is *Henry Dexter White*, which represents an element of the set of ring leaders evoked in the preceding discourse. In (40c), on the other hand, the link is the VP *pass*, which stands in a relation of identity with the anchoring poset.

Although all four major phrasal categories are represented in the corpus, topicalization involving preposed APs is the most constrained of the four. Nonetheless, AP topicalization is possible: An examination of the corpus reveals 17 such tokens. Interestingly, 12 of those 17 tokens (71%) occur as one of a pair of preposings functioning almost as a single utterance or 'information unit' in the sense of Halliday 1967.[16] For the other grammatical categories the reverse is true: The vast majority (419/529, or 79%) are neither preceded nor followed by another preposing. Upon closer examination, we find that the type of topicalization permitting preposed APs typically involves a salient set of two attributes, one of which is affirmed, the other denied, used in tandem to *evaluate* some salient discourse entity. Examples are provided in (41):

(41) a. "In the early days, our productions were cheap and cheerful," says producer John Weaver of London-based Keefco. "We'd go into a seven-light studio, shoot the band in one afternoon and edit as we went along. The client would walk out with a tape that day." Today's tapes may still be cheerful, *but cheap they are not.* The cost of an average video hovers between $35,000 and $45,000 but several performers have splurged lavishly. [=(1d)]

b. N: This is not another vulgar disgusting sexploitation film.
J: *Vulgar it's not. Dumb it is.* Did we see the same movie?
[J. Lyons to N. Gabler, reviewing "Valley Girls" on Sneak Previews]

c. The Philadelphia Fish & Co. is grilling fresh seafood soooooo good the competition is "broiling" mad... *Casual and affordable we are. Expensive we are not.*
[newspaper ad]

---

[16]This figure excludes a functionally distinct type of AP preposing involving the affirmation, suspension, or denial of propositions; see page 50ff.

In each of these examples, a posetcomprising at least two attributes is salient, either by having been evoked in the preceding discourse in the trigger, as in (41a), or by being inferentially related to some salient discourse entity via an entity/attribute relation, as in (41b). In each case, one (or more) of the attributes is affirmed, while another is denied. In (41c), for example, the links of the two preposings (*casual and affordable* and *expensive*) can be seen as representing members of a posetconsisting of the inferrable attributes associated with restaurants.

As noted above, AP topicalizations typically occur in pairs. Consider the examples in (41b)-(41c) with only a single AP topicalization:

(42) a. N: This is not another vulgar disgusting sexploitation film.
J: *#Dumb it is.* Did we see the same movie?

b. The Philadelphia Fish & Co. is grilling fresh seafood soooooo good the competition is "broiling" mad... *#Casual and affordable we are.*

Thus, it appears that AP topicalization is restricted to the explicit contrast of one anchoring poset member with another (not all of which need appear in preposed position). These contrasting attributes are not restricted to adjectives; predicate nominals may also represent contrasting attributes. Consider the following examples involving combinations of preposed APs and NPs:

(43) a. The ratings no doubt will show that some small number of Americans failed to escape and ended up watching the two-hour NBC "World Premiere Movie". *A premiere it may be, but new it's not.* This tale about seven people trapped in a crumbling cavern 300 ft. underground was made at an undetermined time in the 1970's, and wisely left on the shelf.
[*San Francisco Chronicle*, 6/18/83]

b. *Pretty they aren't. But a sweet golden grapefruit taste they have.*
[radio announcer on KYW radio station]

c. "The Killing Fields"
I keep hearing from people who should know better that this adaptation of Sydney Schanberg's article, set against the fall of Cambodia, is the greatest movie ever made. *Gruesome and gut-wrenching it certainly is, but a movie it certainly is not.* It may be all true, but it's not dramatic. There is no consistent point of view on the material.
[*Philadelphia City Paper*, 6/7/85]

These examples of multiple NP and AP topicalizations all involve clear senses of contrast, in the sense that one member of the inferred poset is affirmed while others are denied.[17] In (43c), for example, the trigger *the greatest movie ever made* along with the links *gruesome and gut-wrenching* and *a movie* license the creation of the poset{movie attributes}. Interestingly, a possible attribute of a movie is that it is not (subjectively) 'a movie', in the sense that a movie may be judged to lack certain quintessential properties of movies.

In the case of single AP topicalizations, all of the posetmembers must be explicitly evoked, as in (44):

(44) a. G: All my friends think she's wonderful and generous. Well, she's certainly generous...
H: *Wonderful you're not so sure about*?
[H. O'Neil to G. Ward in conversation]

b. G: I can't stand R. He's stupid, arrogant and totally off-the-wall.
B: *Stupid I wouldn't really say he is.*
[B. Schoenberg to G. Ward in conversation]

Here, a posetof attributes has been explicitly evoked in the context and the speaker is either questioning (as in (44a)) or denying (as in (44b)) one of them. What these data suggest is that AP topicalization is highly constrained in that the members of the attribute poset must be explicitly evoked in the discourse, either in the prior discourse or by the speaker him/herself via multiple topicalizations.

[17]As we will see, NP topicalization involving non-attribute links are less constrained in not requiring any explicit contrast among posetmembers.

Proposition assessment

A more constrained type of topicalization involves the assessment of a proposition's truth value in discourse. We have identified three such types of 'proposition assessment', i.e., three ways in which a speaker may assess a salient or inferrable proposition via preposing. The first two, 'proposition affirmation' and 'proposition suspension', require an explicitly evoked trigger with which the link stands in a relation of identity. That is, the anchor, link and trigger are all coreferential. The third type of proposition assessment, 'proposition denial', involves an inferrable attribute that has typically not been explicitly evoked in the prior context; this type of preposing is generally used for ironic effect.

Proposition affirmation

As argued in Ward 1990, a preposing may be used to affirm a speaker's belief in a proposition explicitly evoked in the discourse. A speaker can be said to affirm a proposition when he or she explicitly commits him- or herself to its truth, as in (45):

(45) At the end of the term I took my first schools; it was necessary to pass, if I was to stay at Oxford, *and pass I did*, after a week in which I forbade Sebastian my rooms and sat up to a late hour, with iced black coffee and charcoal biscuits, cramming myself with the neglected texts. [=(40c)]

As with canonical word order, such propositions are affirmed via the auxiliary element *tense*. If no tense-bearing modal or auxiliary verb is present, then periphrastic *do* supports *tense* in these environments.

In all of the tokens in the corpus, the preposed constituent of proposition affirmation — like preposing in general — serves as a link to the previous discourse. Indeed, the preposed constituent of proposition affirmation must represent (at least part of) a proposition that has been explicitly evoked in the prior context. What distinguishes proposition affirmation and suspension from the other types of preposing is the explicit nature of the anaphoric relation that must obtain. While other types of preposing allow the link to be only implicitly related to the trigger, proposition affirmation and suspension require that the anchor be *explicitly* evoked in the preceding discourse.

Previous accounts of the discourse functions of proposition affirmation (or proposition assessment in general) fail to distinguish it from other preposing constructions (e.g., Hooper & Thompson 1973, Langacker 1974); thus, the specific function of proposition affirmation itself has generally been overlooked.[18] While it will be shown that proposition affirmation does perform the same discourse functions as topicalization in general, its particular discourse functions are more specialized.

Different types of proposition affirmation may be distinguished, depending on the rhetorical relationship that holds between the evoked and affirmed propositions. As argued in Ward 1988 and 1990, one type of proposition affirmation is used for 'logically independent' propositions, i.e. those propositions whose truth is neither semantically entailed by nor presupposed in the prior discourse (Horn 1991). Another type of proposition affirmation is used for propositions that stand in 'rhetorical opposition' to another proposition conceded in the prior discourse (Horn 1991). We shall refer to these two types of proposition affirmation as 'logically independent proposition affirmation' and 'concessive proposition affirmation', respectively. A third type, which we will call 'scalar affirmation', involves the affirmation of a proposition, logically independent *or* dependent, whose predicate is construable as a scale upon which the (referent of the) subject is assigned a high value.

Examples of these three types are provided in (46a)-(46c), respectively. For ease of exposition, we will henceforth refer to the sentence that evokes the relevant proposition as $\mathbf{S_1}$, to the evoked proposition as **p**, and to the sentence that affirms **p** as $\mathbf{S_2}$. In these and all subsequent examples of proposition affirmation, $\mathbf{S_1}$ is in SMALL CAPS (where it is not the only preceding sentence) and $\mathbf{S_2}$ is in *italics*.

(46) a. As members of a Gray Panthers committee, WE WENT TO CANADA TO LEARN, *and learn we did.* We learned the amazing contrast of the philosophy of our neighbor to the North that health care must be and is free and universal, whereas in the United States,

[18]One major exception is Horn 1991, which will be discussed in more detail below.

where we often mistakenly believe we have the best health system around, 35 million people — 15 percent of our population — lack health insurance coverage, according to the Census Bureau. [*Philadelphia Inquirer*, 6/16/85]

b. Waiting in long lines can be infuriating. Waiting in long lines to pay someone else money seems unconscionable. WAITING IN LONG LINES TO PAY SOMEONE ELSE MORE MONEY THAN THEY SEEM TO BE ENTITLED TO IS LUNACY. *But wait in line they did Monday in Chicago and the Cook County suburbs*, partaking in the semi-annual ritual of settling up property taxes by the 6 p.m. deadline. [*Chicago Tribune*, 8/8/89]

c. Asked what he thought about during today's race on a sultry day, [Tour de France winner Greg LeMond] said: "I didn't think. I JUST RODE." *Ride he did.* LeMond won the time trial easily, finishing 33 seconds faster than Thierry Marie, a Frenchman, who was timed in 27:30.
[*New York Times*, 7/23/89]

These three types of proposition affirmation will be discussed in turn.

Logically independent proposition affirmation. Logically independent proposition affirmation involves the affirmation of an explicitly evoked proposition whose truth is neither semantically entailed nor presupposed by the prior discourse. The examples in (47) are of this type:

(47) a. IT WAS NECESSARY TO PASS, if I was to stay at Oxford, *and pass I did...* [=(45)]

b. As members of a Gray Panthers committee, WE WENT TO CANADA TO LEARN, *and learn we did.* [=(46a)]

c. Anti-U.S. feelings run high in Nicaragua, and a rally Nov. 7 in Managua, the capital, provided an opportunity to whip up more

fervor. 'IF YOU DON'T JUMP,' the Sandinistas yell, 'you're a contra,' *and jump they do*.
[*Philadelphia Inquirer*, 12/18/83]

In (47a), **p** — 'I passed' — is first evoked by S_1, interpretable as 'It was necessary (for me) to pass', and then affirmed by S_2 (*and pass I did*). Having to pass an exam does not of course guarantee that one in fact will pass; thus, **p** does not follow from S_1. The affirmation of the logically independent proposition explicitly commits the speaker/writer to that proposition, which is itself evoked but not entailed by S_1. In (47b), the proposition 'we learn' is first evoked by S_1 — *We went to Canada to learn* — and then affirmed by the preposing in S_2 (*and learn we did*). Parallel to (47a), **p** does not follow from S_1: Going someplace to learn does not guarantee that learning will occur. Again, affirmation of **p** with the preposing in (47b) serves to commit the speaker explicitly to an evoked, yet unasserted, proposition. Similarly, in (47c), the proposition 'they jump' is evoked by the negative antecedent of a conditional: *If you don't jump*. Given that a conditional alone does not entail either of its terms, the proposed constraints on independent proposition affirmation are satisfied; S_2 then serves to felicitously affirm the evoked proposition.[19]

Concessive proposition affirmation. A second type of proposition affirmation involves a proposition evoked by S_1 in the context of some countervailing consideration that is conceded in the prior discourse.[20] This type of 'concessive' proposition affirmation is associated with the presence of an adversative discourse connective preceding the preposing, typically *but* or *yet*. Consider (46b), repeated in part below, in which **p** 'they wait in line' is affirmed with *but* after a list of three concessions:

[19]Given that the conditional in (47c) is of the form $\neg\, \mathbf{p} \rightarrow \mathbf{q}$, and given that S_2 affirms the *negation* of the antecedent, i.e. **p**, nothing can be deduced about **q**. However, as is well known, denying the antecedent can implicate the negation of the consequent. So one may infer that the jumpers in (47c) are in fact *not* contras.

[20]The countervailing consideration is typically, but not necessarily, provided in S_1 itself.

(48) Waiting in long lines can be infuriating. Waiting in long lines to pay someone else money seems unconscionable. WAITING IN LONG LINES TO PAY SOMEONE ELSE MORE MONEY THAN THEY SEEM TO BE ENTITLED TO IS LUNACY. *But wait in line they did Monday in Chicago and the Cook County suburbs...* [=(46b)]

That is, despite the fact that waiting in long lines might be infuriating, unconscionable, and even lunatic, depending on the reasons, people in Cook County nonetheless did it. In this way, the preposing in (48) serves to affirm **p** in the presence of countervailing considerations.

As with independent proposition affirmation, the affirmed proposition of concessive affirmation may involve a logically independent proposition (e.g. **p** in (48)). However, this need not be the case; concessive affirmation may also involve a proposition that is entailed or presupposed in the preceding discourse. From a semantic point of view, such a logically dependent proposition is, strictly speaking, redundant, in that its truth has already been established in the discourse.[21] However, as Horn 1991 points out, the affirmation of a logically dependent proposition is not necessarily redundant "provided that it is rhetorically opposed to the content of the first clause" (1991:334). It is this rhetorical opposition between what is conceded and what is affirmed that "motivat[es] the *but* connective and alleviat[es] the redundancy of the clause it introduces" (1991:325). As Levinson notes (1983:120), such an interpretation can be analyzed as a case of Gricean conversational implicature (Grice 1975, 1978). By affirming a logically dependent, and prima facie redundant, proposition **p**, a speaker can flout the maxim of quantity and implicate that 'more than **p**' is intended; in this case, 'more than **p**' corresponds to the rhetorical opposition Horn (1991) notes in connection with proposition affirmation (cf. Horn's 1991 discussion of 'redundant affirmation' and his 'division of pragmatic labor'). Consider (49), in which $\mathbf{S_1}$ presupposes **p** ('he learned her story'):

(49) While he and his mother had often talked about writing her story, he went on, 'the mundane things we do with our lives' had prevented them. IT

[21] This of course assumes a semantics based on truth conditions.

> WAS IRONIC, HE CONTINUED, THAT HE EVENTUALLY LEARNED MORE FROM HIS MOTHER'S PAPERS AND TAPES THAN HE HAD DIRECTLY FROM HER. *But learn her story he did*, and the article is not only her story, about what she and other Jews endured, it is also his story, about the fragile process by which memory is kept alive.
> [*Philadelphia Inquirer*, 5/6/83]

In rhetorical opposition to **p**, which is presupposed in $\mathbf{S_1}$, the speaker in this example concedes the irony of learning more from indirect sources than from direct ones. With the preposing in $\mathbf{S_2}$, the speaker then (re)affirms with concessive affirmation that his mother's story was nonetheless learned — irrespective of the fact that the truth of the proposition has already been established in the prior discourse. Therefore, **p** is not redundant, because the rhetorical opposition present provides additional (inferred) information in context.

Other examples of concessive affirmation are provided in (50):

(50) a. Series EE and HH savings bonds are what the government sells to consumers. In today's inflationary age, they are absolute rip-offs. ONE WONDERS HOW GOVERNMENT OFFICIALS CAN SLEEP AT NIGHT, TAKING WIDOWS' AND ORPHANS' MONEY and paying 6.5% while inflation is running 10% and even the banks are offering 10-15%, albeit on a limited basis through their certificates of deposit. *Yet sell the bonds they do.*
[Donoghue 1981:13-14.]

b. My [Ed Koch's] administration doesn't tolerate violations of the law by developers or anyone else. Twelve extra floors somehow got added to a new building on East 96th Street. THE DEVELOPERS EITHER COULDN'T COUNT OR THEY DIDN'T COUNT ON THE CITY ENFORCING THE LAW. *But enforce the law we did all the way to the United States Supreme Court* — and we won!
[*New York Times*, 8/25/89]

In each of these examples, **p** is affirmed by $\mathbf{S_2}$ despite some countervailing consideration in the prior discourse. In (50a), government officials are said to be selling bonds despite their being 'absolute rip-offs', while in (50b) former New York City mayor Ed Koch reports that real estate developers in Manhattan didn't expect the Koch administration to enforce the city's height restrictions. In these examples of concessive affirmation, and indeed in all of the examples of concessive affirmation in the corpus, the preposing in **S2** is introduced with a conjunction of concession, either *but* or *yet*. As noted by Horn (1991), without such a conjunction, concessive affirmation is infelicitous.[22] Consider, for example, the effect of replacing *yet* in (50a) with a nonconcessive conjunction:

(51) Series EE and HH savings bonds are what the government sells to consumers. In today's inflationary age, they are absolute rip-offs. ONE WONDERS HOW GOVERNMENT OFFICIALS CAN SLEEP AT NIGHT, TAKING WIDOWS' AND ORPHANS' MONEY and paying 6.5% while inflation is running 10% and even the banks are offering 10-15%, albeit on a limited basis through their certificates of deposit. *#And sell the bonds they do.*

Concessive affirmation can therefore be seen as the intersection of two distinct discourse functions: the function of the adversative connective, which signals concession, and the function of the preposing, which conveys affirmation.[23]

Finally, consider (52), where **S1** evokes **p**, 'Tchaikovsky produced music':

(52) Tchaikovsky was one of the most tormented men in musical history. In fact, ONE WONDERS HOW HE MANAGED TO PRODUCE ANY MUSIC AT ALL. *But produce music he did.*

Following Karttunen 1973, inter alia, we assume that *manage* involves an entailment relation, such that 'NP managed to VP' entails 'NP VPd' while implicating that 'to VP' involved difficulty. Furthermore, following Levinson 1983, inter alia, we assume that indirect *wh*-questions involve a presupposition obtained

[22]Of course, if the relevant proposition is also logically independent, as in (48), then independent proposition affirmation is possible (with or without a conjunction of concession). The claim here applies only to cases of concessive affirmation involving logically *dependent* propositions, i.e. those whose truth has already been established in the discourse.

[23]On the discourse function of sentence connectives, see van Dijk 1977, Warner 1985, and Schiffrin 1987, inter alia.

by replacing the *wh*-word (i.e. *how* in (52)) with the appropriate existentially quantified variable. Thus, by uttering $\mathbf{S_1}$, the speaker in (52) presupposes that Tchaikovsky managed to produce music somehow, and concedes that it was difficult for him to do so. By means of the preposing in $\mathbf{S_2}$, then, the speaker affirms that Tchaikovsky produced music despite his being 'one of the most tormented men in musical history'. In this way, **p** is affirmed even though **p** has already been established with $\mathbf{S_1}$.[24]

Scalar affirmation. The third type of proposition affirmation involves the affirmation of a proposition whose predicate is construable as a scale upon which the referent of the subject is assigned a high value. As with concessive proposition affirmation, the proposition affirmed under scalar affirmation may be either dependent or independent. Consider the examples in (53):

(53) a. Asked what he thought about during today's race on a sultry day, [Tour de France winner Greg LeMond] said: 'I didn't think. I JUST RODE.' *Ride he did.* LeMond won the time trial easily, finishing 33 seconds faster than Thierry Marie, a Frenchman, who was timed in 27:30. [=(46c)]

b. Led by police cars with flashing lights and trailed by other vehicles and more police, the seven cyclists were carefully watched for about the first three weeks of their journey [across the Soviet Union]. Neither the Soviets nor the Americans knew how to get rid of the police "shadows." "THEY STOPPED WHEN WE HIT THE MUD," Jenkins said. *And hit mud they did.* And swamps. And paths so small they could barely be followed.
[*Chicago Tribune*, 10/21/89]

c. "This is one of the things that symbolizes the best Evanston has to offer," David Bradford, chairman of the Evanston Human Relations Commissions, said at a public hearing Saturday. "PEOPLE

[24]See Horn 1991 for a discussion of other cases of concessive affirmation (involving canonical word order) in which entailed and presupposed material may be felicitously (i.e. nonredundantly) affirmed.

WILL COME OUT AND TALK ABOUT THINGS." *And talk they did.* For five hours more than 150 residents, police officers and officials, community leaders and politicians filled to capacity the City Council chambers in a public hearing entitled "Crime, The Police and The Community."
[*Chicago Tribune*, 7/17/96]

In these examples, the speaker (in each case, a newspaper reporter) is affirming a proposition that has been uttered by the person about whom the reporter is writing. However, the proposition ($\mathbf{S_1}$) in each case occurs in the context of a direct quotation; it is simply a reported assertion with the reporter taking no stance on its truth. By means of proposition affirmation, the reporter not only explicitly affirms the truth of the proposition, but also conveys that it is true *to a greater extent* than originally reported. That is, proposition affirmation induces a scalar interpretation whereby the entity represented by the subject is assigned a high value on a scale corresponding to the (preposed) predicate. Consider again the examples in (53). In (53a), affirmation conveys more than simply the reporter's belief in the proposition 'he rode'; here, the description of *how* LeMond rode suggests that if a scale of bicycle riding were constructed, based on either skill or racing time, LeMond would be assigned a high value on that scale. Similarly, in the case of (53b), we infer that the reporter believes there was an inordinate amount of mud obstructing the cyclists' path, and in (53c), the reader is licensed to infer that the degree of talking was extraordinary in some sense. Indeed, as the ensuing description reveals, the length of the public hearing (5 hours) and number of people present (150) lends credence to such a scalar interpretation.

It is precisely this exclamative, scalar interpretation that renders the affirmation of a previously asserted proposition informative. As noted earlier for concessive affirmation, this additional interpretation can be analyzed as a flouting of Grice's maxim of quantity: A speaker's redundant affirmation of a proposition **p** can implicate that 'more than **p**' is intended. In this case, 'more than **p**' corresponds to the exclamative interpretation associated with scalar proposition affirmation. It is not surprising, then, that, in the absence of rhetorical opposition, the affirmation of logically dependent propositions is infelicitous when the predicate expressed by **S_1** does not allow a scalar interpretation. Compare (54a) and (54b):

(54) a. I am so proud of Andy for getting a hundred on his exam. *#And get a hundred he did* — it was the highest grade in the class!

b. I am so proud of Andy for passing his exam. *And pass he did* — he got a hundred!

In (54a), **p** ('Andy got a hundred') is presupposed by **S_1**, and is thus logically dependent on it. However, the predicate *get a hundred* expressed by **S_1** does not lend itself to an interpretation as a scale. That is, it is difficult to imagine how one could be assigned a high value on a scale of 'getting a hundred'. With nothing additional to affirm, proposition affirmation is infelicitous in this context. In (54b), where the predicate *pass* does permit a scalar interpretation, scalar affirmation is fully felicitous. Of course, in a logically independent proposition affirmation context, as in (55), the preposing in (54a) is rendered fully felicitous:

(55) Andy claims he got a hundred on his exam. *And get a hundred he did.*

Here **p** is logically independent of **S_1**, licensing the affirmation.

Such scalar interpretations are also possible with the affirmation of logically independent propositions, as in (56):

(56) Kenny Rogers had asked his fans to bring cans to his concerts to feed the hungry in the area. *And bring cans they did.*
[TV news broadcast, 8/29/84]

Here, the proposition affirmed by the preposing in **S_2** is logically independent of **S_1** in that it does not follow from one's being asked to do something that one will in fact do it. However, in addition to the affirmation of **p**, **S_2** here invites a scalar interpretation, i.e. that Kenny Rogers' fans brought an extraordinarily large numbers of cans to the concert.[25] Thus, for logically independent propositions,

[25]Oral tokens of scalar affirmation are generally produced with increased pitch range and nuclear accent on the auxiliary element, attesting to their exclamative nature. Levinson in

all three kinds of affirmation are possible: scalar, non-scalar, and concessive; for logically dependent propositions, whose truth is not at issue, only concessive or scalar affirmation is possible.

Up to now, we have only considered examples of proposition affirmation with preposed VPs. However, this function is not restricted to preposed VPs; consider the examples of preposed AP and NP predicates in (57) and (58), respectively:

(57) a. 'The record store as you know it today won't exist in 5 years,' he says. 'There's not enough profit margin for them to survive. THE REASON I WENT INTO RENTING RECORDS IN THE FIRST PLACE WAS TO PUT US IN A BUSINESS THAT WAS SOLVENT.' *And solvent it is.* Record-renting outfits buy their albums from distributors for about $5.50, rent the LP's two to five times at a price ranging from 99 cents to $2, and then sell the record for $4 to $6.
[*Philadelphia Inquirer*]

b. 'Our hearts are heavy that prayer has become a controversial and divisive issue.' *Controversial it is.*
["ABC World News Tonight"]

(58) a. It's hard to imagine that this tropical little island [Grenada] was a battleground, *but a battleground it was.*
["ABC World News Tonight"]

b. [The hit] gave the Cubs a chance to have a big inning, *and a big inning they had.*
[WGN Cubs Sportscaster, 9/21/89]

---

fact notes that logically dependent propositions may be felicitously reinforced, "but only if the reinforcing phrase contains heavy stress..." (1983:120). However, consider (i)a-b, where accent alone does not render the reinforcement of the logically dependent proposition felicitous, regardless of word order:

(i)a. #John managed to win and he *did* win.

b. #John managed to win and win he *did.*

Moreover, 'heavy stress' (i.e. nuclear accent) is also possible, and in fact common, in cases of logically *independent* proposition affirmation; thus accent alone is not a sufficient condition for felicitous scalar affirmation.

It is clear that these examples with preposed AP and NP predicates are functionally equivalent to preposed VPs. In (57a), for example, the record salesman states (in $\mathbf{S_1}$) that he wanted to put himself into a solvent business. Of course, it does not follow from this that his business would actually *be* solvent, hence the felicitous use of the AP preposing in $\mathbf{S_2}$ to affirm this proposition. With the NP preposing in (58a) the newscaster affirms **p** ('Grenada was a battleground') despite the countervailing consideration that Grenada is (merely) a 'tropical little island'.

Before we turn to the second type of proposition assessment, it should be noted that the construction can also be used to affirm propositions that do not involve morphological identity; however, some kind of morphological relation is required. Consider the example in (59):

(59) On a recent sun-splashed Saturday afternoon at American University, a Coors beer truck lumbered up to the campus amphitheater where about a thousand students were taking in a rock concert. INSIDE THE COORS TRUCK WAS BEER FOR THE STUDENTS' CONSUMPTION. *Consume they did* — not only 15 kegs of beer, which they guzzled like soda pop, but also the free Coors posters which they seized as works of art to adorn their dorm walls.
[*Philadelphia Inquirer*, 10/7/83]

Here, the preposing in $\mathbf{S_2}$ (*Consume they did*) is used to affirm a proposition which is logically independent of the nominal in $\mathbf{S_1}$ (*the students' consumption*); however, the morphological relation between the derived nominal in $\mathbf{S_1}$ and the verb in $\mathbf{S_2}$ allows us to consider the former as 'explicitly evoking' the latter. Consider the effect of substituting a morphologically distinct near-synonym for *consume*:

(60) Inside the Coors truck was beer for the students' consumption. *#Drink they did...*

In fact, no matter how close the semantic relation between $\mathbf{S_1}$ and the affirmed proposition in $\mathbf{S_2}$, the lack of a morphological relation between the two will render the proposition affirmation infelicitous, as the examples in (61) show:

(61) a. John didn't mean to insult his aunt. *#But upset her he did.*

b. I told my boss I was going to quit today. *#And resign I did.*

c. Betty was exhausted after staying up all night. *#So take a nap she did.*

Note that these examples of proposition affirmation are felicitous in canonical word order. Thus, the requirement that the proposition affirmed via proposition affirmation be explicitly evoked in the discourse seems to tolerate differences in surface morphological form, but, in the absence of any morphological relation, disallows both close synonyms and simple pragmatic inferences. No other English preposing construction is similarly constrained.

Proposition suspension

The second type of proposition assessment involves the suspension of a speaker's commitment to an explicitly evoked proposition. Crucial to proposition suspension is the presence of the connective *if*, which, as we shall see, serves both to introduce and to conditionalize the preposing. In contrast to proposition affirmation, the evoked proposition must be logically dependent on the preceding discourse. Consider first the suspended entailment in (62a), and the suspended presupposition in (62b):

(62) a. Mark submitted his report late, *if submit it he did.*

b. It's odd that Diane said that, *if say it she did.*

In both of these examples, the speaker suspends a commitment to **p**, which follows from $\mathbf{S_1}$, while maintaining a belief, expressed in $\mathbf{S_1}$, that a particular condition attaches to **p**.

In his dissertation, Horn notes (1972:14) that in the case of presuppositions involving quantifiers (e.g. *only* and *even*), 'a presupposition may be suspended only if the resulting sentence may be true in a wider range of cases than is the initial sentence with its presupposition intact.' This principle can be straightforwardly extended to cover cases of proposition suspension. Consider, for example, the suspended proposition in (62a) above. The preposing in $\mathbf{S_2}$ serves to conditionalize **p** and $\mathbf{S_1}$, resulting in 'If Mark submitted his report, then he submitted it late'. This conditional is of course true if the antecedent is false, irrespective of the truth of the consequent. Therefore, even if **p** is false — that is, if Mark did *not* submit his report — the entire conditional ($\mathbf{p} \rightarrow \mathbf{S_1}$) is still true. Under the same circumstances, the nonsuspended 'Mark submitted his report late' would be truth-valueless in light of the failed presupposition. Proposition suspension thus serves to suspend a proposition, pace Horn, such that the resulting conditional is true in a wider range of circumstances than (the proposition corresponding to) $\mathbf{S_1}$ alone with the presupposition intact.

In more recent work, Horn (1991) claims that 'a presupposition will be felicitously suspended, filtered, or reinforced just in case its content is rhetorically — and in particular argumentatively — distinct from the presupposing clause'. In this way, Horn attempts to provide a unified account of felicitous presupposition suspension and reinforceability: Both are possible only in the context of rhetorical opposition. However, it would appear that presupposition suspension, unlike presupposition reinforceability, is in fact possible even in the absence of any rhetorical opposition. Consider the examples in (63):

(63) a. I'm pleased that dogs eat cheese, *if eat cheese they do*. [cf. Horn 1991, ex. 21a]

b. I know why Ellen said that, *if say it she did*. [cf. Horn 1991, ex. 21c]

The felicity of these examples, if felicitous they are, is problematic for Horn's conditions under which a presupposition may be suspended or reinforced, since the suspension of the presuppositions in (63) occurs in the absence of any rhetorical opposition. As evidence that rhetorical opposition is absent in these examples, consider substituting the contrastive reinforcer *but* for the suspender *if*:

(64) a. I'm pleased that DOGS EAT CHEESE, *#but eat cheese they do.*

b. I realize that ELLEN SAID THAT, *#but say it she did.*

From the infelicity of *but* in these examples — Horn's crucial diagnostic for rhetorical opposition — we can conclude that felicitous proposition suspension requires no rhetorical opposition.

Other examples of felicitous suspensions involving propositions that are logically dependent, yet not rhetorically opposed, are provided in (65):

(65) a. OJ killed his wife with a blunt object, *if kill her he did.*

b. John drinks alone, *if drink he does.*

c. Barbara stole the money for Pat, *if steal it she did.*

In each of these examples, the suspended proposition is entailed by $\mathbf{S_1}$. The suspended proposition of $\mathbf{S_2}$ serves as an antecedent to a conditional of which $\mathbf{S_1}$ is the consequent. Proposition suspension serves to render the entire conditional true even when **p** is false; without the suspension, $\mathbf{S_1}$ would be false in this situation. When $\mathbf{S_1}$ contains no propositional content distinct from that of **p**, infelicity results, as seen in (66):

(66) a. OJ killed his wife, *#if kill her he did.*

b. John drinks, *#if drink he does.*

c. Barbara stole the money, *#if steal it she did.*

When $\mathbf{S_1}$ and **p** are nondistinct, there is nothing for the preposing of $\mathbf{S_2}$ to suspend that would not also include all that is asserted by $\mathbf{S_1}$. Thus, examples like those in (66) constitute logical tautologies and, as such, are uninformative. These examples of infelicitous proposition suspension correspond to the infelicitous example of scalar affirmation in (54a) above: In neither case does $\mathbf{S_2}$ contribute any new information to the discourse. Thus, felicitous proposition affirmation and suspension both require that $\mathbf{S_1}$ and $\mathbf{S_2}$ be distinct; in the case of suspension, $\mathbf{S_1}$ must convey more than is suspended by $\mathbf{S_2}$, while in the case of affirmation, $\mathbf{S_2}$ must affirm more than is conveyed by $\mathbf{S_1}$. We may conclude that proposition suspension, then, is in fact sensitive to Horn's earlier (1972) principle of felicitous suspension, i.e. that presuppositions are suspended only in the direction of increased universality.[26]

[26]On the basis of various syntactic and semantic differences, Horn (1972) distinguishes between 'true antecedent-of-conditional' *if* clauses (of the sort involved in proposition suspension) and what he calls 'suspender *if* clauses', (e.g. *if at all*, *if anyone*). Though there may be differences,

Proposition denial

Proposition denial, used by speakers to deny a salient proposition in the discourse for ironic effect, is the most constrained type of proposition assessment. In cases of proposition denial involving understatement, or *meiosis*, an ironic interpretation results, in part, from the use of the preposed word order itself. That is, such preposing induces an ironic interpretation which would not necessarily be induced by the corresponding non-preposed utterance. Our account is based, in part, on Sperber & Wilson's (1986) analysis of irony as a type of 'echoic mention'.

First consider the examples of proposition denial provided in (67):

(67) a. When Erving threw down a flying jam, Iavaroni and Mark McNamara exchanged grinning high-fives of delight at the end of the bench. And during a timeout, Iavaroni leaped from his seat to lead cheers with a Joe College burst of "Let's go, Red!" *A jaded pro, he is not.* After seven months of being exposed to his excitability and enthusiasm, the Sixers don't even blink anymore at his verbal gusts.
[*Philadelphia Inquirer*, 4/26/83]

b. *The average American family of four they are not.* But for one week the Secretary of Agriculture tried to live like one.
["ABC World News Tonight"]

c. And Lee Corso, the former Indiana football coach, is simply miscast in the broadcast booth. An example of Corso's inappropriate efforts at analyzing came earlier in the season when, listening to boos at Giants Stadium, he informed viewers that "you couldn't pay me to coach" the Generals. Corso's enthusiasm also seems to lack purpose; *John Madden he's not.*
[*New York Times*, 5/3/83]

Horn is mistaken in claiming that antecedent *if* clauses do not serve to suspend presuppositions and entailments; indeed, this analysis demonstrates that the suspension accomplished by such clauses follows straightforwardly from Horn's 1972 analysis.

d. The NBA's new collective-bargaining agreement sounds as though it was written by the same people who put together the Internal Revenue Service's long form. *Simple it is not.*
[*The Arizona Republic*, 4/3/83]

e. *Light as a feather this bird is not.* The small rock hopper, being weighed by a keeper at the zoo in Duisburg, W. Germany, tips the scales at more than a pound. Standing in the, er, wings, is a group of penguins waiting their turn. Various birds and animals were weighed for record-keeping purposes.
[*Philadelphia Inquirer*, 2/21/83; caption]

f. *Like Clockwork It Wasn't...* [series of photos]
In the course of his duties, William P. Clark, the President's national security adviser, dispatches carrier groups and thousands of troops to Central America and other distant points without a hitch. Yesterday morning, however, he had difficulty dispatching himself from the Capitol, where he had appeared for a closed Senate briefing on Central America, to the White House. His limousine was mysteriously missing.
[*New York Times*, 7/28/83]

First, note that the preposed predicate of proposition denial is in each case an NP (as in (67a)-(67c)), an AP (as in (67d)-(67e)), or, more rarely, a PP (as in (67f)).[27] In fact, preposed VPs are grammatically excluded from proposition denial, as evidenced in (68):

(68) A: How's your new boss?
B: **Win a popularity contest he wouldn't.*

Second, note that the examples in (67) are all evaluative in that they express a subjective — often negative — opinion on the part of the speaker. Furthermore, they are intended to be amusing; informants tend to characterize preposings of

[27] The pragmatic difference between proposition denial with preposed NPs and APs and other (structurally identical) types of NP and AP topicalization is discussed below.

this type as 'colorful' or 'sarcastic', and some even comment that they sound 'Yiddish'.[28]

In what follows, we demonstrate how this type of preposing is both related to and distinct from the other types of preposing discussed earlier. Specifically, we will argue that proposition denial is used to evaluate a salient entity in the discourse with respect to some evoked or inferrable attribute. The 'humorous tone' or 'colorful quality' usually associated with proposition denial results from its discourse function of conveying irony in such evaluative contexts. This discourse function can be accounted for in a straightforward fashion by appealing to the general theory of irony presented in Sperber & Wilson 1986.

As evidenced by examples (67a) through (67e), the link in a proposition denial stands in a salient entity/attribute poset relation to the discourse trigger. In each of these examples, the speaker may be said to be evaluating the referent of the subject NP with respect to the attribute represented by the preposed constituent; the attribute in question must either be explicitly mentioned or inferrable. Consider (69), where the relevant attribute, in this case 'physical appearance', is neither evoked nor inferrable:

(69) A: I don't think the TV repairman knows what he's doing.

a. B_1: #Handsome he's not.

b. B_2: #A sex symbol he's not.

c. B_3: #Mel Gibson he's not.

In the context of A's statement, one is hard-pressed to see how the repairman's physical appearance is relevant to the discussion of his ability to repair television sets. Compare A's utterance in (69) with that in (70):

(70) A: The TV repairman keeps looking in the mirror.

[28] In *Hooray for Yiddish!*, Rosten claims that preposings of this type are used "for purposes of irony or emphasis" (1982:21). While the full extent of the Yiddish substratum effect remains unknown, we do know that Yiddish-influenced English differs from the standard language in certain respects; see the discussion of Yiddish-movement on page 90ff.

In response to this utterance, any of B's responses in (69) would be felicitous; from A's comment about the TV repairman looking in the mirror, the relevant attribute can be inferred.

It is rare for the relevant attribute of proposition denial to be explicitly evoked; it is far more likely to be inferred on the basis of the prior discourse, as in (71):

(71) a. I shall also long cherish Mickey Rooney's appearance to receive a special Oscar in recognition of his 60 years as a performer. *Humble he wasn't*, but why should he be? As he told us rather curtly, he'd been the world's biggest box office star at 19 and, at 40, unable to get work. As he accepted the award as his due, he also named all of the other awards he'd received recently, just in case the academy members thought they were doing him a favor. [*New York Times*, 4/17/83]

b. Lately [immigrants to LA] have seemed to hanker not so much for jobs as for a sunny, sexy LA way of life, as have the growing number of French and British. The international hordes now streaming in from the west and south have, in contrast, no-nonsense ideas about what they want: a chance to work hard and make money. *Laid back they are not*. The newcomers seem almost eager to endure adversity in pursuit of their American dreams, not unlike the teeming masses at the turn of the century. [*Time*, 6/13/83]

In (71a), we can assume the speaker believes that recipients of special Oscars generally possess the attribute 'humility'. The link *humble* thus represents one of the inferrable attributes associated with such individuals. In (71b), it is not unreasonable to expect Los Angeles inhabitants to possess the attribute 'laid-back', given the well-known stereotypes about California in general, and Los Angeles in particular.

It is also possible for the link itself, in combination with the prior discourse, to license the inference to the relevant attribute. Consider the preposed indefinite NPs in (72):

(72) a. But why is life like a glass of tea, you ask. As the old joke goes: How should I know? *A philosopher I'm not.*
[*New York Times* movie review]

b. *A saint I'm not,* Miss Jones, but I do have a heart.
[from the comic strip "Juliet Jones"; a woman involved in an embezzlement scheme, now remorseful, decides to help Juliet Jones prevent the crime.]

c. *An Eagle Scout he ain't.*
["M*A*S*H"; Trapper John is trying to return a Korean girl to her family, which keeps selling her to American soldiers. He arranges to meet with her 'manager', who turns out to be her twelve-year-old brother. Trapper John's first glimpse of him is one in which he is smoking a cigar, sipping a martini, and cursing.]

In these examples, the attribute with respect to which the referent is being evaluated must be inferred on the basis of not only the prior context but also the link itself. In (72a), the speaker's meaning-of-life query 'Why is life like a glass of tea?' creates the expectation that the speaker will go on to answer the question, and is thus in possession of the attribute 'wise'. A non-referential interpretation of the link *a philosopher*, in conjunction with the aforementioned query, evokes this attribute and relates it to the set of philosopher attributes. Similarly, in (72b), the link *a saint* exemplifies the attribute 'saintliness' or 'goodness' which Miss Jones expects at least herself to possess. In (72c), one might expect a 12-year-old boy to possess the attribute 'wholesome', which is evoked via the link *an Eagle Scout*. Thus, the referent of the link in (72c) is not any particular Eagle Scout, or even the class of Eagle Scouts, but rather the attribute crucially associated with that class and related to it via a readily accessible poset ordering.

Another way in which the link itself may license the inference to the anchoring poset is through the use of a definite NP (typically a proper name) whose referent can be seen as the epitome of the relevant attribute. Following Ward 1983, we call this type 'epitomization'. The link of epitomization is related to the anchoring poset via an entity/attribute relation, while at the same time representing the highest value on a scale defined by that attribute. Examples of epitomization are provided in (73):

(73) a. *Mount Everest it wasn't*, but Engineering School sophomore Benno Matschinsky prepares to rappel from the South St. Bridge yesterday afternoon, and then falls graciously with a safety rope toward the ground.
[*The Daily Pennsylvanian*, 4/18/83; caption]

b. BASKET CASE
A charmingly tasteless bloodbath of a film about a young man carting his deformed brother around in a picnic basket. However, it takes more than that wicker latch and an occasional pack of hot dogs to curb the creature's homicidal habits. *"Potemkin" it's not*; but, nonetheless, a bonafide classic in the ranks of Guilty Pleasures.
[Theater of the Living Arts movie schedule]

c. The triumphant mood is broken when an usher from the movie theater next door strolls over. "You're blocking our marquee" he bellows in my ear, making it clear that I should move on — hastily.
Carnegie Hall it isn't, but for an amateur musician, a bustling sidewalk can be as good a place as any to begin.
[*Wall Street Journal*, 10/7/83]

In (73a), the relevant attribute — 'mountain height' — stands in an entity/attribute poset relation to the link *Mt. Everest*. This attribute is clearly salient in light of the photograph in which a student, wearing mountain climbing gear, is seen dangling from a bridge. For the reporter, Mt. Everest also represents the highest value on the scale defined by this attribute. Thus, the preposed constituent of epitomization is performing two functions in discourse: It serves as the link to the prior discourse via an entity/attribute relation while at the same time representing the epitome of that attribute. In (73b), the epitomized attribute is 'film-classic', evoked in the film review, and in (73c), it is 'musician-success'. Thus, for all three types of proposition denial, the link represents a salient attribute of some evoked entity; the three types differ only in the way in which that attribute is evoked.

One of the ways in which proposition denial with ironic effect differs from the corresponding canonical-word-order variant is that the preposed constituent of proposition denial necessarily receives a non-referential interpretation, while the canonical-word-order variant may receive either. To illustrate the non-referential nature of the preposed link of proposition denial, we can construct a context in which the referential interpretation is forced, and the denial is consequently inappropriate. First, consider (74):

(74) Joan Crawford she's not.
[emcee at a Halloween costume party contest, referring to one of the contestants in tacky drag]

Here, the link *Joan Crawford* epitomizes glamour, an attribute which the costume party contestant is (unsuccessfully) attempting to possess.

Now imagine that A and B are at a Halloween costume party and that A is looking for the one individual who is masquerading as Joan Crawford. A is told to look in a certain room and, in doing so, encounters B:

(75) A: Excuse me, but you're not Joan Crawford.
B: She'll be right back.

In (75), A can refer to the individual masquerading as Joan Crawford that night as *Joan Crawford.* However, in the same context, the preposed (76) is decidedly odd:

(76) A: Excuse me, but #Joan Crawford you're not.

In this example, *Joan Crawford* receives a non-referential interpretation, which, in the context described, is infelicitous. Upon hearing *Joan Crawford you're not* in this context, B is likely to interpret the utterance ironically, inferring that A is actually evaluating B him-/herself (or B's costume) with respect to glamour, the attribute epitomized by Joan Crawford.

As additional evidence that the proper names used in epitomization do not refer directly to individuals, consider the following examples:

(77) a. Tanya: Well, one thing's for sure. *Another Jack Nicklaus he ain't.* ["Charlie's Angels", 5/6/84; Tanya watches a golfer miss the ball entirely]

b. Tabitha: I understand why you want to have a baby boy. Some people like little boys better than little girls.
[exit Tabitha]
Darren: What do you think about that?
Samantha: Well, *Dr. Spock we're not.*
["Bewitched", 7/26/83]

c. Jane Fonda he's not.
["Overnight"; L. Ellerbee describing Reagan's article on keeping fit in *Parade* magazine]

In (77a), the proper name is preceded by an indefinite quantifier; in (77b), the proper name does not agree with the copula in number; and there is even a mismatch of gender in (77c). These examples illustrate that the proper name of epitomization is not being used to refer directly to the individual denoted by the name, but rather refers to some salient attribute which that individual epitomizes.

Certain preposings can actually be ambiguous between an ironic and non-ironic interpretation, as in (78):

(78) A: What do you think of John?
B: He's a very successful, but humble guy.
A: Successful, yes. *But humble he's not.*

In this example, B evokes a set of attributes — {successful, humble} — to describe the individual in question. Speaker A affirms one of the set members — 'successful' — but denies 'humble'. In this way, the utterance functions as a regular topicalization. However, as we have seen, the preposing in (78) could also be used to convey irony if *humble* is taken to be a scalar value on the scale 'humility'. Under an ironic interpretation, the speaker implicates that John is not only not humble, but downright conceited. Note that these two functions overlap just when there is an evoked set of attributes of which the preposed attribute is seen as a member. Without such a set, or if the proposition in question is not evaluative, the utterance will not be ambiguous.

Unlike the type of proposition denial that explicitly mentions the attribute with respect to which the entity is being evaluated (e.g., the ironic interpretation of (78)), epitomization involves an indirect reference to that attribute via the preposed link. Felicitous epitomization requires that the speaker believe, or at least intend to convey, that the referent of the link represents the epitome or exemplar of a salient attribute. Consider (79):

(79) A: So, how do you like living in Denver? Is there a lot to do?
B: *New York it's not.*

Here, New York seems like an appropriate candidate to serve as an epitome of urban centers. Now consider the following epitomization based on an average or even above-average scalar value:

(80) A: So, how do you like living in Denver? Is there a lot to do?
B: *#Atlanta it's not.*

In the absence of special contextual circumstances, B's response might be considered odd just because Atlanta does not generally epitomize urban activities. It's not that Atlanta represents a low value on this scale; what makes it a poor epitome is simply that it is not generally believed to represent an especially high value for this attribute.

Such a belief, of course, is highly subjective, as illustrated in (81):

(81) C: Is he cute?
G: *Robert Redford he's not.*
C: Oh right. You like blondes.
[G. Danley to C. Davis in conversation]

In this exchange, C is reacting to and implicitly disagreeing with G's selection of Robert Redford as the epitome of the *handsome* scale.

While two speakers may disagree about whether some entity in fact represents the epitome of the attribute in question, it is self-evident that the speaker must minimally believe that his or her hearer knows of the entity in question.[29] Consider, for example, B's response in (82) if (B believes that) A is a non-linguist and has never heard of *Syntactic Structures*:

(82) A: What did you think of his monograph?
B: #Syntactic Structures *it's not.*

Felicitous epitomization, then, requires that the link be mutually known, as well as the attribute scale upon which that value lies. However, if a speaker errs and selects a link which turns out to be unknown to his or her hearer, the hearer will nonetheless be able to draw an inference *on the basis of the preposing itself.* Epitomization, unlike other preposing types, drives a particular interpretation which is to some degree independent of the proposition conveyed therein. Upon hearing a token of epitomization, a hearer for whom the link is unknown can still draw the inference that the link epitomizes some salient attribute. Thus, even if a non-linguist who has never heard of *Syntactic Structures* were to hear (82), that person could still infer that the speaker believes that there is something extraordinary about that work, an inference which would not necessarily be drawn from the corresponding canonical-word-order variant, as seen in (83):

(83) A: What did you think of his monograph?
B: It's not *Syntactic Structures.*

In this example, A would not necessarily infer that *Syntactic Structures* represents, for B, a maximum value, although such an interpretation is still possible.

Semantically, epitomization conveys a trivially true assertion; pragmatically, however, it is far more informative. The ironic nature of epitomization serves not only to deny that the referent of the subject possesses the attribute associated with the link, but also to convey that the entity represents a low value on the attribute scale in question. How low on the scale the entity is taken to lie is, of course, context-dependent; however, it appears that the more extraordinary the

[29] This condition could be stated in terms of Clark and Marshall's (1981) 'cultural copresence' or Prince's (1992) 'hearer-old' information status: that which the speaker assumes the hearer already knows but is not necessarily thinking about at the time of the utterance.

referent of the link, the less low the referent of the subject NP is taken to be. Consider the 'super-epitomes' in (84):

(84) a. All this took shape under the watchful eye of Representative Geraldine A. Ferraro of Queens, chairman of the overall committee. The fact that she is a potential Vice Presidential candidate was not lost on anyone. Early in the proceedings she confessed "*Superwoman I'm not*," but ran the talky platform with a firm hand. [*New York Times*, 6/24/84]

b. Einstein he's not.

In (84a), the ultra-high value referenced by the link *Superwoman* does not lead us to infer that Ferraro is a weakling. Rather, we infer that she views herself as 'simply human'. Similarly, (84b) could be uttered by someone who believes the referent of *he* to be of average, or even above-average, intelligence, compared to Einstein's legendary genius.

The same type of understatement involved in epitomization also occurs with certain cases of proposition denial involving non-preposed superlatives. Consider the examples in (85):

(85) a. It wasn't the most exciting movie I've seen.

b. This is not the happiest day of my life.

c. He's not the smartest guy.

In these examples an ironic interpretation is certainly possible. Ideally we would like the same pragmatic account of the meiosis in (85) to be able to account for the various types of proposition denial under discussion here as well. Grice (1975) analyzes so-called figurative language, i.e. irony, metaphor, meiosis, and hyperbole, as 'conversational implicature' resulting from a speaker's deliberate flouting of the maxim of quality. For example, a speaker's utterance is viewed as ironic when it is (mutually) believed by speaker and hearer to be false. Upon hearing such an utterance, Grice reasons, the hearer infers that the speaker cannot actually believe the proposition conveyed and must therefore be conveying "some obviously related (i.e. contradictory) proposition" (1975:53). In this way, a speaker who utters, for example, *What a great idea that is!* can implicate that the idea in question is *not* a great one, assuming that it is mutually believed that the speaker does not believe that the idea was, in fact, great.

Sperber & Wilson (1981, 1986) take issue with Grice's analysis of irony. First, as Grice himself notes in a later article (1978:124), not all patently false sentences are ironic. Consider (86), which conveys a transparently false proposition:

(86) $18 - 6 = 37$

It is difficult to imagine a context in which (86) would receive an ironic interpretation. Second, Grice's account renders every ironic utterance totally uninformative. Given that a speaker's ironic intentions are recognized as such only by someone who must *already* know that the speaker holds a belief opposite to that conveyed by the literal meaning of the sentence, why would a speaker then implicate what he must believe his hearer already knows? Third, Sperber & Wilson note that an implicature-based account does not account for *why* a speaker would choose an ironic utterance over the corresponding non-ironic one.

Instead, Sperber & Wilson (1981, 1986) view irony as a type of 'echoic mention'. Specifically, they claim that ironic utterances mention a proposition by conveying a particular attitude or opinion of the speaker about that proposition. Ironic utterances are those in which a speaker echoes some proposition in such a way as to "suggest that he finds it untrue, inappropriate, or irrelevant" (1981:307). In the case of ironic proposition denial, however, the echoed proposition is not untrue; indeed, as illustrated in the examples provided above, the proposition conveyed by preposing is in each case literally true. What is being mentioned in the case of proposition denial is the corresponding affirmative proposition, which the speaker denies — in fact ridicules — as being entirely inappropriate.

Sperber & Wilson's echoic-mention approach to irony also accounts for the fact that so many tokens of proposition denial are used to effect insults or criticisms. If the function of irony is to echo a proposition in the discourse for the purpose of ridiculing it, then proposition denial can also have this effect. In addition, the fact that many examples involve a standard speaker's use of *ain't* can be accounted for in Sperber & Wilson's account. Irony often involves register and voice quality shifts as the speaker echoes the attitude or speaking style of someone other than the speaker (or of the speaker on a previous occasion). In the case of proposition denial, this involves echoing the non-standard speakers with whom the form *ain't* is associated. Note the difference between the functionally ambiguous (78) above and the equivalent with *ain't*:

(87) A: What do you think of John?
B: He's a very successful, but humble guy.
A: Successful, yes. *But humble he ain't.* [cf. (78)]

The use of *ain't* in this exchange disambiguates the utterance and forces an ironic interpretation.

As further confirmation of the ironic nature of this kind of proposition denial, consider the fact that, in general, it is easier to use irony for critical rather than laudatory effects:

(88) a. It wasn't the least interesting movie I've seen.
b. This is not the saddest day of my life.
c. He's not the stupidest guy.

Such examples are not generally used ironically as meiosis to convey that the entity in question ranks *high* on the relevant scale. Similarly, proposition denial is more felicitous when the link represents a high, rather than low, value on the relevant scale. Consider (89):

(89) a. A: Do you think Bill is a nice guy?
B: *#Saddam Hussein he's not.*
b. A: What do you think of Glendale?
B: *#Cleveland it's not.*
c. A: I hear Pat's new boyfriend isn't too attractive.
B: *#Quasimodo he's not.*

In (89a), for example, one who holds the opinion that Saddam Hussein occupies a low value on the *nice* scale would not be likely to infer that Bill is an extraordinarily nice guy on the basis of the epitomization.

Topicalization and definiteness

There have been a number of attempts to place restrictions on the morphological and/or semantic types of constituents that can serve as links in topicalization. For example, it has been claimed (Hankamer 1979, Feinstein 1980) that topicalization in the standard language is restricted either exclusively or primarily to morphologically definite NPs.[30] For example, consider Hankamer's (1979) claim that "topicalization moves constituents to the left when they have been previously mentioned, but *cannot* be presupposed (i.e. when there is not enough information in the discourse to predict or 'recover' them)" [emphasis in the original] (1979:198); and later, in a footnote, he adds: "Topicalization can only prepose constituents which have occurred in previous discourse [...] E.g., an indefinite NP can't be preposed by Topicalization" (1979:217, footnote 12).

As Ward 1988 shows, however, Hankamer's claim regarding the impossibility of preposing indefinites cannot be maintained. Consider the examples in (90):

(90) a. G: Do you think you'd be more nervous in a job talk or a job interview?
S: *A job talk I think you'd have somewhat more control over.*
[S. Pintzuk to G. Ward in conversation]

b. I'll have to introduce two principles. *One I'm going to introduce now* and *one I'm going to introduce later.*
[T. Wasow in lecture]

c. [Grandpa and Herman Munster are trying to find a buried treasure in their backyard by means of a map, which makes reference to an oak tree.]
Persimmon trees we got. Cypress trees we got. Oak trees we haven't got.
[Grandpa on "The Munsters"]

[30]The 'standard language' qualification is here in light of the fact that the aforementioned studies (Hankamer 1979 and Feinstein 1980) do allow for preposed indefinite NPs in 'Yiddish-English' dialects. See discussion on page 90ff.

Indeed, indefinites constitute almost 30% (270/915) of the preposings in the corpus. If the 131 non-NP preposings are excluded from the sample, the proportion of indefinite preposings increases to over a third of the corpus (270/784 or 34%). In fact, one of the more common preposed constituents is the indefinite NP quantifier *some* (as in *Some I like*). One could argue that Hankamer and Feinstein were considering only those indefinites with the indefinite article *a/an*; however, the corpus contains 67 tokens of preposed NPs containing the indefinite article.

Along the same lines, Kuno (1972) claims that indefinite NPs cannot be preposed. For Kuno, an NP preposed by topicalization constitutes the 'theme' of the sentence, and thematic NPs must be either anaphoric or generic (1972:301), where 'anaphoric' is defined as representing an entity already 'in the registry of discourse', either because it has been mentioned previously or because it is in the 'permanent registry'. However, this claim is both too strong in that it disallows topicalizations like the one in (91a), where the preposed NP is neither anaphoric nor generic in Kuno's sense, and too weak in that it would allow the infelicitous topicalization in (91b), where the entity represented by the preposed NP is in the 'permanent registry':[31]

(91) a. I became a waitress because I needed money fast and you don't get it in an office. My husband and I broke up. [...] The fast buck, your tips. *The first ten-dollar bill that I got as a tip, a Viking guy gave to me.* He was a very robust, terrific atheist.
[=Ward & Prince 1991, ex. 4a]

b. Oh, I just heard some good news — *#Harvard University I got into.*
[=Ward & Prince 1991, ex. 4b]

Kuno further associates the information status of the entity an NP represents with (morphological) definiteness by stating that indefinite NPs represent 'new, unpredictable information' (1972:304), at least so long as they do not have stressed quantifiers (1972:301). Therefore, it follows that (non-generic) indefinite NPs

[31] In fact, of the 270 preposed indefinites in the corpus, only 42 can be interpreted generically, leaving 228 tokens that are problematic for Kuno's claim.

which do not have a stressed quantifier may not be felicitously topicalized. This, however, is not borne out by the data, as evidenced by (90c).

It has also been claimed that only specific indefinites can felicitously occur in the marked position in syntactic constructions such as topicalization (Davison 1984:814); on the other hand, Gundel (1974) claims that preposed indefinite NPs in 'topic topicalization' are limited to a *nonspecific* interpretation (1974:187). However, neither claim holds up under scrutiny. For example, the following preposings, contra Davison, permit a nonspecific interpretation:

(92) a. To illustrate with a simple analogy, consider a person who knows arithmetic, who has mastered the concept of numbers. In principle, he is now capable of carrying out or determining the accuracy of any computation. *Some computation he may not be able to carry out in his head.* Paper and pencil are required to extend his memory. But the person does not have to learn something new to carry out a more complex computation, using paper and pencil.
[Chomsky 1980:221]

b. I'm expropriating 'text' sort of as a technical term. *Some other environment I wouldn't call a text.*
[S. Weinstein at Penn Sloan Cognitive Science Group]

c. A: Here's your change. [handing customer a penny]
B: No thanks. You can keep it.
C: What if it was a nickel?
B: *A nickel I'd keep.*
[service encounter at 7-11]

Ward 1988 found that 56 tokens of preposing (6% of the total) involved nonspecific links and 68 (7%) involved generics. If the 235 preposings whose specificity is irrelevant (e.g., non-NPs) are excluded, then the percentage of nonspecifics and generics increases to 8% (56/680) and 10% (68/680) of the corpus, respectively. Needless to say, neither figure is low enough to support the claim that only NPs that can be interpreted specifically can be preposed.

Davison (1984:828) also claims that quantified indefinite NPs are 'not particularly felicitous' when preposed.[32] However, consider the examples in (93a) through (93d), containing the indefinite quantifiers *several*, *most*, *a lot*, and *some*, respectively:

(93) a. *Several of these questions I will try to answer* — but, let me emphasize, from a personal rather than a general viewpoint. [Nixon 1962:xiii]

b. America wants to know: Did she buy a whole new wardrobe for school? 'Not really. I have a great deal of clothes.... *Most of my stuff, my mom gets at Alexander's*,' she laughs. [*Philadelphia Inquirer*, 11/6/83]

c. You know what another problem is today? The upper echelon of the management hasn't the faintest idea of what's going on in the business. I report the likes and dislikes of the workers. *A lot of them I get along with* and I tell them, 'The guys are right and the system's no good, it stinks, get rid of it.' [Terkel 1974:290]

d. I've never been held up. We have a foot alarm, one that you just tip with your toe. At the other place, we had a button you push, which was immediately under the counter. *Some people, you get a funny feeling about*. Like, I don't think that's his passbook, it's probably stolen. [Terkel 1974:347]

Thus, the felicity of preposing a given NP is also independent of its quantificational status.

Of the 556 tokens of preposed specific NPs in the corpus, 114 (21%) were found to be morphologically indefinite. This would seem to constitute clear counter-evidence to Gundel's (1974) claim that only a nonspecific interpretation

[32]Davison restricts her claim regarding infelicitous quantified indefinites to those with 'neutral' intonation and 'collective' interpretations. However, the counterexamples below in fact satisfy these conditions.

of a preposed indefinite NP is possible for 'topic topicalization'. In particular, Gundel argues that a preposed NP (of topic topicalization) cannot felicitously contain, for example, the word *certain* or a non-restrictive relative clause. Such unambiguously marked specific indefinite NPs are no doubt rare, independent of word order. However, consider the following examples of this type of preposed NP:

(94) a. She found that certain kinds of things she just couldn't recognize. [J. Hirschberg in conversation]

b. Most places, it's your full name on the window. Some places just have Miss or Mrs. So-and-So. I prefer giving my whole name so people can call me Nancy. [laughs] They feel a little more comfortable. *Certain officers you refer to by their first names.* Other people you don't.
[Terkel 1974:351]

c. Three terms will have to be defined before we can proceed. *One, which involves the notion 'presupposition', I'll have to hold off on presenting.* The others I can present right away.
[colloquium speaker, University of Pennsylvania]

These examples contain the indicators of specificity which Gundel explicitly disallows for topic topicalization. Thus, the preposed constituent of topicalization is not limited with respect to definiteness or specificity.

As pointed out in Ward & Prince 1991, what these previous analyses share is an attempt to account for the same general observation, namely that NPs representing entities brand-new to the discourse are not felicitously topicalized. What is relevant, however, is neither the morphological/lexical features of the NP nor its specificity, but rather the relationship that must hold between the entity in question and other entities in the discourse model. While these categories are clearly related, the relationship is not isomorphic and the three must be kept distinct.

We can accommodate the intuitions that led previous researchers to posit various restrictions on the types of NPs that can be preposed by recasting the constraint in terms of the theory being presented here. We have argued that the preposed constituent must constitute a discourse-old link within the discourse. As is well known, an entity that is brand-new in the discourse is typically represented by an indefinite NP. By 'brand-new', we mean here entities that have not been mentioned, are assumed not to be already known to the interlocutor, and are not inferentially related to entities that have been evoked in the discourse model (Prince 1981a). Now, it follows from the constraint on preposing presented above that the preposed NP cannot represent a brand-new discourse entity, and, therefore, the class of indefinite NPs representing them will of course be infelicitous when topicalized.

However, it is not the case that all indefinite NPs represent brand-new entities; when the entities they represent are related to the prior discourse by a salient poset relation, then and only then may they be felicitously topicalized. For example, indefinite NPs may represent nonspecific entities already evoked, as in (90a); they may represent members of evoked sets, as in (90b); they may represent parts of evoked entities, as in (93b), and so on, and as seen in these examples, all of these can be topicalized. Thus, as argued in Ward & Prince 1991, definiteness and topicalization are in fact independent. The relative infrequency (and alleged ungrammaticality) of indefinite links can be attributed to the fact that NPs with the indefinite singular article do not often stand in a salient poset relation with other entities in the discourse model, since the indefinite article is usually used when the entity to which it refers is new in the discourse and *unrelated* to other entities in the discourse. However, this is only a tendency; what is relevant for the topicalization of an NP is not its intrinsic morphological/lexical/semantic properties but rather the relation of the entity it represents to other entities in the discourse structure.

Focus Preposing

Recall that what distinguishes topicalization from other preposing constructions is that the preposed constituent of topicalization does not contain the focus of the utterance. In this section, we examine the discourse properties of focus preposing, the class of constructions in which the focus is contained within the preposed link. Consider the examples in (95):

(95) a. I made a lot of sweetbreads. *A couple of pounds I think I made for her.*
[C. Ward in conversation]

b. I: Are there black kids in that school now?
S: Not many. I had two really good friends. *Damon and Jimmy their names were.*
[Temple University undergraduate to interviewer in sociolinguistic interview]

c. I promised my father — *on Christmas Eve it was* — to kill a Frenchman at the first opportunity I had. [=(16a)]

In each of these examples, the preposed constituent contains the focus of the utterance; notice also that the preposed focus is intonationally marked with a nuclear accent. As with topicalization, the link of focus preposing can stand in a wide range of linking relations to the prior discourse; these will be discussed in detail below.

General constraints

In each of the examples of focus preposing in (95), the link is inferentially related to the anchor via a salient linking relation other than identity. In (95a), for example, by replacing the preposed focus with a variable of the appropriate type, we obtain the OP in (96):

(96) I think I made X amount of sweetbreads for her, where X is a member of the poset {amounts}.

The OP in (96) is salient in view of the previous utterance that *a lot of* sweetbreads had been made. In conjunction with this OP, the link of the preposing — *a couple of pounds* — serves to evoke the salient anchor {amounts}. The link is related to this anchor via a set/subset linking relation. In more general terms, our data suggest that whenever an OP involves mention of a relevant yet unspecified quantity (of time, space, objects, people, etc.) focus preposing supports a preposed focus that instantiates the amount in question. Consider the additional examples in (97):

(97) a. There's some fresh coffee in the kitchen. *A whole pot I made.*
OP = I made X amount of coffee, where X is a member of the poset {amounts}.

b. I stopped off at the Cash Station on my way home. *Two hundred dollars I withdrew.*
OP = I withdrew X amount of money, where X is a member of the poset {amounts}.

c. Bill's parents visited last month. *An entire week they were here.*
OP = They were here X amount of time, where X is a member of the poset {amounts}.

In (97a), the mention of fresh coffee renders salient the OP that some amount of coffee was made; this along with the link — *a whole pot* — renders the anchor {amounts} salient. The instantiation of the variable in the OP, then, is a member of this set. Similarly, in (97b), the mention of stopping at a Cash Station licenses the OP that some amount of money was withdrawn, while in (97c) mention of a parental visit licenses the OP that the parents were there for some amount of time.

The relevant OP for (95b) is given in (98):

(98) Their names were X, where X is a member of the poset {names}.

Given that one expects people to have names, this OP is clearly salient in the discourse. The link of the focus preposing — *Damon and Jimmy* — together with the trigger — *two really good friends* — evokes the anchoring set {names}, of which the link is a member. Interestingly, there are many tokens of focus preposing in the corpus containing predicates with *name* or *call.* It seems that mere mention of a new object or entity can render salient the OP that that entity is called something. Consider the wide range of things that we assume have names:

(99) Bill has a new theory/car/dog/boat/ailment/book. *'Foo' he calls it.*

In (95c), on the other hand, the relevant OP is 'It [the promising event] was (on) X, where X is a member of {times}'. This OP is salient given the prior mention of the Lieutenant's promise and the fact that events, especially important ones, are remembered as having occurred on a particular day. Again, the link (*Christmas Eve*) and the trigger (the promising event) evoke the anchoring poset {times}.

Alternatively, the trigger itself may represent a member of the anchoring poset along with the link of the preposed constituent. The trigger may represent either a higher, lower, or alternate value in the relevant poset. First, consider cases of triggers representing alternate values, as in (100):

(100) a. Waitress: Did you want tea?
Customer: *Coffee I ordered*, I think.
[customer to waitress at Deluxe Diner]

b. I think she was Japanese. No — *Korean she was.*
[M. Pollack in conversation]

c. J: What was the name of that film with Jessica Lange who plays that crazy actress?
M: Fanny? No, no. Um... Damn, I know I know it... *"Frances" it was called.*
[M. Greenberg to J. Rosoff in conversation]

In (100a), for example, the link and the trigger represent alternate values in the inferred anchoring poset {beverages}, rendered salient in light of the waitress' query regarding the customer's beverage order. The anchor, then, can be inferred on the basis of the trigger (*tea*) and the link (*coffee*).[33] Note in the absence of a salient or inferrable poset, infelicity results, as in (101):

(101) I was in a nightclub last night. *#An interesting guy I met.* [cf. I was in a nightclub last night. I met an interesting guy.]

[33]Some focus substitutions in the corpus have the flavor (and intonation) of a repair, as in (100b), but the vast majority do not.

Here, mere reference to a nightclub does not provide a sufficient trigger to construct the anchor necessary to support the focus preposing. That is, no appropriate anchor can be identified on the basis of the context (being in a nightclub) and the link (*an interesting guy*), and the preposing is therefore infelicitous.

In addition to representing an alternate value, the trigger can represent a value that is either higher or lower than that of the link. Consider first the examples of higher-value triggers in (102):

(102) a. G: Have you finished it yet?
S: *Half of it I've read.*
[S. Pintzuk to G. Ward in conversation]

b. Colonel Khaddafy, you said you were planning on sending planes — *M-16s I believe they were* — to Sudan...
["ABC World News Tonight"]

In (102a), the trigger *it* and link *half of it* are ordered by a part/whole relation, with the trigger constituting a higher value in the poset {units of a book}. Similarly, in (102b), the trigger *planes* constitutes a higher value in the poset {planes} than that of the link *M-16s*, where the salient poset is ordered by a type/subtype relation.

The trigger may also represent a lower value than does the link, as illustrated in (103):

(103) a. G: Do you still have last week's New Yorker?
M: No, I threw it out. *All of them I threw out.*
[M. Scott to G. Ward in conversation]

b. He resented my staying out late Saturday night. It seems that *everything I do he resents.*

In both of these examples, the trigger represents a lower value in a poset ordered by a set/subset relation. In (103a), the trigger and link together evoke the poset consisting of all New Yorker magazines, while in (103b), the trigger (*my staying out late*) and link (*everything I do*) are values in the poset consisting of the things the speaker does. Thus, the link of focus preposing can be related to the anchoring poset via a number of linking relations. Where the trigger itself is a member of the poset, the link can represent a higher, lower, or alternate value in relation to the trigger.

Echoing

Ward 1988 describes another type of focus preposing called 'echoing', in which the link of the preposing is being called into question. As with focus preposing in general, the link and focus of echoing are one and the same; however, unlike other types of focus preposing, the link of echoing typically represents a poset member that has been explicitly evoked in the prior discourse. Preposings of this type are used by speakers to convey their lack of commitment as to whether the link constitutes an appropriate instantiation of the focus variable within the open proposition.

A speaker may wish to convey such a lack of commitment either because he or she is uncertain about the appropriateness of the link or because he or she is doubtful about it. Uncertainty can be paraphrased as 'It is *not* the case that the speaker believes the link is an appropriate instantiation of the focus variable', whereas doubt can be paraphrased as 'It *is* the case that the speaker believes the link is an *in*appropriate instantiation.' The notion of 'lack of speaker commitment' subsumes these two possibilities.[34] First, consider a case of echoing that involves speaker uncertainty, as in (104):

(104) C: Cheeseburger, large fries, and a large Coke.
[5 minutes elapse]
E: *Large Coke you ordered?*
[Burger King employee to customer]

Here, the link *large Coke* is related to the anchor {beverages} via a type/subtype relation. The speaker conveys his lack of commitment by expressing uncertainty about the customer's drink order, and requesting confirmation of it. That is, the speaker is not certain that the link is the correct instantiation of the variable in

[34]See Ward & Hirschberg 1988 for a discussion of the notion 'lack of speaker commitment' as it relates to a particular intonational contour.

the OP 'You ordered X', and conveys that uncertainty with an echoing. One obvious reason for questioning a preceding utterance is simply that the speaker is unsure of having heard it correctly. However, there are other reasons as well, as we will show below.

The other type of echoing conveys speaker doubt. Consider (105):

(105) A: I sure wish Newt Gingrich would decide to run for President.
B: *Newt Gingrich you'd vote for!?*

In this example, the speaker expresses disbelief at the hearer's choice of presidential candidate. That is, the speaker believes that the link (*Newt Gingrich*) is *not* an appropriate instantiation of the variable in the OP.

In the case of both speaker uncertainty and speaker doubt, the link in an echoing typically represents a poset member that has been explicitly evoked in the prior discourse and whose appropriateness the speaker is either questioning or challenging. However, not all cases of echoing involve explicitly evoked links. Consider the examples in (106):

(106) a. A: There's isn't a winter sport that Andy doesn't like.
B: *Hockey he likes?*

b. A: Diane gets along with all her colleagues.
B: *David she gets along with?*

c. A: I've been everywhere in the Mideast.
B: *Iraq you've been to*?

In (106a), the link (*hockey*) has not been explicitly evoked in the prior discourse, although it can be related to the anchoring poset {winter sports} explicitly evoked by the trigger. Although hockey is clearly a member of this poset, B may nonetheless have reason to question A's assertion. In (106b), the speaker might use echoing to convey her surprise that Diane can get along with someone as difficult as David; here again the link constitutes an unevoked member of the anchoring poset. Similarly, in (106c), the speaker doubts A's (implicit yet entailed) assertion that she has traveled to Iraq, a member of the anchoring poset.

Whether a speaker uses echoing to question the trigger itself or an entailed poset member depends on the context. Compare B's two responses in (107):

(107) A: Did you know Rocky next door's got a poodle?
B1: *A poodle he's got?*
B2: *A dog he's got?*

If Rocky's having a dog per se is surprising, e.g. in the event that, say, dogs are not allowed in the building, then B2's utterance is felicitous. If, however, there's something unexpected about Rocky having a poodle (as opposed to some other breed), then B1 is felicitous and B2 is odd.

For those cases of echoing that are based on a relation of identity between link and trigger, exact lexical identity is not required. Unlike proposition affirmation, echoing may be licensed by relations of coreference or synonymy between the link and trigger. Consider the examples of synonymy and coreference in (108a) and (108b), respectively:

(108) a. A: The terrorists will not even release an expectant woman.
B: What? *A pregnant woman they won't release*?

b. A: I voted for the winning presidential candidate in 1992.
B: *Clinton you voted for*?

In (108a), the link *a pregnant woman* is synonymous with the trigger *an expectant woman*. Similarly, in (108b), the link *Clinton* is coreferential with the trigger *the winning presidential candidate in 1992*. While the link itself is a linguistic entity in our framework, what it represents (in all non-metalinguistic uses) is a *non-linguistic* entity in the discourse model. Thus, we would expect semantically and referentially equivalent links to relate to the anchor in precisely the same way as do lexical repetitions.

Yiddish-movement

The last type of focus preposing, Yiddish-movement, is unique among preposing types in that it is dialectally restricted. It occurs in those dialects of English which have been influenced to some extent by a Yiddish substratum. While the full effect of Yiddish on contemporary American English is unknown, there is evidence to suggest that preposing is one area in which Yiddish has influenced the English of certain American English speech communities (cf. Feinstein 1980, Prince 1981b). Examples of Yiddish-movement are provided in (109):

(109) a. Then came bald Uncle Hymie, one fist shaking violently in the air — *like Lenin he looked*! And then the mob of aunts and uncles and elder cousins, swarming between the two so as to keep them from grinding one another into a little heap of Jewish dust.
[Roth 1959:63]

b. Butter! She's dreaming about butter. *Recipes she dreams while the world zips*. He closed his eyes and pounded himself down into an old man's sleep.
[Roth 1969:149]

c. "You've got clean underwear?"
"I'm washing it at night. I'm okay, Aunt Gladys."
"By hand you can't get it clean."
"It's clean enough. Look, Aunt Gladys, I'm having a wonderful time."
"*Shmutz he lives in and I shouldn't worry*!"
[Roth 1969:54]

At first glance, it might appear that Yiddish-movement is completely unconstrained, but an examination of the data reveals that this is not the case.

Prince (1981b) compares Yiddish-movement to other types of focus preposing (her 'Focus Movement') and notes that, although they are similar, Yiddish-movement is less constrained: "The NP (of Yiddish-movement), which receives tonic stress, represents new or, in the case of rhetorical redundancy, given information. The open proposition resulting from the replacement of the NP in the proposition by a variable represents minimally generally known/plausible information" (1981b:260). So, for (109a) above, the relevant OP would be 'He looked like someone', which, although not salient in the discourse, represents plausible information. The preposed focus, *Lenin*, represents brand-new information in discourse.

Thus, we see that Yiddish-movement is less constrained than other focus preposing constructions in two significant ways: First, as seen in (109a), the preposed constituent need not constitute a link within the discourse. Consider also (110):

(110) A: How's your son?
B: Don't ask! *A sportscar he wants!*
[=Prince 1981b, ex. 43a]

Here, the preposed constituent, *a sportscar*, is hearer-new and completely unrelated to anything in the prior discourse.

Second, Yiddish-movement is less constrained than other focus proposings in that the relevant OP need not be salient, but merely generally known or plausible. Compare (110) above with (111):

(111) A: How's your son?
B: Don't ask! *#A sportscar he stole!*
[=Prince 1981b, ex. 43b]

In (110), the OP 'he wants X' can be safely assumed to be general shared knowledge (albeit not salient at the time of the preposing). However, it cannot be assumed in (111) that 'he stole X' is generally known. Thus, Yiddish-movement does impose a requirement of plausibility on the OP, whereas in the case of other focus preposings the OP must be salient.[35]

It would seem, then, that for speakers of Yiddish-English, Yiddish-movement and other focus preposings are not distinct types of focus preposing, but rather a

[35]In addition to the pragmatic differences between Yiddish-movement and other focus preposings, Ward 1988 notes some syntactic differences as well. Yiddish-movement permits preposing of certain verbal prepositions which standard English generally does not allow. Some examples are provided in (i):

(i)a. For a girl like that you shouldn't wait.
b. To me you should listen.
c. On him you rely?
d. Like Lenin he looked.
e. For him I don't care.

Another difference is the well-known ability of Yiddish-movement to prepose negative-polarity items:

single construction that is less constrained than Standard English focus preposing. Given that the set of discourse environments which permit felicitous focus preposing in standard English is a proper subset of the environments which permit felicitous Yiddish-movement (since one can assume that all salient propositions are generally known or plausible, but not vice versa), then what standard speakers designate as Yiddish-movement is actually the difference between the set of focus preposings with *plausible* OPs and those with the *salient* OPs required for Standard English focus preposing. If the OP is clearly salient, then it satisfies the conditions for focus preposing in standard English. If the OP is merely plausible/knowable, then it is seen (by non-Yiddish-English speakers) as Yiddish-movement.[36]

Left-Dislocation

In each of the constructions examined thus far, the preposed constituent serves as a link to the previous discourse.[37] In this section, we briefly examine another construction — left-dislocation — that is superficially similar to the preposing constructions we have been investigating. What distinguishes left-dislocation is the presence of a referential pronoun in the marked constituent's canonical position. Consider (112):

(112) I bet she had a nervous breakdown. That's not a good thing. *Gallstones, you have them out and they're out.* But a nervous breakdown, it's very bad.
[Roth 1969:162]

Here, the direct object pronoun *them* is coreferential with the sentence-initial constituent *gallstones*. Moreover, left-dislocation is not only syntactically dis-

(ii)a. A finger he wouldn't lift!
b. A bite she wouldn't eat!

The above examples are unacceptable in Standard English.

[36]See Prince 1988d, 1994, where Yiddish-movement is analyzed as a case of pragmatic borrowing.

[37]The only exception is Yiddish-movement, as described in the previous section.

tinct from preposing, but is functionally distinct as well. As we have seen, preposing constructions constitute a functionally unified class in that the preposed constituent consistently represents information standing in a contextually licensed partially ordered set relationship with information evoked in or inferrable from the prior context. On the other hand, no such requirement holds for left-dislocation. Thus, the formal distinction between the two types of construction corresponds to a functional distinction, while the formal similarity within the class of preposing constructions corresponds to a functional similarity.

Prince (1997) argues that there are in fact three types of left-dislocation (LD), distinguishable on functional grounds. Type I LD is what Prince calls 'simplifying LDs':

> A 'simplifying' Left-Dislocation serves to simplify the discourse processing of Discourse-new entities by removing them from a syntactic position disfavored for Discourse-new entities and creating a separate processing unit for them. Once that unit is processed and they have become Discourse-old, they may comfortably occur in their positions within the clause as pronouns. (1997:124)

That is, LDs of this type are reserved for entities that are new to the discourse and that would otherwise be introduced in a non-favored (i.e. subject) position. Consider the example in (113):

(113) My sister got stabbed. She died. Two of my sisters were living together on 18th Street. They had gone to bed, and this man, their girlfriend's husband, came in. He started fussing with my sister and she started to scream. *The landlady, she went up and he laid her out.* So sister went to get a washcloth to put on her, he stabbed her in the back...
[*Welcomat*, 12/2/81]

Here, the landlady is new to the discourse (and presumably to the hearer as well); however, the speaker is introducing her via an NP in subject position — a position disfavored for introducing new information. The dislocated NP creates a new information unit and thus, according to Prince, eases processing. The other two types of LD — triggering a poset inference and amnestying an island violation — typically do, according to Prince, involve discourse-old information.

Prince is not alone in claiming that at least some types of LD serve to introduce new entities into the discourse: Gundel (1974, 1985), Rodman (1974), and Halliday (1967) propose similar functions. More recently, Geluykens (1992) argues that the primary function of left-dislocation is 'referent-highlighting', i.e. "the introduction of a referent which is for some reason communicatively salient" (158).[38]

Thus, we find that most previous functional studies of left-dislocation posit that the dislocated constituent may represent discourse-new information. This stands in stark contrast to true preposing constructions, in which the preposed constituent must represent a discourse-old link to the prior discourse.

Summary

In this chapter, we have examined a broad range of sentence-types in which a lexically governed phrasal constituent appears in a marked preverbal position. Our corpus-based study has revealed that such preposing, like other marked syntactic constructions, serves an information-packaging function. First, preposing effects the instantiation of a salient or inferrable open proposition; second, the preposed constituent represents a discourse-old link that serves to situate the information presented in the current utterance with respect to the prior context. We have argued that such links are related to previously evoked information via a partially ordered set (poset) relationship.

In addition, we have identified and analyzed two major types of preposing in English: focus preposing and topicalization, distinguishable on the basis of whether or not the focused constituent appears in preposed position. In the case of focus preposing, the preposed focus constitutes the link to the prior discourse, while in the case of topicalization the focus remains in canonical position, with the (non-focused) preposed constituent providing the link. On the other hand, these properties do not hold for left-dislocation, in which a pronoun that is

[38]For reviews of Geluykens (1992), see Ward 1995 and Birner 1996b.

coreferential with the marked constituent appears in that constituent's canonical position. This formal distinction was shown to correspond to a functional one, while the formal similarity found within the class of preposing constructions was shown to correspond to a functional similarity.

Chapter 3

Postposing

While, as we have seen in Chapter 2, preposing requires that the marked constituent represent information that is 'given' in the sense of being discourse-old, in this chapter we will see that postposing requires its marked constituent to represent information that is 'new' in some sense, although the type of newness in question will be shown to vary by construction. The postposing constructions we will focus on in this chapter are existential and presentational *there*-insertion. It has long been recognized that the felicity of *there*-insertion is sensitive to the information status of the postverbal NP (Erdmann 1976; Rando & Napoli 1978; Ziv 1982a; Penhallurick 1984; Holmback 1984; Lumsden 1988; Prince 1992; McNally 1992; Abbott 1992, 1993; Ward & Birner 1994b, 1995; inter alia). However, most previous studies have focused on *there*-sentences with *be* as the main verb. Others (e.g., Aissen 1975, Larson 1988, and Rochemont & Culicover 1990) have argued that there are two structurally distinct types of *there*-insertion: 'existential' *there*, restricted to main-verb *be*, and 'presentational' *there*, restricted to verbs of 'appearance' or 'emergence' (Levin 1993). Existential *there* is exemplified in (114), while presentational *there* is exemplified in (115):

(114) a. There's a problem with our analysis.
[B. Birner to G. Ward in conversation]

b. I would like to concentrate on Florida more than anything else to show you what we see there now. *Between 1981 and 1983, there were nine bombings and seven attempted bombings and one kidnapping carried out by terrorist groups or alleged terrorist groups in the Florida area.* All 17 of these incidents were in Miami, Florida.
[Challenger Commission transcripts, 2/7/86]

(115) a. Daniel told me that *shortly after Grumman arrived at Wideview Chalet there arrived also a man named Sleeman.*
[Upfield 1946:246]

b. *Not far from Avenue de Villiers there lived a foreign doctor, a specialist, I understood, in midwifery and gynecology.* He was a coarse and cynical fellow who had called me in consultation a couple of times, not so much to be enlightened by my superior knowledge as to shift some of his responsibility on my shoulders.
[=(3b)]

In this chapter we will argue that presentational *there*-sentences are also functionally distinct from existential *there*-sentences.[1] We will argue that, independently of any structural differences that may exist between them, the two types of *there*-insertion are pragmatically distinct with respect to the information status of the postverbal NP (henceforth PVNP).

[1]For terminological convenience and continuity, we will retain the terms 'existential *there*' and 'presentational *there*', while taking no stand on their theoretical accuracy. The functional constraints we will propose for these constructions do not make reference to such notions as 'existence' or 'presentation'; it is nonetheless an open question whether these terms might be argued to map onto the constraints in an interesting or useful way. Notice also that what we are calling 'presentational' *there*-sentences may contain what previous researchers have termed 'existential' verbs, such as *lived* in (115b). This apparent inconsistency is due to the use of the terms 'existential' and 'presentational' in the literature for two rather different purposes; both terms are used on the one hand to denote a construction and on the other a class of verbs. Given our definitions of these terms, however, no mapping between verb type and construction type is intended and none should be inferred.

We will show that, on the one hand, these two sentence-types share a common discourse constraint in that each requires the postposed NP to represent information that is unfamiliar in some sense, while on the other hand they differ in the nature of this unfamiliarity — specifically, whether the information must be (believed to be) new to the discourse or new to the hearer. Thus, postposing serves an information-packaging function in that it serves to place constituents representing unfamiliar information in postverbal position; however, this constraint is realized differently by different postposing constructions. Moreover, this constraint on postposing will be contrasted with that of another sentence-type involving the noncanonical placement of an NP in postverbal position, namely right-dislocation. Unlike postposed NPs, the marked NP in a right-dislocation represents information that is familiar within the discourse; concomitantly, a pronoun coreferential with the marked constituent appears in this constituent's canonical position. Hence, in all cases with no coreferential element in canonical position, the postposed subject represents unfamiliar information, while in right-dislocation, containing a coreferential pronoun, the marked constituent represents familiar information. This difference in function can be attributed to the anaphoric pronoun of right-dislocation. Given that the marked NP in a right-dislocation is coreferential with the pronoun, and given that the pronoun is anaphoric and therefore represents a discourse-old entity, it follows that the marked NP must also represent this same discourse-old entity. Thus, it is not accidental that right-dislocation does not require the marked NP to represent new information; the presence of the pronoun in fact precludes such a possibility.

General Constraints

Many previous pragmatic accounts of *there*-sentences have maintained that they are 'presentational' or 'presentative' in function; however, what these terms mean varies from account to account. For example, Hetzron (1971) identifies English *there*-sentences as performing a presentative function, by which he means "[calling] special attention to one element of the sentence (whatever may happen to it in the course of the event expressed by the sentence) for recall in the subsequent context. This recall may be needed because the element is going to be talked about again, or because it is contrasted with something to be mentioned later, or, more generally, because what is going to be said later is, in some manner, relevant to the element in question" (1971:86). In a similar vein, Jespersen 1969 suggests that existential *there* "generally indicates (vaguely) the existence of something on which fuller information is to follow" (1969:130), and Kirkwood (1977) argues that existentials "are a direct means of introducing referents into the discourse and of enlarging the stock of knowledge of particulars shared by speaker and hearer (about them)" (1977:59). However, the notion that *there*-sentences serve to highlight the NP for further elaboration conflicts with other accounts, in which it is argued that *there*-sentences serve to 'demote' or 'defocus' the referent of the NP (Davison 1984, Kirsner 1979).

Such approaches also differ from those based on the status of the postverbal NP as representing information that is new in some sense. For example, Penhallurick (1984) maintains that *there*-insertion with a preposed locative PP is a variety of inversion in which *there* may appear if both the locative and the postverbal NP represent new information, or "when something is out of sight or less concrete, factors which make for harder processing" (1984:50). In this latter approach, Penhallurick follows Bolinger (1977), who argues that existential *there* is an extension of locative *there*, and that whereas inversion "presents something on the immediate stage (brings something literally or figuratively BEFORE OUR PRESENCE)," *there*-insertion "presents something to our minds (brings a piece of knowledge into consciousness)" (1977:91-94). Thus, Bolinger treats *there*-insertion as presentational in the sense of bringing something into the hearer's awareness. He goes on to state that "[s]omething can be brought into awareness by relating it to a concrete scene or to an abstract one (existence). Location and existence are two extremes, but there is no dividing line between them" (1977:99). Similarly, Hannay (1985) presents a study of existential *there* within the framework of Functional Grammar and finds that it serves a presentative function, where by 'presentative' he means that the speaker is explicitly introducing an entity into the world of discourse. (Hannay's account is discussed further on page 113ff.)

Others take the 'presentational' nature of *there*-sentences to reflect the placement of 'nonthematic' information in postverbal position; however, here too there is variation regarding what constitutes 'thematic' information. Pettinari (1980) argues that *there*-sentences serve to remove 'nonthematic' information from subject position, where thematic information is taken to be that which is most relevant to the goal of the communicative event. Bresnan & Kanerva (1989) also take *there*-insertion to be presentational in nature, arguing that "in the special context of presentational focus..., an atypical subject low on the thematic hierarchy (either a locative or expletive) appears" (1989:37); however, here the thematic hierarchy in question is based on thematic roles (such as agent and location). Finally, Breivik (1981) likewise states that *there*-sentences are presentative, by which he means that they serve to present new information into the discourse. The concept of new information as used by Breivik is based on the Prague School notion of communicative dynamism; here, information in sentence-final position (such as the PVNP of a *there*-sentence) is taken to be nonthematic, and one way in which material may be nonthematic is to be unfamiliar. In other cases, Breivik claims, *there*-insertion may serve to place 'heavy' (i.e., lengthy or structurally complex) subjects in sentence-final position. Thus, even among those who take the 'presentational' nature of *there*-sentences to reflect constraints on thematicity, there is little consensus on what thematicity itself is or reflects.

In sum, a wide variety of functional accounts have been proposed for English *there*-sentences, yet even those accounts that identify the PVNP as representing new information disagree on how 'newness' is to be defined — whether in terms of being out of sight (e.g., Penhallurick 1984), out of mind (e.g., Bolinger 1977), outside the world of discourse (e.g., Hannay 1985), or lacking in thematicity (which itself is defined in a wide variety of ways). Our data confirm the intuition that the PVNP in a *there*-sentence represents new information; however, they also reveal that existential and presentational *there* make reference to quite distinct notions of newness.

Existential 'there'

Recent corpus-based studies have shown that existential *there*-sentences are sensitive to hearer-familiarity as opposed to discourse-familiarity. That is, as argued in Prince 1988b, 1992 and Ward & Birner 1995, the postverbal NP in an existential *there*-sentence is required to represent information that the speaker believes is not already familiar to the hearer. Consider (116):

(116) a. *"There's a warm relationship, a great respect and trust"* between [United Air Lines]'s chairman, Stephen M. Wolf, and Sir Colin Marshall, British Air's chief executive officer, according to a person familiar with both sides. [=(3a)]

b. Weather is by no means being excluded. My opinion is that that might be a very major factor. During the month of January, I believe, before this launch *there was also something like seven inches of rain down at Kennedy.*
[Challenger Commission transcripts, 2/7/86]

c. What can happen is a hangup such as Rocky Smith ran into, as the independent hauler was traversing Chicago with a load of machinery that just had to get to a factory by morning. *"There was this truck in front of me carrying giant steel coils, and potholes all over the place,"* he remembers. "This guy swerves all of a sudden to avoid a big hole." He hit it anyway.
[*Wall Street Journal*, 8/30/89]

In (116a), the referent of the PVNP *a warm relationship...* is being presented to the reader as new information; similarly, in (116b) the PVNP *something like seven inches of rain* represents hearer-new information. Finally, in (116c) the truck mentioned in the PVNP is new to the hearer; for this reason, despite the fact that the PVNP is morphologically definite, it is nonetheless felicitous in the existential (see below).

If the PVNP represents hearer-old information, on the other hand, the use of existential *there* is infelicitous. Thus, consider (117):

(117) a. I have some interesting news for you. *#At today's press conference there was President Clinton.*

b. President Clinton appeared at the podium accompanied by three senators and Margaret Thatcher. *#Behind him there was the Vice President.*

The PVNPs in these examples represent entities that are new to the discourse yet presumably familiar to the hearer, and in both cases the existential *there*-sentence is unacceptable. Similarly, we would expect *there*-sentences with discourse-old PVNPs to be infelicitous, given that discourse-old entities are necessarily also hearer-old. This prediction is borne out, as evidenced in (118):

(118) a. A: Hey, have you heard from Jim Alterman lately? I haven't seen him for years.
B: Yes, actually. *#On the panel today there was Jim Alterman.*

b. President Clinton appeared at the podium accompanied by three senators and Margaret Thatcher. *#Behind him there was Thatcher.*

Here, the PVNPs represent entities that are discourse-old, and the *there*-sentences are infelicitous. Thus, whenever an NP represents a hearer-old entity, regardless of its discourse-status, it may not be felicitously postposed in an existential *there*-sentence.

This explains the difference in felicity between minimally distinct utterances such as those in (119):

(119) a. A: I'm home. Anything interesting happen today?
B: Not really. *There's a dog running loose somewhere in the neighborhood.*

b. A: Have you seen the dog or the cat around?
B: Not lately. *#There's the dog running loose somewhere in the neighborhood.*

c. A: Have you seen the dog or the cat around?
B: Not lately. *The dog is running loose somewhere in the neighborhood.*

In (119a), where the dog being referred to is hearer-new, the use of the existential is acceptable. However, in (119b), where the dog is hearer-old, the use of the existential is infelicitous. Notice that the canonical-word-order variant in (119c) is felicitous.

One might suppose that the problem with the infelicitous examples in (117)-(119b) is not the hearer-status of the referent of the PVNP, but rather the presence of a definite NP in postverbal position. Indeed, hearer-new information is typically, although not necessarily, represented by morphologically indefinite NPs, as illustrated above in (116).[2] This correlation has led many researchers to claim that definites are grammatically and categorically excluded from postverbal position in existential *there*-sentences (Milsark 1974, 1977; Jenkins 1975; Guéron 1980; Safir 1985; Szabolsci 1986; Reuland & ter 1987; Belletti 1988; Larson 1988; Lasnik 1992; Freeze 1992; inter alia). However, it has been observed by many others that definites do in fact appear regularly and felicitously in existential *there*-sentences (Erdmann 1976; Rando & Napoli 1978; Woisetschlaeger 1983; Penhallurick 1984; Holmback 1984; Hannay 1985; Lakoff 1987; Lumsden 1988; Prince 1988b, 1992; McNally 1992; Abbott 1992, 1993; inter alia). As argued in Ward & Birner 1994b, 1995, definite NPs may appear felicitously in this position just in case they represent hearer-new information. Consider (120):

(120) A: I'm home. Anything interesting happen today?
B: Not really. *There's the funniest-looking dog running loose somewhere in the neighborhood.*

Here, the definite NP *the funniest-looking dog* is fully felicitous in the existential. Notice, however, that here the NP is being used to refer to an entity that, although realized with a definite, is nonetheless hearer-new. That is, *the funniest-looking dog* is not used to refer to a particular dog that the hearer is expected to know of. Thus, as we will argue in more detail below, it is not definiteness per se that is responsible for the infelicity of an example such as (119b), but rather the fact that definite PVNPs typically represent hearer-old information. It is in fact this tendency for such information to be realized by a definite NP that has led to the illusion that definite PVNPs are themselves disallowed in existentials.

[2]The status of so-called 'indefinite *this*', illustrated in (116c), is discussed below.

Notice also that it is hearer-status, and not discourse-status, that is relevant for the felicity of existential *there*-sentences. That is, information that is new to the discourse is nonetheless infelicitous in postverbal position in an existential *there*-sentence if it is known to the hearer, as in (121):

(121) a. President Clinton appeared at the podium accompanied by three senators and Margaret Thatcher. *#Behind him there was the Vice President.* [=(117b)]

b. #At the NOW convention last week there was Hillary Clinton.

In (121a), given that the Vice President can be assumed to be familiar to the hearer, the existential is infelicitous; likewise, in a context where Hillary Clinton is new to the discourse but assumed to be known to the hearer, (121b) is infelicitous. If the felicitous use of an existential required only that its PVNP represent information that is discourse-new, we would expect that both of these examples of hearer-old, discourse-new PVNPs would be acceptable. Notice that the felicity of such hearer-old PVNPs in existentials does not improve when they represent discourse-old information; if anything, they become worse:

(122) a. President Clinton appeared at the podium accompanied by three senators and Margaret Thatcher. *#Behind him there was Thatcher.* [=(118b)]

b. Hillary Clinton and Tipper Gore have been travelling extensively over the past few months. *#At the NOW convention last week there was Hillary Clinton.*

The canonical-word-order variant, of course, is fully felicitous regardless of whether the relevant entity has been evoked in the prior discourse.

Given that both hearer-old, discourse-new PVNPs and hearer-old, discourse-old PVNPs are infelicitous in existential *there*-sentences, we are left with the situation shown in Table 3.1. As shown both in (119b) and in (122) above, if the PVNP is both hearer-old and discourse-old, the existential is infelicitous. Moreover, as shown in (121), if the PVNP is hearer-old but discourse-new, the existential is still infelicitous. The reverse case, an NP that is hearer-new yet

Table 3.1: *Hearer-Status vs. Discourse-Status of PVNPs*

	HEARER-OLD	HEARER-NEW
DISCOURSE-OLD	infelicitous	does not occur
DISCOURSE-NEW	infelicitous	felicitous

discourse-old, presumably does not occur in any syntactic context (existential or otherwise), given that an entity that has been introduced into the discourse can be assumed to have been introduced into the hearer's knowledge store as well. Finally, a PVNP that is both hearer-new and discourse-new is felicitous in an existential *there*-sentence. That is, in all cases where the PVNP is hearer-old, it is infelicitous in the existential, regardless of its discourse-status; however, in all (logically possible) cases where it is hearer-new, it is felicitous in the existential. Thus, it is newness with respect to the hearer's knowledge that is required for the felicitous use of existential *there*-sentences.

Presentational 'there'

As noted above, a number of previous syntactic analyses of English *there*-sentences (Aissen 1975, Larson 1988, Rochemont & Culicover 1990, inter alia) have argued that so-called presentational *there*-sentences are structurally distinct from existential *there*-sentences.[3] The most obvious difference between the two is that, in contrast to existential *there*-sentences, presentational *there*-sentences contain a main verb other than *be*. Correlated with this formal difference is a functional one: The two sentence-types are subject to distinct pragmatic constraints on the information status of the PVNP. Based upon an analysis of a corpus of over 400 naturally occurring tokens, we have found that presentational *there* differs from existential *there* in being sensitive to the discourse-status, rather than the hearer-status, of the PVNP. Specifically, the felicitous use of a presentational

[3]See also Breivik 1990, Ball 1991, and McNally (to appear) for arguments that the two constructions are not historically related.

there-sentence requires that its PVNP represent information that is new to the discourse.[4]

In the vast majority of cases, the PVNP in a presentational *there*-sentence is both hearer-new and discourse-new. Thus, consider the examples in (123):

(123) a. After they had travelled on for weeks and weeks past more bays and headlands and rivers and villages than Shasta could remember, *there came a moonlit night when they started their journey at evening, having slept during the day.* They had left the downs behind them and were crossing a wide plain with a forest about half a mile away on their left.
[Lewis 1954:23]

b. The volume of engine sound became louder and louder. Motorcycle police, a whole battalion (or whatever unit they come in) neared — took over the road — there must have been twenty of them. *Behind them there appeared police vans and police buses, one, two, four, six, eight of each.* And then, at last, behind these, the American military vehicles began to appear.
[Wakefield 1991:94]

c. Why would Honda locate in Alliston? Why did Toyota pick Cambridge? Why did GM-Suzuki pick Ingersoll? The answer is, first, that the Canadian labour force is well educated and capable of operating the sophisticated equipment of modern industry. *Second, in the Province of Ontario and in the communities of Alliston, in Waterloo Region and Oxford County, there exists a tremendous work ethic.* We recognize it. The workers recognize it. More important, industry recognizes it, too.
[token provided by D. Yarowsky, AT&T Bell Laboratories]

Note that the main verbs in these examples — *came* in (123a), *appeared* in (123b), and *exists* in (123c) — are prototypical verbs of appearance and emergence (Levin

[4] See page 273ff for discussion of a construction in Yiddish that appears to be subject to the same constraint.

1993), and thus are also prototypical in presentational *there*-sentences. Moreover, in each case the PVNP represents information that is new to the discourse. That is, the moonlit night in (123a) has not been evoked previously in the discourse, nor have the police vans and police buses in (123b) or the work ethic in (123c). Thus, all of the PVNPs in these examples represent discourse-new information.

However, in each of these examples the entity represented by the PVNP is new to the hearer as well as to the discourse — i.e., it is hearer-new as well as discourse-new. Nonetheless, there do exist cases that distinguish between the two, specifically those tokens involving information that is new to the discourse yet presumably known to the hearer. In examining such tokens, we find that presentational *there* is less restrictive than existential *there* in that it admits PVNPs that are hearer-old as long as they are discourse-new. Consider the examples in (124):

(124) a. *There only lacked the moon*; but a growing pallor in the sky suggested the moon might soon be coming.
[adapted from Erdmann 1976:138]

b. Famous men came — engineers, scientists, industrialists; and *eventually, in their turn, there came Jimmy the Screwsman and Napoleon Bonaparte...*
[Upfield 1950:2]

In these examples, the referent of the PVNP is one that is familiar to the hearer yet new to the discourse. In (124a) the moon has not been evoked previously in the discourse, yet it is clearly hearer-old in that the speaker may reasonably assume that the moon is known to the hearer. Similarly, in (124b), the PVNP represents individuals that are already familiar to the reader. Thus, while both types of *there*-sentences allow hearer-new, discourse-new PVNPs, they do so for different reasons: Existential *there*-sentences, being sensitive to hearer-status, require the PVNP to represent hearer-new information, while presentational *there*-sentences, being sensitive to discourse-status, require the PVNP to represent discourse-new information.

If the PVNP in a presentational *there*-sentence represents information that is discourse-old (and therefore also hearer-old), the utterance is infelicitous; thus, consider (125)-(126):

(125) a. Suddenly there ran out of the woods the man we had seen at the picnic.
[=Aissen 1975:2, ex. 12]

b. For a brief moment we could see among the trees a man and a woman picking flowers. *#Suddenly there ran out of the woods the man we had seen.* [cf. The man we had seen suddenly ran out of the woods.]

(126) a. President Clinton appeared at the podium accompanied by three senators and Margaret Thatcher. *Behind him there stood the Vice President.*

b. President Clinton appeared at the podium accompanied by three senators and Margaret Thatcher. *#Behind him there stood Thatcher.* [cf. Thatcher stood behind him.]

In each of the (a) examples, the referent of the PVNP represents information that is presumably familiar to the hearer, and the utterance is felicitous; in each of the (b) examples, this same entity has been evoked in the prior discourse, and use of the presentational *there*-sentence is infelicitous (while canonical word order is fully acceptable). Thus, in each case it is the referent's status as discourse-old information that renders the utterance infelicitous, not its status as hearer-old information, since the corresponding examples of hearer-old but discourse-new entities in the (a) variants are felicitous. Unlike the PVNPs of existential *there*-sentences, then, those of presentational *there*-sentences are sensitive to the discourse-status of their referents.

A comparison of existential and presentational 'there'

We have seen that existential *there*-insertion requires the PVNP to represent hearer-new information, while presentational *there*-insertion requires the PVNP to represent discourse-new information. Very frequently, of course, the two statuses coincide. For example, any entity that is hearer-new is also necessarily discourse-new; if it were discourse-old, it would necessarily be (assumed to be) known to the hearer (given that a speaker assumes the hearer is attending to the discourse). While it is not correspondingly the case that discourse-new information is necessarily hearer-new, in fact discourse-new information is very commonly also hearer-new. Thus, consider again the presentational *there*-sentences in (123), repeated here as (127):

(127) a. After they had travelled on for weeks and weeks past more bays and headlands and rivers and villages than Shasta could remember, *there came a moonlit night when they started their journey at evening, having slept during the day.* They had left the downs behind them and were crossing a wide plain with a forest about half a mile away on their left. [=(123a)]

b. The volume of engine sound became louder and louder. Motorcycle police, a whole battalion (or whatever unit they come in) neared — took over the road — there must have been twenty of them. *Behind them there appeared police vans and police buses, one, two, four, six, eight of each.* And then, at last, behind these, the American military vehicles began to appear. [=(123b)]

c. Why would Honda locate in Alliston? Why did Toyota pick Cambridge? Why did GM-Suzuki pick Ingersoll? The answer is, first, that the Canadian labour force is well educated and capable of operating the sophisticated equipment of modern industry. *Second, in the Province of Ontario and in the communities of Alliston, in Waterloo Region and Oxford County, there exists a tremendous work ethic.* We recognize it. The workers recognize it. More important, industry recognizes it, too. [=(123c)]

In (127a) the particular moonlit night in question is not only new to the discourse but can also be assumed to be entirely new to the hearer. Similarly, in (127b) the police vans and buses evoked in the PVNP can also be assumed to be new to both discourse and hearer. Finally, in (127c) the work ethic that exists in the areas in question can be considered to be new not only to the discourse but also to the hearer.

Given that these constituents all represent hearer-new information in context, we would predict that existential *there* in the same context would be equally felicitous, and indeed this prediction is borne out. Thus, consider the corresponding discourses with existential *there*:

(128) a. After they had travelled on for weeks and weeks past more bays and headlands and rivers and villages than Shasta could remember, *there was a moonlit night when they started their journey at evening, having slept during the day.*

b. The volume of engine sound became louder and louder. Motorcycle police, a whole battalion (or whatever unit they come in) neared — took over the road — there must have been twenty of them. *Behind them there were police vans and police buses, one, two, four, six, eight of each.*

c. Why would Honda locate in Alliston? Why did Toyota pick Cambridge? Why did GM-Suzuki pick Ingersoll? The answer is, first, that the Canadian labour force is well educated and capable of operating the sophisticated equipment of modern industry. *Second, in the Province of Ontario and in the communities of Alliston, in Waterloo Region and Oxford County, there is a tremendous work ethic.*

The fact that these discourses are equally felicitous with either presentational or existential *there* is due to the large area of overlap between the constraints to which the two constructions are subject.

Similarly, both types of *there*-sentences disallow PVNPs representing discourse-old information. Consider the examples in (129):

(129) a. A: Hey, have you heard from Jim Alterman lately? I haven't seen him for years.

B: Yes, actually. *#Before the committee today there was/appeared Jim Alterman.*

b. President Clinton appeared at the podium accompanied by three senators and Margaret Thatcher. *#Behind him there was/stood Thatcher.* [=(118b), (126b)]

The PVNPs in these examples represent information that is discourse-old, and therefore also hearer-old, and hence are infelicitous in either presentational or existential *there*-sentences.

Where discourse-status and hearer-status diverge, however, different distributions are found for existential and presentational *there*-sentences. As noted above, entities that are hearer-new are necessarily also discourse-new; thus, the only cases where the two statuses diverge are those in which an entity is both discourse-new and hearer-old. PVNPs representing such entities would be predicted to be felicitous in presentational *there*-insertion due to the entity's status as discourse-new, but would be predicted to be infelicitous in existential *there*-insertion due to the entity's status as hearer-old. This prediction is borne out, as seen in the presentational *there*-sentences in (130a) and (131a) and the corresponding existential *there*-sentences in (130b) and (131b):

(130) a. I have some interesting news for you. *At today's press conference there appeared President Clinton.*

b. I have some interesting news for you. *#At today's press conference there was President Clinton.* [=(117a)]

(131) a. President Clinton appeared at the podium accompanied by three senators and Margaret Thatcher. *Behind him there stood the Vice President.* [=(126a)]

b. President Clinton appeared at the podium accompanied by three senators and Margaret Thatcher. *#Behind him there was the Vice President.* [=(117b)]

Here, the PVNPs *President Clinton* and *the Vice President* represent information that is new to the discourse yet presumably known to the hearer; as such, they are felicitous in presentational *there*-sentences but disallowed in existential *there*-sentences.

We have seen, then, that when the PVNP represents information that is both discourse-new and hearer-new, both presentational and existential *there*-sentences are felicitous; likewise, when the PVNP represents information that is both discourse-old and hearer-old, both presentational and existential *there*-sentences are infelicitous. Finally, when the PVNP represents information that is discourse-new but hearer-old, presentational *there*-insertion is felicitous while existential *there*-insertion is not. Thus, the distribution of these constructions in discourse is exactly that which is predicted by the functional constraints we have proposed.

Definites in 'There'-Sentences

It is well known that certain *there*-sentences with definite PVNPs are either infelicitous, anomalous, or ungrammatical, depending on whether one attributes their unacceptability to pragmatic, semantic, or syntactic factors. For example, consider again the PVNPs in (119b) and (119c), repeated here as (132a) and (132b), respectively:

(132) Have you seen the dog or the cat around?

a. Not lately. *#There's the dog running loose somewhere in the neighborhood.* [=(119b)]

b. Not lately. The dog is running loose somewhere in the neighborhood. [=(119c)]

In (132a), the existential *there*-sentence with the definite PVNP *the dog* is ill-formed, although the canonical-word-order variant in (132b) is fully acceptable. What is at issue is the source of the restriction, i.e. what makes the existential in (132a) unacceptable.

The so-called 'definiteness effect'

As noted above, it has frequently been claimed that *there*-sentences disallow a lexically definite postverbal NP; this restriction has come to be known as the 'definiteness restriction' or 'definiteness effect' (Milsark 1974, 1977; Jenkins 1975; Guéron 1980; Safir 1985; Szabolsci 1986; Reuland & ter Meulen 1987; Belletti 1988; Larson 1988; Lasnik 1992; Freeze 1992; inter alia). However, it has been observed by many others that this restriction is far from absolute (Erdmann 1976; Rando & Napoli 1978; Woisetschlaeger 1983; Penhallurick 1984; Holmback 1984; Hannay 1985; Lakoff 1987; Lumsden 1988; Prince 1992; McNally 1992; Abbott 1992, 1993; inter alia). Indeed, the wide range of definite postverbal NPs that occur in *there*-sentences and their sensitivity to contextual constraints argue for a pragmatic account of the phenomenon.[5] We will show that the alleged restriction against definite PVNPs in *there*-sentences is epiphenomenal, the result of an imperfect correlation between the cognitive status to which definiteness is sensitive and that to which postverbal position in *there*-sentences is sensitive (Ward & Birner 1995).

As Prince (1992) notes, much confusion surrounds the use of the term 'definite'; at times, it is taken to denote a formal property of determiners or NPs, but at other times it is taken to denote a conceptual category (cf. Bolinger's (1977) distinction between 'semantic definiteness' and 'grammatical definiteness'). It is clear, however, that the class of formally definite NPs (i.e. proper names, personal pronouns, and NPs containing definite or possessive determiners (e.g. *the*, *this*, *those*, *our*, *her*) or certain quantifiers (e.g. *all*, *every*)) is not categorically excluded from postverbal position in *there*-sentences. Attempts to account for the extensive counterexamples to the definiteness effect frequently take definiteness to be a cognitive category rather than a formal one, formulating the restrictions on *there*-sentences in terms of the information status of the discourse entity to which the PVNP is used to refer, rather than in terms of the NP itself. Thus, the infelicity of examples like (132a) above is said to result from the general

[5]Thus, we take issue with Safir's claim that 'it is only through the mediation of formal syntactic properties, particularly syntactic chains and the theory of indexing, that the distribution of the definiteness effect can be predicted in an explanatory way' (1985:171).

incompatibility of placing given information in a position reserved for new information. That is, the use of a definite NP is said to require that its referent be known, given, or inferrable in context, and this information status is incompatible with a pragmatic condition on *there*-sentences requiring the PVNP to represent an unfamiliar, or new, discourse entity. Previous studies, however, differ in their characterization of what it means for an entity to be new.

For example, Rando & Napoli (1978) argue that the correct restriction on *there*-sentences is not that the PVNP must not be formally definite, but rather that it must be 'non-anaphoric'. For Rando & Napoli, anaphoricity is defined in terms of what is familiar to both speaker and hearer (Kuno 1972). Under this view, then, postverbal NPs in *there*-sentences must represent unfamiliar entities. One type of apparent counterexample to Rando & Napoli's proposal (which they themselves discuss) is the 'list sentence', illustrated in (133):

(133) Q. What's worth visiting here?
A. *There's the park, a very nice restaurant, and the library.*
[=Rando & Napoli 1978, ex. 4]

To account for the well-formedness of such formally definite postverbal NPs in *there*-sentences, Rando & Napoli argue that in these cases the requirement of non-anaphoricity applies to the list itself and not to the individual items on it. However, as Abbott (1992) and others have noted, anaphoric NPs may also be fully felicitous in non-list *there*-sentences. Consider the examples in (134):

(134) a. A: Don't forget that Kim will be bringing a salad.
B: Oh right — *there is that.*
[=Abbott 1992, ex. 15]

b. Ms. Trapnell: Was there any discussion in figuring out what was going to be put on this chart, was there any discussion about creating the chart in such a way that it continued to reflect the concerns?
Mr. Russell: You have to realize that I wasn't in there for the full time of this chart preparation. In reading the chart, there were still some concerns there and some admissions, and I do recall

discussions that, yes, we do expect more blow-by. But the system, the O-ring sealing system in the joint should still work. *But yeah, there were the reservations which are reflected on the chart here that, yeah, we're definitely not going in a better direction.* I think that was realized, and I can't remember if that was stated exactly that way or not, but I got the impression that that was realized. [Challenger Commission transcripts, 3/19/86]

In (134a), *that* is clearly anaphoric; likewise, (134b), *the reservations* is anaphoric to the preceding discussion of concerns, and in neither case does a list seem to be involved.

Abbott (1992, 1993) argues against Rando & Napoli's treatment, arguing instead that such sentences are 'contextualized existentials', and require only an appropriate licensing context for felicity. Consider for example (135):

(135) A: I guess we've called everybody.
B: No, *there's still Mary and John.*
[=Abbott 1993, ex. 5]

With respect to the existential here, Abbott says "the utterer does not seem to be asserting the existence of a list with Mary and John on it, but rather simply drawing the addressee's attention to the existence of Mary and John as filling the predicational slot 'people for us to call' " (1993:43). Instead, Abbott argues for a unified account of *there*-sentences under which their function is "to draw the addressee's attention to the existence and/or location of the entity or entities denoted by the focus [postverbal] NP" (1993:41). Abbott observes that while it will generally be anomalous to assert the existence of an entity presumed to be familiar to the addressee, it will not be anomalous if the existence of this entity is pointed out as a response to a request for entities of a certain type or fulfilling a certain role. Consider (136):

(136) A: What could I give my sister for her birthday?
B: *There's John's book on birdwatching.*
[=Abbott 1992, ex. 22a,c adapted from Lumsden 1988:224]

For Abbott, “use of the anaphoric definite implies the speaker is assuming the addressee is familiar with the referent” (1992:10). In a context where one has been asked to supply an entity to fill a certain role, as in (136), use of a contextualized existential “becomes a polite way to suggest that [familiar] entity as suitable for the purposes at hand” (1992:10). However, consider (137):

(137) The worst one that existed was 10 thousandths on the single O-ring on the Titan, and there are 20 of the five-segment. That was the earliest version. There were four of the seven-segment, which never went into production, but was just a development; and then two five-and-a-half segments, which was a way of getting a little additional performance. And I believe every one of them flying now is the five-and-a-half-segment device. And there is not any evidence, but *there was this 10 thousandths*.
[Challenger Commission transcripts, 2/10/86]

Here, the PVNP *this 10 thousandths* represents information that has been evoked four sentences earlier, and the speaker does not seem to be drawing the hearer's attention to this entity as filling a particular role.

Holmback (1984) bases her analysis of definites in *there*-sentences on Hawkins' (1978, 1991) theory of definiteness, whereby definite descriptions require ‘inclusive reference’, i.e. reference to the totality of objects (within some pragmatically-defined set) satisfying the definite description. Under this view, entities need not be familiar or known for successful definite reference, merely ‘uniquely identifiable’ (Gundel et al. 1990, 1993; cf. Abbott 1993, Birner & Ward 1994). Thus, for Holmback, the ‘definiteness effect’ is simply the consequence of the general incompatibility between the presentational meaning of a *there*-sentence and the following inclusiveness condition on definite descriptions: “[T]he description must be such that it can be seen to refer inclusively independent of the immediate context in order for an existential [*there*-sentence] to have a definite description as [postverbal NP]” (1984:209). To illustrate, consider the examples in (138):

(138) a. There were both major political parties represented at the conference.
[=Holmback 1984, ex. 35]

b. There is the village idiot at the front door. [=Holmback 1984, ex. 49b]

In each case, the definite description contains sufficient information for a hearer to uniquely identify the intended referent on first mention, thus satisfying the inclusiveness condition on definite reference.

While we agree with Holmback that the definiteness effect is the consequence of a (partial) incompatibility between conditions licensing *there*-sentences and those licensing definites, we take issue with her claim that *there*-sentences have a presentational meaning. The following examples of definite PVNPs in *there*-sentences, for example, cannot be interpreted as presentational:

(139) a. There was that deaf comedienne I was telling you about on TV today.

b. I'd love to get away from my job, the kids, the bills... I've thought of chucking it all and going to Hawaii. *But there are the kids to consider.*

c. Like voters everywhere, Montanans are in a resentful mood, and Marlenee is adept at exploiting that resentment...

To add to his troubles, Williams used to be chairman of the subcommittee overseeing grants to the National Endowment for the Arts, and he firmly defended the agency against charges that it funded 'obscene' art works.

That's what won him the support of Keillor, who said, 'It's a measure of the man when he's courageous when it's not absolutely required of him.'

But it has inspired the opposition of national conservatives, including Pat Robertson, who referred to Williams as 'Pornography Pat.'

Then there is that resentment.

[*Chicago Tribune*, 9/4/92]

In none of these examples is the referent of the PVNP being introduced into the discourse.

Hannay (1985) also discusses a number of types of definite NPs that occur in *there*-sentences; to account for their distribution, he argues that it is "inappropriate to assert the existence of a state of affairs if the Subject term of the predication which designates that state of affairs is also the Topic, i.e. what the predication is about in the given setting" (1985:130). A PVNP in a *there*-sentence that asserts the existence of a state of affairs may be definite, then, just in case it not does not represent the sentence topic. However, it is not the case that definite NPs that are topics are categorically excluded from *there*-sentences, as shown in (140):

(140) I think there was one flight where we had one problem. It wasn't ours, but *there was that one flight*. Other than that, I believe the answer to the remaining flights is yes.
[Challenger Commission transcripts, 4/2/86]

Although the determination of sentence topics is notoriously difficult (see Ward 1988 for discussion), it seems intuitively clear that the PVNP in the *there*-sentence in (140) constitutes the sentence topic. Moreover, it passes Gundel's (1974) classic 'what about x' test:

(141) A: What about that one flight you mentioned?
B: It wasn't ours, *but there was that one flight.*

Thus, we conclude that the NP *that one flight* in (140) represents the sentence topic; nonetheless, it appears felicitously in postverbal position.

Lumsden (1988), following Milsark (1974), argues for a distinction between 'strong' and 'weak' quantified expressions, with only the latter being possible PVNPs in *there*-sentences. However, Lumsden's proposed restriction on *there*-sentences, unlike Milsark's, is a hearer-based, interpretive one rather than a formal one. Under Lumsden's analysis, if the hearer expects the set of objects being quantified over to be "in some form already accessible to him" (1988:144), then the interpretation is 'strong' and outside the province of *there*-sentences. However, it is unclear what is meant by a set of objects being "in some form already accessible"; as Prince (1981a, 1992) notes, there are a variety of information statuses covering given and new information. More importantly, Lumsden argues against approaching the definiteness effect (his 'quantification effect') as a unitary phenomenon, and instead distinguishes between enumerative (list) and non-enumerative *there*-sentences. We consider this distinction unnecessary, and will instead present a unified account of *there*-sentences based on a single pragmatic principle which we believe captures the intuition behind Lumsden's analysis.

Definites in existential 'there'-sentences

As we have seen, although many researchers have attempted to account for the distribution of definite PVNPs in *there*-sentences, there has been little consensus among these accounts. Nonetheless, an examination of our corpus confirms that all cases of acceptable *there*-sentences with definite PVNPs can be accounted for by our independently motivated constraint: Specifically, the PVNP in a *there*-sentence must represent an entity that is not presumed by the speaker to constitute shared knowledge; i.e., the PVNP must be hearer-new. As we will show, however, it is possible for an entity to be treated by the speaker as being hearer-old in one respect yet hearer-new in another. Moreover, we will show that an entity's status as hearer-old or hearer-new is independent of whether it may be felicitously realized by a definite NP. We will discuss a number of circumstances in which an entity may be both hearer-new and nonetheless felicitously realized by a definite NP.

As Prince (1992) observes, a definite PVNP is permitted in a *there*-sentence just in case it represents an entity that the speaker believes is not already known to the hearer. Examples of such hearer-new, formally definite NPs are found in (142):

(142) a. There were the same people at both conferences.
[=Prince 1992, ex. 5a]

b. There was the usual crowd at the beach.
[=Prince 1992, ex. 5b]

c. There was the stupidest article on the reading list.
[=Prince 1992, ex. 5c]

Although the PVNPs in (142) are all formally definite, Prince notes that in all cases the entities they represent are assumed to be new to the hearer. For this reason, they are acceptable in postverbal position in *there*-sentences.[6]

Our analysis of the English existential is based on a corpus of 100 naturally occurring existential *there*-sentences with definite PVNPs.[7] We found that, indeed, the entity represented by the PVNP in an existential *there*-sentence always constitutes hearer-new information; however, in certain circumstances this entity may nonetheless be realized by a definite, due to a mismatch between hearer-new status and the constraint on felicitous use of the definite.

As noted above, Holmback (1984) follows Hawkins (1978, 1991) in taking definite descriptions to require inclusive reference, i.e. reference to the totality of objects satisfying the definite description. Under this view, the definite description must render the entity uniquely identifiable for the hearer (Gundel et al. 1990, 1993; Birner & Ward 1994; cf. Du Bois 1980, Abbott 1993). The term

---

[6]McNally 1992 basically accepts Prince's novelty condition for most types of definite NPs, but argues that necessarily quantificational NPs are categorically excluded from postverbal position. McNally (to appear) qualifies this claim somewhat, arguing that "all and only those necessarily quantificational NPs whose descriptive content ranges over nonparticulars (e.g. kinds, sorts, varieties, etc.)" are acceptable in postverbal position. However, consider the following examples:

(i)a. I think that's probably still a NASA job because of the number of contractors involved. *In firing room two, there's every contractor we've got, just about, over there.*
[Challenger Commission transcripts, 3/4/86]

b. *There's everything you want in the spare room.* Use that bathroom. I use the back one, have all my things there...
[Golding 1984:170]

c. There were both major political parties represented at the conference. [=(138a)]

In each of these examples, the PVNP is necessarily quantificational, but in neither case does its descriptive content range over nonparticulars in McNally's sense; nonetheless, the PVNP in each example represents a hearer-new entity and, as we would predict, the use of existential *there* is felicitous. In addition, McNally (1992) argues that the novelty condition may be blocked for bare NPs in list contexts, whereas we will argue below that such contexts are not exceptional and can be straightforwardly handled by our unified account.

[7]In this case, the corpus consists entirely of tokens drawn from the Challenger Commission transcripts.

'uniquely identifiable', however, is misleading in that it suggests that a hearer must be able to identify the actual object in the world. We would argue that what is required for felicitous use of the definite article (and most uses of other definites[8]) is that the speaker must believe that the hearer is able to *individuate* the referent in question from all others within the discourse model. For example, if the speaker utters the NP *the man sitting next to me on the train*, what is required is not that the hearer be able to identify this man on any other basis (e.g., provide his name, or pick him out of a lineup), but rather that the hearer be able, on the basis of this NP, to individuate this man from all other entities in the discourse model. That is, the utterance of this NP in context must provide enough information for the hearer to distinguish this individual from all others. Thus, for the NP *the man sitting next to me on the train* to be felicitously uttered, the speaker must believe that the hearer a) has no other entity in his or her model of the current discourse which is describable by this NP, and b) has no reason to believe there exists another entity (or entities) describable by this NP in the relevant world of discourse. Since the requirement that the entity be identifiable in the real world (or in some preexisting set of discourse entities) cannot account for a felicitous first-mention use of phrases such as *the man sitting next to me on the train*, we will abandon the term 'uniquely identifiable' in favor of the more specific 'individuable within the discourse model', which we take to be a more accurate characterization of the constraint on definiteness.

Thus, an empirical study of existential *there*-sentences in context not only provides evidence against the notion of a definiteness effect, but also helps to clarify the pragmatic constraints on both definiteness and existentials. We have identified five distinct cases in which formally definite yet hearer-new PVNPs may felicitously occur in *there*-sentences (Ward & Birner 1995). In each case, the definiteness of the NP is licensed by the individuability of the referent, while the existential is licensed by its status as hearer-new information. These five classes of definite PVNP, categorized by the relationship holding between the referent of the PVNP and its context, are listed in (143):

---

[8]One class of exceptions would be what we call 'false definites', which despite their form serve to introduce a new referent into the discourse model, as discussed below.

(143) I Hearer-old entities treated as hearer-new
II Hearer-new tokens of hearer-old types
III Hearer-old entities newly instantiating a variable
IV Hearer-new entities with individuating descriptions
V False definites

These classes, while not necessarily exhaustive, illustrate the variety of ways in which a definite NP may represent a hearer-new entity and thus satisfy the constraint on existentials. We will discuss each of these categories in turn.

Hearer-old entities treated as hearer-new

First, certain entities that have been evoked earlier in the discourse may nonetheless be treated by a speaker as hearer-new if the speaker has grounds to believe the entity may have been forgotten. Thus, as noted by Bolinger (1977), Hannay (1985), Lakoff (1987), and Abbott (1993), inter alia, existentials with definite PVNPs can serve as "reminders", as illustrated in (144):

(144) a. Almanzo liked haying-time. From dawn till long after dark every day he was busy, always doing different things. It was like play, and morning and afternoon *there was the cold egg-nog*. [Wilder 1933:232]

b. Like voters everywhere, Montanans are in a resentful mood, and Marlenee is adept at exploiting that resentment...

To add to his troubles, Williams used to be chairman of the subcommittee overseeing grants to the National Endowment for the Arts, and he firmly defended the agency against charges that it funded 'obscene' art works.

That's what won him the support of Keillor, who said, 'It's a measure of the man when he's courageous when it's not absolutely required of him.'

But it has inspired the opposition of national conservatives, including Pat Robertson, who referred to Williams as 'Pornography Pat.'

Then there is that resentment. [=(139c)]

c. Mr. Rummel: Well, didn't the designer of the orbiter, the manufacturer, develop maintenance requirements and documentation as part of the design obligation?
Mr. Collins: Yes, sir. And that is what we showed in the very first part, before the Pan Am study. *There were those other orbiter maintenance and requirement specifications*, which not only did processing of the vehicle, but in flow testing, pad testing, and what have you, but also accomplished or was in lieu of an inspection plan.
[Challenger Commission transcripts, 3/31/86]

Although the cold egg-nog in (144a) is evoked two pages earlier, there are sufficient grounds for the writer to believe that the entity has been (temporarily) forgotten by the reader, thus licensing her to reintroduce it and treat it as hearer-new (see Hawkins 1978, Lakoff 1987). Similarly, the resentment in (144b) and the specifications in (144c) have each been evoked sufficiently earlier in the discourse to license the speaker's treatment of them as hearer-new information. Note that in (144c), *those other orbiter maintenance and requirement specifications* is not coreferential with the maintenance requirements and documentation asked about in the previous speaker's turn; on the contrary, the use of the word *other* in combination with the distal deictic indicates that in fact a different set of specifications is being referred to here. And indeed, examining the entire document, one finds that the reference is to specifications mentioned much earlier in the text (1,277 lines, to be exact):

(145) To go back through just a little of the history, the operational maintenance and requirement specification document had requirements for inspections in there from the first, before the first flight, which covered specific known and suspected problem areas, usually based on previous maintenance findings and inspections, schedule tailored to item of concern.

Thus, in each case, the use of the existential in conjunction with the definite reflects the treatment of the referent as simultaneously hearer-new and individuable. It is this mixed marking that leads the hearer to interpret the utterance as a reminder — i.e., to infer that even though the entity appears to be hearer-new, it nonetheless constitutes shared knowledge. Note that an indefinite in this context would misleadingly instruct the hearer to construct a brand-new discourse entity for what is in fact a previously evoked referent.

The 'reminder' flavor of such tokens is particularly evident in examples such as that in (146):

(146) Caspian's hand had gone to his sword hilt, when Lucy said, "And you've almost promised Ramandu's daughter to go back."

Caspian paused. "Well, yes. *There is that,*" he said. He stood irresolute for a moment and then shouted out to the ship in general.
[Lewis 1952:209]

Here, Caspian has clearly forgotten his promise, and the *there*-sentence serves to echo Lucy's reminder that the promise exists. Thus, the *there*-sentence on the one hand treats the promise as new information, and on the other hand, via the definite, acknowledges it as individuable based on 'prior co-presence' (Clark & Marshall 1981).

Note also the use of demonstratives in the PVNPs in (144b)-(144c). Although the existential in each case would be equally felicitous with *the* replacing the demonstrative, the demonstrative conveys not only that the NP denotes an entity which is individuable in context, but also that this entity is assumed to be part of the interlocutors' private shared knowledge store, based again on assumed co-presence. Thus, consider the following pairs:

(147) a. Those neighbors have been circulating petitions.

b. The neighbors have been circulating petitions.

(148) a. That fence fell down yesterday.

b. The fence fell down yesterday.

The felicitous use of (147a) requires that there be specific neighbors whose existence constitutes shared knowledge for the speaker and hearer (Gundel et al. 1990, 1993); for example, the speaker may have complained to the hearer about these neighbors before. In (147b), on the other hand, the neighbors in question needn't constitute previously shared knowledge; the use of the NP will evoke the culturally inferrable neighbors one is typically assumed to have. Similarly, the use of (148a) conveys that the fence in question is a specific one of which the speaker and hearer share prior knowledge, while the fence referred to in (148b) may be the generally inferrable fence that might plausibly be assumed to surround one's home.

Since it would be odd to remind a hearer of the fact that people have neighbors, *the neighbors* is infelicitous as the PVNP in a 'reminder' *there*-sentence, as shown in (149):

(149) #There were the neighbors at the City Council meeting yesterday.

The demonstrative, on the other hand, is not thus constrained:

(150) There were those neighbors at the City Council meeting yesterday.

Here, the use of the demonstrative signals that the neighbors under discussion constitute shared knowledge, while the existential acknowledges their current status as unfamiliar information. It is this apparent clash that results in a sense of reminder — conveying, in effect, 'you used to know about them, remember?'

Hearer-new tokens of hearer-old types

A definite PVNP is also possible in an existential *there*-sentence when it represents a new instance of a known type; such cases are well attested in the literature (Jenkins 1975; Erdmann 1976; Hannay 1985; Lakoff 1987; Lumsden 1988; Prince 1988b, 1992; Abbott 1993; inter alia). In many cases, an adjective within the NP indicates that the NP denotes a type that is either known (e.g. *same, usual, regular, traditional, obligatory,* and *expected*) or inferrable (e.g. *ideal*, *correct*, *perfect*, *necessary*, and *required*), as in (151) and (152), respectively:

(151) a. The Woody Allen-Mia Farrow breakup, and Woody's declaration of love for one of Mia's adopted daughters, seems to have everyone's attention. *There are the usual sleazy reasons for that, of*

course — the visceral thrill of seeing the extremely private couple's dirt in the street, etc.
[*San Francisco Chronicle*, 8/24/92]

b. Mr. Lee: Aren't you contractually required to perform a hazard analysis? I thought that was in all of our contracts. Aren't you?
Dr. Peller: Yes, we do perform a hazard analysis. It's very similar to what Rocketdyne has done because we've got the same guidelines put out by NASA, which go across the board. And unfortunately, by the way, without the instructions for what information you wish to hear today, they mention the FMEAs and the CIL and did not mention the hazard analysis. So the charts aren't physically in my presentation, but I could have them by tomorrow.
Mr. Lee: I believe they are contractually required. *There is the same requirement placed on all our contractors to perform a hazard analysis, I believe.*
[Challenger Commission transcripts, 4/3/86]

(152) a. The real trouble is, of course, that there isn't the necessary intelligence.
[Erdmann 1976:276]

b. There is the perfect man for Mary in my 210 class.
[=Holmback 1984, ex. 25]

In each of these examples, the PVNP has dual reference, both to a type and a token (Peirce 1931-58; see also Lyons 1977, Nunberg 1979, inter alia). The definite is licensed by the unique individuation of the (hearer-old) type, while the existential is licensed by the hearer-new status of the current instantiation of that type.

Such dual reference also commonly occurs in non-*there*-insertion contexts, as shown in (153):

(153) Fellow-linguists — I'm going to be running the traditional sessions to do problems in comparative reconstruction this term. Scheduling constraints

are already pretty tight...
[D. Ringe, electronic bulletin board posting]

Here, the NP *the traditional sessions* simultaneously specifies both a type and a token. The adjective *traditional* applies to the (hearer-old) type, while the predicate *going to be running* applies to the (hearer-new) instantiation of that type. Thus, the sessions (as a type) are presumed to be familiar; what is hearer-new is the instantiation of these sessions that will occur this term. And as we would predict, this NP is felicitous in a *there*-sentence:

(154) There will be the traditional sessions to do problems in comparative reconstruction this term.

Thus, the PVNP in such *there*-sentences has essentially two distinct referents simultaneously: the hearer-old type and the hearer-new token.[9] Consider (155):

(155) There was the usual crowd at the beach today.[10]

Notice that the group identified as 'the usual crowd' need not always consist of the same set of members; the phrase may felicitously be used to refer to a group of people whose membership varies. Consider (156):

(156) *There was the usual crowd at the beach today.* They were there yesterday too.

Here, the speaker is not referring only to the current instantiation of the crowd, since it is not just today's instantiation that is specified by *they*; (156) may be equally appropriate if several members of today's beach crowd differed from yesterday's.

Nor can the phrase be said to refer only to the entire group. As illustrated in (157), the speaker can go on to describe other attributes holding only of the current instantiation:

---

[9]Ziv (1982b) discusses a similar type/token effect on definiteness in a related construction (*yeŝ*) in Colloquial Modern Hebrew.

[10]As Barbara Abbott points out (p.c.), there is an ambiguity associated with *usual*: (155) can mean either that the same general crowd was at the beach again today, or else it can mean that there was a crowd at the beach today, as usual. It is the first reading that concerns us here.

(157) *There was the usual crowd at the beach today.* They were playing volleyball and eating pizza, and today for the first time they sat around a fire and roasted marshmallows.

Here, the PVNP is not being used to refer only to the type, since sitting around the fire and roasting marshmallows is only being predicated of today's instantiation. Moreover, it cannot be the case that *the usual crowd* is simply ambiguous between the 'type' and 'token' interpretations, because both readings may apply to a single utterance simultaneously:

(158) *There was the usual crowd at the beach today.* They were there yesterday too. Today for the first time they sat around a fire and roasted marshmallows.

Thus, the PVNP in these examples has dual reference, to both a type and a token. The definite is licensed by the status of the type as individuable (i.e., distinguishable from all other types), while the existential is licensed by the hearer-new status of this particular instantiation of the type.[11]

Note also that an explicit adjectival marker isn't necessary; the instantiation of a known type may be indicated instead by the use of a demonstrative:

(159) a. And there was this problem with *all* of his analyses of *there*.

b. And there was the same problem with *all* of his analyses of *there*.

[11]Indeed, to the extent that uniqueness is an integral part of the lexical meaning of the adjective, the use of an indefinite in conjunction with that adjective will be unacceptable:

(i)a. The usual crowd was at the beach.

b. The same crowd was at the beach.

c. ?A usual crowd was at the beach.

d. ?A same crowd was at the beach.

Obligatory or *expected*, on the other hand, may be used with an indefinite to indicate that the referent of the NP is not unique, since uniqueness is not inherent in the meaning of these terms:

(ii)a. An obligatory meeting was held at the beach.

b. An expected crowd was at the beach.

In (iia), the obligatory nature of the meeting in question does not necessarily render its type unique and therefore individuable in the sense that *usual* does above; likewise for the expected crowd in (iib).

(160) a. There was never that situation in America. [=Hannay 1985, ex. 32a]

b. There was never the same situation in America.

In these examples, the use of the demonstrative indicates the relationship of a specific hearer-new token to a previously evoked type (cf. Hannay 1985).

While the examples discussed above involve the instantiation of a previously known type, adjectives such as *ideal*, *correct*, *perfect*, *necessary*, and *required* indicate the instantiation of an inferrable type. In (161), for example, the precise amount of money needed to proceed with the project needn't be previously known; given a project, it is inferrable that some amount of funds will be necessary.

(161) There weren't the funds necessary for the project. [=Abbott 1992, ex. 31a; adapted from Bolinger 1977, ex. 359]

It is this inferrable type that is individuable and licenses the use of the definite. However, the current instantiation of that inferrable type — i.e., the amount of money needed for this particular project — is hearer-new, licensing the use of the existential.

Hearer-old entities newly instantiating a variable

The third class of definite PVNP corresponds to the so-called 'list' interpretation that has been widely acknowledged to tolerate definite NPs in *there*-sentences (Milsark 1974, 1977; Rando & Napoli 1978; Lakoff 1987; Lumsden 1988; Abbott 1992, 1993; inter alia). It consists of one or more hearer-old entities newly instantiating a variable, as in (162):

(162) a. And there's two components in [Division H], which is the operations division: the people that do the flight activity planning procedures work, provide for the crew activity planning and the time line support and integrated procedures development and overall flight data file management; *and then there is the payload support folks*, who provide for customer operations integration and support

of their onboard interfaces.
[Challenger Commission transcripts, 4/8/86]

b. A: What could I give my sister for her birthday?
B: There's John's book on birdwatching. [=(136)]

In each of these examples, the PVNP represents information that is already familiar to the hearer. For example, *the payload support folks* in (162a) denotes a hearer-old group of people comprising one of the previously mentioned components in Division H. In (162b), the PVNP represents a book with which the hearer is presumably familiar. Thus, in both cases, the entities in question are individuable, i.e., distinguishable from all others, thereby licensing the definite.

However, in both cases, the PVNP also serves to instantiate the variable of a salient or inferrable open proposition and, as such, constitutes hearer-new information within that OP. As discussed in Chapter 1, an open proposition represents salient or inferrable information, and is obtained by replacing the constituent bearing nuclear accent with a variable in the semantic representation of the sentence. The element instantiating the variable constitutes the new information, or focus, of the utterance. In (162a) above, for example, *there's two components in Division H* evokes an OP of the form:

(163) X is a member of {components in Division H}.

Here, X is a variable, one instantiation of which is represented by the PVNP *the payload support folks* in the existential. This entity, although familiar, is nonetheless hearer-new with respect to its role as a component in Division H. If, as has often been claimed, *there*-sentences are existential in force, one could say that the OP sets up a narrower context into which the entity is to be introduced as new; here it is the context of Division H components. Thus, the entity is hearer-new, but only within the context established by the OP (cf. Hannay 1985, Abbott 1992).

Unless such an OP is salient or inferrable, a list *there*-sentence with a hearer-old PVNP, as in (164), is infelicitous:

(164) a. What a great time I had last night! *#There was/were John, Mary, Fred, Susan, Hilda, Xavier, and Ethel at this party I went to.* We

danced for hours. [cf. John, Mary, Fred, Susan, Hilda, Xavier, and Ethel were at this party I went to.]

b. A: Who was at the party last night?
B: *There was John, Mary, Fred, Susan, Hilda, Xavier, and Ethel.*

The infelicity of (164a) demonstrates that it is not the enumerative nature of the PVNP that renders it felicitous in a *there*-sentence, but rather its status as instantiating the variable in a salient or inferrable OP. In the presence of the relevant OP (roughly, 'X was at the party'), as in (164b), the use of the existential is fully felicitous. In fact, the PVNP needn't represent a member of a list at all, as illustrated in (162b) above.

While there need be no list, a speaker may use a *there*-sentence involving an OP to implicate that there may be other possible instantiations as well, i.e. that the items mentioned do not exhaust the set of possibilities. Thus, consider the contrast between (165a) and (165b):

(165) a. A: What should I get for John's birthday?
B: There's the bird-watching book that he mentioned.
B´: The bird-watching book that he mentioned.

b. A: What did you get for John's birthday?
B: #There's the bird-watching book that he mentioned.
B´: The bird-watching book that he mentioned.

In (165a), B's use of a *there*-sentence conveys that she believes that there are other possibilities worth considering. Without the *there*-sentence, as in B´, A would be licensed to infer that B's response was exhaustive. In (165b), on the other hand, it would be inappropriate for B to convey that there are other possible, yet unstated, instantiations to the OP in question; B would certainly be in a position to know all true instantiations of the OP. Therefore, in a context in which B purchased only one gift, as in (165b), the *there*-sentence is infelicitous.

Note that the implicature of additional instantiations may be explicitly canceled in a *there*-sentence, as illustrated in (166):

(166) a. A: What's on the office desk?
B: There's the telephone, but nothing else.
[OP: X is on the office desk.]

b. [Khalili] joined the staff of the Rehabilitation Institute of Chicago, a nationally prominent 20-story medical facility, which at the time was just a handful of doctors working in a former warehouse at Ohio Street and McClurg Court. "At times, *there were just the two of us*, and he and I had to see all the patients," recalled Dr. Henry Betts, the institute's medical director and chief executive officer.
[OP: X was on the staff of the Rehabilitation Institute.]
[*Chicago Tribune*]

In each of these examples, the PVNP represents a hearer-old entity newly instantiating the variable in an OP; hence, it is hearer-new in the restricted context of the OP, rendering the existential felicitous. However, in both cases, the speaker explicitly cancels the implicature of non-exhaustiveness that would otherwise be conveyed by the *there*-sentence. Consider these examples without the explicit markers of exhaustiveness:

(167) a. A: What's on the office desk?
B: #There's the telephone.

b. [Khalili] joined the staff of the Rehabilitation Institute of Chicago, a nationally prominent 20-story medical facility, which at the time was just a handful of doctors working in a former warehouse at Ohio Street and McClurg Court. "At times, *#there were the two of us*, and he and I had to see all the patients," recalled Dr. Henry Betts, the institute's medical director and chief executive officer.

In each of these examples, the speaker is using a *there*-sentence to evoke a set whose membership is exhausted by the entity (or entities) represented by the PVNP; with no explicit cancellation of the implicature of non-exhaustiveness associated with the *there*-sentence, infelicity results. In contexts where there are no other relevant instantiations of the OP (such as those in (167) and (165b) above), and no explicit cancellation (as in (166)), use of a *there*-sentence is disallowed.

Hearer-new entities with individuating descriptions

Unlike definite PVNPs that instantiate a variable, those containing individuating descriptions do not depend on the prior context for their felicity; in fact, such NPs are equally felicitous outside of *there*-sentences in first-mention contexts. Consider each of the tokens in (168) in a context where the referent of the direct object NP is entirely hearer-new:

(168) a. The current stock market fluctuations give rise to the added risk that when interest rates fall, mortgages will be prepaid, thereby reducing the Portfolio's future income stream.

b. Postponing the investigation will increase the chance that we'll uncover something additional that is significant.

Although the referents of *the added risk that...* and *the chance that...* in these examples may be new to the hearer, the description provided by the NP in each case is sufficient to fully and uniquely individuate the chance or risk in question, licensing the use of the definite (see Birner & Ward 1994).

Since such NPs may felicitously represent hearer-new entities in non-existential sentences, it is unsurprising that they may also appear felicitously as the PVNP in an existential:

(169) a. In addition to interest-rate risk, there is the added risk that when interest rates fall, mortgages will be prepaid, thereby reducing the Portfolio's future income stream.
[Vanguard Financial Center Newsletter]

b. In addition, as the review continues, there is always the chance that we'll uncover something additional that is significant.
[Challenger Commission transcripts, 3/18/86]

In (169a), although this particular risk is assumed to constitute new information for the hearer, the description provided in the NP is sufficient to completely individuate the risk in question, hence the felicity of the definite (cf. Holmback

1984). Similarly, in (169b), the chance in question is hearer-new but individuated by the embedded clause within the NP itself.

Also unsurprisingly, such sentences tend to be infelicitous when negated:

(170) a. #There isn't the added risk that when interest rates fall, mortgages will be prepaid, thereby reducing the Portfolio's future income stream.

b. #In addition, as the review continues, there isn't the chance that we'll uncover something additional that is significant.

Such sentences are unacceptable because it is generally odd to deny the existence of an entity that is simultaneously being introduced and individuated via a definite; that is, why individuate a new entity only to deny its existence? This accounts for the contrast in acceptability between (170) and (171):

(171) a. There weren't the necessary funds to complete the project. [cf. (161)

b. There wasn't the usual crowd at the beach today. [cf. (155)]

In (171a), the inferrable type *necessary funds* is hearer-old, hence the felicity of denying the existence of an instantiation of that type; similarly, in (171b), *the usual crowd* represents a hearer-old type. In (170), however, the entities represented by the PVNPs are new at every level; consequently, it is pointless, and therefore infelicitous, to both individuate them and deny their existence. It is for this reason that negating *there*-sentences of this type results in infelicity, while negating *there*-sentences that involve hearer-new tokens of hearer-old types is fully felicitous.

This analysis also accounts for the contrast between (172a) and (172b):

(172) a. In Kittredge's latest book there is the claim that syntactic structure is inferrable from pragmatic principles.

b. #In Kittredge's latest book there is the claim about the interaction of syntax and pragmatics.

Since there are many possible claims that could be made about the interaction of syntax and pragmatics, the PVNP in (172b) does not represent an individuable claim, and therefore is infelicitous as a definite.

Other cases in which a PVNP may represent an entity that is both hearer-new and individuated by this NP (and where it is therefore both definite and acceptable in an existential *there*-sentence) include superlatives, deictics, and cataphoric references, as in (173a)-(173c), respectively:

(173) a. There was the tallest boy in my history class at the party last night.

b. You can see the runway and the HUD that overlays the Edwards runway, and *then there is this line which comes out to the outer glide slope aim point.* It is hard to see the PAPIs there because of the lights that are here.
[Challenger Commission transcripts, 4/9/86]

c. There are the following reasons for this bizarre effect...

In (173a), the superlative NP *the tallest boy in my history class* is sufficient to individuate a new entity that the hearer is being instructed to add to his or her discourse model. In (173b) the speaker refers to a line while gesturing toward it; the gesture serves to individuate the new entity represented by the PVNP. Finally, in (173c) *the following reasons* individuates the hearer-new set of reasons in question; it's the set of reasons about to be presented. Similar to this are examples like that in (174), where the referent of *those* is individuated in the relative clause:

(174) There are those who would claim that computers will take over the earth within the next decade.

Again, the individuation licenses the definite, while the hearer-new status of the PVNP licenses the existential; that is, although the hearer is being instructed to add a new entity to his or her model, that entity is provided with a sufficiently rich description to render it individuable within the model.

A final type of hearer-new entity with an individuating description involves a particular sort of inferential relationship that provides the individuation of the PVNP. This class corresponds to Woisetschlaeger's (1983) 'conceptual generics', exemplified in (175):

(175) a. The child crowed. Small feet ran. *There was the sound of a smart slap, and a wail, which subsided quickly.*
[Thane 1943:35]

b. There was the wedding picture of a young black couple among his papers.
[=Woisetschlaeger 1983, ex. 15f]

In these examples, *the sound of a smart slap* and *the wedding picture of a young black couple* constitute 'containing inferrables' in the sense of Prince 1981a. A containing inferrable is a special case of an inferrable entity in which 'what is inferenced off of is properly contained within the Inferrable NP itself' (Prince 1981a:236). That is, the entity represented by the inferrable constituent can be inferred from some other constituent syntactically contained within it, which triggers the inference. Thus, in (175a) the NP *a smart slap* triggers the inference to *the sound of a smart slap*, which syntactically contains it. Given that a slap has a characteristic sound associated with it, the sound is inferrable from the slap. Similarly, in (175b) the trigger *a young black couple* gives rise to the inferrable *wedding picture of a young black couple*, since a married couple is typically associated with a characteristic wedding picture (cf. Lumsden 1988, McNally 1992). In this way, the sound in (175a) and the wedding picture in (175b) are individuated by virtue of their relationship to the trigger, which in turn licenses the use of the definite article. Notice that when no such inferential relationship holds, the definite fails:

(176) a. #There was the large picture of a young black couple among his papers.

b. #The large picture of a young black couple was among his papers.

c. There was a large picture of a young black couple among his papers.

Since couples typically have no characteristic large picture associated with them, (176a) is less acceptable than (175b). Note that the corresponding sentence without *there* (as in (176b)) is equally unacceptable, while the corresponding *there*-sentence with an indefinite PVNP (as in (176c)) is fine. Thus, the inferential relationship between the containing inferrable and the trigger provides the individuation that in turn licenses the use of the definite.

Nonetheless, the containing inferrables in (175) can be considered hearer-new. Birner 1996c shows that the discourse-status of a containing inferrable is dependent on the discourse-status of the trigger; when the trigger is discourse-old, the entire containing inferrable is treated as discourse-old, whereas when the trigger is discourse-new, the entire containing inferrable is treated as discourse-new. Similarly, the evidence from *there*-sentences shows that when the trigger is hearer-new, as in (175), the entire containing inferrable is treated as hearer-new and therefore may felicitously appear in postverbal position in an existential.

Likewise, when the trigger is hearer-old, the entire containing inferrable is treated as hearer-old and is thus infelicitous in postverbal position in a *there*-sentence:

(177) #There was the wedding picture of the Clintons on his table.

We would moreover predict that the trigger can felicitously be definite in exactly the same cases in which any other PVNP in an existential can be definite — i.e., when it represents hearer-new information, as in (178):

(178) There was the sound of the traditional cork-popping as the clock struck midnight.

Here, the trigger *the traditional cork-popping* is definite because the adjective *traditional* individuates an inferrable type; however, the current instantiation of this type is hearer-new. The sound, since it is inferrable from the current instantiation of the type, is in turn individuable and therefore realizable as a definite, yet inherits the hearer-new status of the trigger.

False definites

Finally, we have identified a number of formally definite NPs that behave functionally like indefinites and, as such, may appear felicitously in *there*-sentences. For example, it has been noted that the demonstrative *this* can be used felicitously to non-deictically introduce a hearer-new entity (Prince 1981c, Wald 1983; cf. Givón 1984). Consider (179):

(179) a. One day last year on a cold, clear, crisp afternoon, I saw *this huge sheet of ice* in the street.
[Terkel 1974:505]

b. There once was *this sharp Chicago alderman who also happened to be a crook.*
[*Chicago Tribune*]

c. "There was *this truck* in front of me carrying giant steel coils, and potholes all over the place," he remembers.
[*Wall Street Journal*, 8/30/89]

The italicized NP in each of these examples is used to refer to an entity that the speaker believes is unknown to the hearer.

Whereas the use of a demonstrative typically requires that the speaker assume the hearer is in a position to identify the referent, the use of *this* exemplified in (179) assumes the hearer is not in such a position, and instead instructs the hearer to add a new entity to his or her model of the discourse. As we would expect, demonstratives used in this way are fully felicitous in PVNPs in existential *there*-sentences:

(180) One day last year on a cold, clear, crisp afternoon, there was this huge sheet of ice in the street.

Whether one wishes to call *this* in (179a) and (180) definite or indefinite depends on whether definiteness is considered to be a formal or a cognitive category (cf. Prince 1992). Under a functional or cognitive characterization of definiteness as a category reserved for those discourse entities that a speaker has reason to believe are individuable in context, such NPs would not be definites at all; indeed, they provide a strong motivation for treating definiteness as a cognitive category that maps imperfectly onto the formally defined class of definite NPs within a particular language.

The lexical form *this*, categorized formally as definite, has two distinct uses: It may be used to instruct the hearer to locate (or construct) an individuable discourse entity (a use shared by most other formal definites), or alternatively it may be used to indicate that there is no such individuable entity available to the hearer. Where the PVNP contains anaphoric *this*, as in (181), infelicity results:

(181) One day last year on a cold, clear, crisp afternoon, I saw a huge sheet of ice in the street. *#There was this sheet of ice there all day.*

Here, where the PVNP is being used anaphorically to refer to the previously mentioned and hence individuated ice, the *there*-sentence is infelicitous. In the case of (180), however, the entity being referred to is not individuated by the NP; there may be any number of other entities in the context that are describable by *huge sheet of ice*, and the corresponding *there*-sentence is felicitous. We will use the term 'false definite' to refer to a formal definite used to represent an entity not assumed to be individuated by the use of the NP in context.

Although *this* is by far the most widely discussed member of this class, there are other types of false definites that occur in *there*-sentences, as illustrated in (182):

(182) a. *There are all sorts of variations on term insurance:* policies structured to pay off your mortgage debt, term riders tacked on to permanent insurance, and many others.
[*Wall Street Journal*, 10/20/89]

b. It isn't up as much as many cyclical stocks are, and *there's every reason to believe that over the next several years demand will continue for the computer hardware and data processing equipment that IBM makes.*
[*Wall Street Journal*, 9/18/89]

In (182a), *all sorts of* is not being used to mean literally 'every sort of', but rather is being used colloquially to mean, in effect, 'a lot of'. Similarly, in (182b), *every reason to believe...* doesn't denote literally each one of a set of reasons, but rather something more like 'good reason' or 'many reasons'. When definites are used 'indefinitely' in this way, i.e. to represent entities not assumed to be individuable within the context, they may felicitously appear in existential *there*-sentences. Notice that when the meaning is truly exhaustive, as with *each*, the PVNP is disallowed in a *there*-sentence:

(183) #There is each reason to believe that demand will continue.

None of the false definites, then, are being used to refer to an entity that the speaker believes is individuable to the hearer. Note that a false definite can be felicitously replaced by an indefinite in the same context, but not by a true definite. Compare the examples in (182) with those below:

(184) a. There are some variations on term insurance.

b. #There are the variations on term insurance.

(185) a. There is a reason to believe that demand will continue.

b. #There is the reason to believe that demand will continue.

The (a) variants in these examples are rough paraphrases of the corresponding sentences in (182) (and are correspondingly felicitous), while the (b) variants are not (and are correspondingly infelicitous). Since the PVNPs in (182) are formally definite yet cognitively indefinite, they constitute false definites in the same sense as does *this* in (180). In each case, the PVNP represents a hearer-new entity, rendering it felicitous in the existential.

Definites in presentational 'there'-sentences

As noted above, presentational *there*-sentences constrain their PVNP to represent information that is discourse-new. Since discourse-new information may be either hearer-old or hearer-new, it is unsurprising that definites may felicitously appear in postverbal position in presentationals, as in (125a)-(126a), repeated here as (186a)-(186b):

(186) a. Suddenly there ran out of the woods the man we had seen at the picnic. [=(125a)]

b. President Clinton appeared at the podium accompanied by three senators and Margaret Thatcher. *Behind him there stood the Vice President.* [=(126a)]

In each of the presentational *there*-sentences in (186), the PVNP represents information that is hearer-old yet discourse-new, licensing its appearance in the presentational; its hearer-old status, moreover, renders it individuable, licensing the definite.

Of course, as discussed above with respect to existential *there*-sentences, it is not only hearer-old information that can be definite; hearer-new information may also be definite when (and only when) the speaker believes it to be individuable by the hearer on the basis of the NP in question. Since this mismatch between hearer-status and individuability is independent of any particular syntactic construction, we would expect to find in presentational *there*-sentences the same sorts of hearer-new (and thus necessarily discourse-new) yet definite PVNPs that we find in existential *there*-sentences. This prediction is borne out, as illustrated in (187):

(187) a. The first to be seen of the Wirragatta homestead by anyone following the creek track from the Broken Hill road were the stockyards; and then, as he swung round a sharp bend in what had become the Wirragatta River, *there came into view the trade ships, the men's quarters, then the office-store building, and finally the large bungalow surrounded by orange-trees, which in turn were confined by a white-painted wicket fence.*
[Upfield 1937:55]

b. The visitors here are a doctor who keeps zapping himself with a burglar-fighting stun gun, and Moon Unit's best friend, a lovable flake played by Bess Meyer. The two women like to wear goofy hats. The credits say that three writers were required to create this tableau. Okay, but it has only one good line. The line is: "So?" *There remains the burning question of whether the Zappas, offspring of rock star Frank Zappa and occasional guest veejays on MTV, can act.*
[AP Newswire 1990]

c. They were in a wide and perfectly circular enclosure, protected by a high wall of green turf. A pool of perfectly still water, so full that the water was almost exactly level with the ground, lay before him. *At one end of the pool, completely overshadowing it with its branches, there grew the hugest and most beautiful tree that Shasta had ever seen.* Beyond the pool was a little low house of stone roofed with deep and ancient thatch.
[Lewis 1954:139-140]

In each of these examples, the PVNP represents information that is hearer-new (and therefore also discourse-new) yet individuable, and each corresponds to one of the categories discussed above for definites in existentials. In (187a), for example, the PVNP represents a hearer-new instantiation of a variable; the open proposition 'X came into view' is licensed by the preceding description of what could be seen from various vantage points. Although the various things that came into view are themselves familiar to the reader, the identification of those items as instantiations of the variable constitutes information that is both hearer-new and discourse-new. The PVNP in (187b) is definite because it represents an entity that is individuated by virtue of having been explicitly and completely identified within the NP; nonetheless, the referent is assumed to be both hearer-new and discourse-new. Similarly, in (187c), the NP *the hugest and most beautiful tree that Shasta had ever seen* individuates the tree in question despite its being both hearer- and discourse-new.

Thus, we find two types of definite PVNPs in presentational *there*-sentences: those with hearer-old, individuable PVNPs (as in (186)), and those with hearer-new, individuable PVNPs (as in (187)). In all cases, however, the PVNP represents discourse-new information.

Summary of definites in 'there'-sentences

We have seen that the wide range of definite PVNPs found in both existential and presentational *there*-sentences precludes any non-circular formulation of a definiteness effect based on formal considerations alone. However, previous functional analyses have also failed to account for all of the problematic data in a unified way.

Our empirical study of the contexts in which definite PVNPs may appear in *there*-sentences has shown that when independent constraints on the status of the PVNP are satisfied, the distribution of definites falls out naturally with no need to stipulate a further 'definiteness effect'. Specifically, the PVNP in an existential *there*-sentence must represent an entity which is hearer-new, while the PVNP in a presentational *there*-sentence must represent an entity which is discourse-new. Definiteness, on the other hand, requires the referent of the NP to be individuable by the hearer. Typically this individuability is due to prior shared knowledge; for this reason, many NPs that are definite, and thus individuable in context, will also be hearer-old and/or discourse-old, and thus infelicitous as a postverbal NP in a *there*-sentence. This infelicity has been variously termed the definiteness restriction, quantification effect, and definiteness effect in the formal syntax and semantics literature, on the erroneous assumption that this ill-formedness is due to the definiteness of the PVNP. As we have shown, however, the infelicity in the use of such sentences instead arises from a close but imperfect correlation between the cognitive status to which definiteness is sensitive and that to which postverbal position in *there*-sentences is sensitive. Based on a study of natural language data, we have identified at least five contexts in which the postverbal NP in an existential *there*-sentence may felicitously be definite; what all have in common is the hearer-new status of an individuable discourse entity.[12] The same types of definite PVNP also appear in presentational *there*-sentences; but here, since the constraint is on the discourse-status of the PVNP rather than its hearer-status, we also find definite PVNPs that are hearer-old yet discourse-new. In such cases, the individuability that licenses the definite may be due to the hearer-old status of the referent, while its felicity in the presentational *there*-sentence is due to its status as discourse-new. Whether our findings extend to other languages remains to be seen; what is certain is that the alleged restriction against definite postverbal NPs in *there*-sentences is an epiphenomenon, and the much-discussed 'definiteness effect' a misnomer.

[12]The one exception, of course, is indefinite *this*.

Right-Dislocation

Likė existential and presentational *there*-insertion, right-dislocation involves the noncanonical placement of an argument of the verb in postverbal position. However, in contrast to both existential and presentational *there*-insertion, right-dislocation does not require the postverbal NP to represent new information. Consider the right-dislocations in (188):

(188) a. Below the waterfall (and this was the most astonishing sight of all), a whole mass of enormous glass pipes were dangling down into the river from somewhere high up in the ceiling! *They really were* ENORMOUS, *those pipes.* There must have been a dozen of them at least, and they were sucking up the brownish muddy water from the river and carrying it away to goodness knows where. [=(4a)]

b. Can't write much, as I've been away from here for a week and have to keep up appearances, but did Diana mention the desk drama? Dad took your old desk over to her house to have it sent out, but he didn't check to see what was in it, and forgot that I had been keeping all my vital documents in there — like my tax returns and paystubs and bank statements. Luckily Diana thought "that stuff looked important" so she took it out before giving the desk over to the movers. Phew! *She's a smart cookie, that Diana.* [=(4b)]

c. Clinton has set aside time for a private meeting with Trimble, the only political leader he is seeing on a one-to-one basis. That apparently is designed to offset the 2 1/2 hours he will spend in Londonderry accompanied by John Hume, leader of the mainly Catholic Social Democratic and Labor Party.

Trimble said he doesn't expect any attempt by Clinton at arm-twisting, as the president didn't engage in anything like that when they met in Washington.

All sides are emphasizing that there will be no American attempt at mediation. The British have made clear in the past that they see no need for such help in dealing with British problems, and their view is well understood in Washington.

"It's a massive plus, this visit," said a senior official in London. "It's a huge compliment to Ulster. This thing's going to run a long time."

[*Chicago Tribune*, 11/27/95]

d. *It's very delicate, the lawn.* You don't want to over-water, really. [father in the movie "Honey, I Shrunk the Kids"]

In each of these examples, the sentence-final constituent represents information that has been evoked, either explicitly or implicitly, in the prior discourse. For example, *those pipes* in (188a) and *that Diana* in (188b) represent entities that have been explicitly evoked in the immediately prior discourse, while in (188c) the NP *this visit* represents the global topic of the discourse. Similarly, in (188d) the speaker (whose ant-sized children are lost somewhere in the lawn) has just screamed to two people to get off the grass and then raced to turn off the sprinklers; thus, the lawn is highly salient in this context. Since, in each case, the relevant information is both hearer-old and discourse-old, right-dislocation cannot be viewed as marking information that is new, either to the discourse or to the hearer, and thus differs crucially from existential and presentation *there*-insertion on functional grounds.

General constraints

An examination of naturally occurring data indicates that right-dislocation not only permits, but in fact requires, the dislocated NP to represent information that is given in some sense. As illustrated in (189a), this construction disallows new information in dislocated position:

(189) a. Below the waterfall (and this was the most astonishing sight of all), a whole mass of enormous glass pipes were dangling down into the river from somewhere high up in the ceiling! *#They really were* ENORMOUS, *some of the boulders in the river.* Nonetheless, they were sucked up into the pipes along with the brownish muddy water.

b. [...] Some of the boulders in the river really were enormous. Nonetheless, they were sucked up into the pipes along with the brownish muddy water.

In (189a), the presentation of new information in dislocated position renders the utterance infelicitous, although the canonical non-dislocated variant in (189b) is felicitous in the same context.

The functions posited by previous researchers for right-dislocation, in fact, generally assume either that the dislocated NP represents information that is to some extent given or inferrable within the discourse, or that it represents an effort by the speaker to repair a defective reference. The first approach is exemplified by Davison (1984), who argues that right-dislocation marks the referent of the dislocated NP as a topic, and thus also as having a 'discourse antecedent' (1984:802). Tomlin (1986), exemplifying the second approach, maintains that right-dislocation's primary function is "to self-correct potentially defective texts" (1986:62), with the speaker initially believing that the pronoun will be sufficient to enable the hearer to identify the referent, but then anticipating a possible communicative breakdown and providing a more explicit referring expression in order to forestall failure of reference. Similarly, Geluykens (1987) argues that right-dislocations (in his terminology, 'tails') represent a repair mechanism for self-initiated correction of a potentially unclear reference (see also Givón 1976). However, in cases like those in (188), it is not plausible to consider the right-dislocation to be correcting for a possible reference failure. In (188a), for example, the identity of the referent of *they* in the right-dislocation is clear; not only do the pipes represent the only entity realized by a plural in the previous sentence, but they are also presumably the most salient entity in the discourse at the time the pronoun is uttered. Likewise, in (188b) Diana is the only female mentioned in the prior discourse, and thus the only available referent for the pronoun *she*. Geluykens suggests that such cases may be functionally distinct from right-dislocations used for repair purposes; however, he offers no account of such cases, maintaining only that the majority of right-dislocations serve as repairs.

Ziv & Grosz (1994), on the other hand, draw a sharp distinction between repairs (or 'afterthoughts') and right-dislocations on the basis of distinct syntactic and intonational properties. Afterthoughts, they argue, are characterized by a pause before the final NP, while right-dislocations consist of a single intonation contour. Similarly, they argue that the two constructions have distinct functions, with the function of afterthoughts being corrective while the function of right-dislocation is organizational. In right-dislocation proper, according to Ziv & Grosz, an entity which has previously been situationally or textually evoked (Prince 1981a) is brought to the top of the 'Cf list' (Grosz et al. 1983); that is, it becomes the most salient entity available for subsequent reference. Following Lambrecht (1981), Ziv & Grosz argue that right-dislocation instructs the hearer to search the context for the intended referent. They argue, however, that "if the immediately preceding utterance includes a reference to the entity in question right-dislocation is not felicitous" (1994:190), except when (a) the entity is merely inferrable from, but has not been explicitly evoked in, the prior utterance, or (b) the dislocated NP is predicative rather than purely referential (e.g., when it expresses additional descriptive or emotive content). But the data do not support this claim; as we have seen in (188), the dislocated NP may in fact felicitously represent information that is immediately accessible and currently topical, even when it has been explicitly mentioned in the immediately prior utterance, is referential, and expresses no further descriptive or emotive content. That is, the dislocated NP not only must represent discourse-old information, but may in fact represent currently salient and topical information.

Crucially, this information status is precisely the one that is disallowed by both existential and presentational *there*-insertion; neither construction permits the PVNP to represent information that is both hearer-old and discourse-old, and it follows that neither type of *there*-insertion permits the PVNP to represent the most recently evoked and most topical information in the discourse. Moreover, what all of the above accounts of right-dislocation share is a prohibition on the appearance of brand-new information in dislocated position, where 'brand-new' refers to information that has not been evoked either textually or situationally, is not inferrable from the prior discourse, and is not believed to be otherwise within the hearer's knowledge store (Prince 1981a). And this, importantly, is also the one information status that is not only allowed but in fact prototypical for PVNPs in both existential and presentational *there*-insertion (which differ from each other only in terms of the nature of the newness upon which their felicity depends). Thus, it is clear that the functional restriction on the dislocated NP in right-dislocation differs radically from that imposed on the PVNP in existential and presentational *there*-insertion.

Notice, however, that it is not sufficient for felicitous right-dislocation that the dislocated NP represent hearer-old information; information that is hearer-old yet discourse-new is disallowed in right-dislocated position. Consider (190):

(190) a. I hear the Art Institute has a new exhibit on 19th Century post-Impressionism. *#He was a genius, that Van Gogh.* [cf. That Van Gogh was a genius.]

b. A: What would you like to do for lunch?
B: I'm not sure. *#It's really awful, Pizza Hut.* Let's not go there. [cf. Pizza Hut is really awful.]

In (190a) *that Van Gogh* represents information that is known to the hearer but new to the discourse, and the right-dislocation is infelicitous. Likewise, in (190b) the infelicitously dislocated *Pizza Hut* represents information that is hearer-old but discourse-new. (Notice also that the corresponding canonical-word-order sentence in each case is felicitous in the same context.) In a context in which the dislocated constituent represents discourse-old information, however, the right-dislocation becomes felicitous:

(191) a. I just saw the newly discovered Van Gogh painting at the Art Institute; apparently he painted it when he was only 11 years old. *He was a genius, that Van Gogh.*

b. A: Want to come to Pizza Hut with us? They have a lunch special this week.
B: No, thanks. *It's really awful, Pizza Hut.* Are you sure you want to go there?

Here, the dislocated constituents represent information that has been explicitly evoked in the discourse, and the right-dislocations are entirely felicitous. Thus, what is required for felicitous right-dislocation is not simply that the dislocated constituent represent hearer-old information, but that it represent information that is discourse-old (Ward & Birner 1996).

A comparison of right-dislocation and postposing

We have seen that existential *there*-insertion, presentational *there*-insertion, and right-dislocation are subject to distinct constraints on the information status of the NP in noncanonical position. However, the pragmatic constraints to which these constructions are sensitive do show a significant pattern.

First, notice that our analysis predicts different distributions for the constructions in question. For example, we have seen that while existential *there*-insertion disallows hearer-old, discourse-new information in postverbal position, presentational *there*-insertion does not. Nonetheless, both types of *there*-insertion serve to postpose information that is unfamiliar in some sense, either within the discourse or within the hearer's knowledge store. This function does not apply to right-dislocation, which requires instead that the dislocated NP represent discourse-old information. There exist other important distinctions between right-dislocation and *there*-insertion, however. Both involve a constituent placed in a marked position to the right of its canonical sentence position, and both place some other word in the canonical position of the marked constituent. However, right-dislocation differs from *there*-insertion in permitting the dislocation of constituents other than the subject, as illustrated in (192):

(192) a. He's a pain in the ass, that guy.

b. I can't stand him, that guy.

c. I'd like to wring his neck, that guy.

In (192a), the dislocated NP *that guy* is coreferential with the subject pronoun *he*, whereas in (192b), it is coreferential with the direct object pronoun *him*, and in (192c) it is coreferential with the genitive *his*. In contrast, the noncanonically placed constituent of *there*-insertion must correspond to the canonical-word-order subject.

More importantly, right-dislocation and *there*-sentences differ crucially in the referential status of the lexical item occupying the canonical-word-order position of the noncanonically positioned constituent. In right-dislocation, that position is occupied by a referential pronoun, whereas in both types of *there*-insertion, it is occupied by non-referential expletive *there*. To see this, consider (193):

(193) a. I looked on the table. There I saw a bagel.

b. There are two kinds of bagels I like.

In (193a), *there* is referential, being coreferential with *on the table* in the previous utterance; it also necessarily receives a pitch accent. In (193b), *there* is not referential; instead it is interpreted as an expletive and is correspondingly deaccented. Notice that in (193a) it is impossible to interpret *there* as an expletive, and the sentence as a token of *there*-insertion, due to the fact that the subject position in the sentence is filled by *I*, precluding an interpretation of *there* as filling the subject position (as it does in *there*-insertion). In (193b), on the other hand, the interpretation of *there* as an expletive is forced by the absence of any apparent antecedent, and the utterance is interpreted as a *there*-insertion.[13]

Notice also that in some cases an utterance may be ambiguous between the referential and the non-referential (i.e., *there*-insertion) reading:

(194) On the table there was a bagel.

Here there are two readings available.[14] On the *there*-insertion reading, *there* is a dummy element and is correspondingly deaccented. On the referential reading, *there* is used to refer to a particular place and receives a pitch accent; on this reading, the sentence is an inversion corresponding to the canonical-word-order variant *A bagel was on the table there*. In oral tokens, then, intonation

[13] Of course, changing the context to provide a highly salient location as a potential antecedent could change the interpretation to be referential, e.g. if a person staring at a table containing bagels utters *THERE are two kinds of bagels I like!*

[14] There is actually a third reading, in which the preposed PP is left-dislocated and coreferential with the subject *there*; this reading is not relevant to the present discussion.

disambiguates between the referential and nonreferential readings of potentially ambiguous uses of *there*.

Presentational *there*-insertion gives rise to the same ambiguity:

(195) On the table there remained a bagel.

Since sentences such as those in (194) and (195) exhibit a clear ambiguity between the referential and the *there*-insertion readings, with corresponding differences in intonation, we can conclude that in the *there*-insertion reading, *there* is non-referential.

Right-dislocation, on the other hand, differs from *there*-insertion in that it contains a referential pronoun. That is, in right-dislocation a pronoun that is coreferential with the dislocated NP appears in that NP's canonical position. Consider the right-dislocation in (196):

(196) She's a smart cookie, that Diana.

Here, *she* clearly is coreferential with the dislocated *that Diana*, as evidenced by the number and person agreement. Thus, in right-dislocation the pronominal is necessarily coreferential with the dislocated constituent.

Corresponding to this syntactic difference between right-dislocation and *there*-insertion is a functional difference; as we have seen, right-dislocation is subject to an entirely different pragmatic constraint. In both types of *there*-insertion, where no element coreferential with the logical subject appears in syntactic subject position, the postposed subject is constrained to represent unfamiliar information, while in right-dislocation, containing a pronoun coreferential with the dislocated constituent in its canonical position, the dislocated constituent is constrained to represent familiar, and in fact discourse-old, information.

Moreover, it is precisely the presence of this pronoun that motivates the functional distinction between *there*-insertion and right-dislocation. In right-dislocation, the pronoun is required to represent a discourse-old entity, as do referential pronouns in general. Since it is coreferential with the dislocated NP, that NP must also represent discourse-old information. Thus, it is not accidental that right-dislocation does not serve to keep unfamiliar information out of subject position; the presence of the pronoun actually rules out such a function.

Summary

We have seen that both types of *there*-insertion require the postposed NP to represent information that is unfamiliar in some sense, though the type of unfamiliarity required differs: Existential *there*-sentences require the PVNP to represent information that is new to the hearer, while presentational *there*-sentences only require the PVNP to represent information that is new to the discourse. Thus, presentational *there*-sentences are less constrained, in that they allow PVNPs whose referents are discourse-new but hearer-old; such PVNPs are disallowed in existential *there*-sentences, which require their PVNP to represent information that is hearer-new.

Various previous studies have proposed that *there*-sentences are subject to a definiteness effect, whereby formally definite NPs are disallowed in postverbal position. However, we have identified five specific types of formally definite yet hearer-new NPs that may appear felicitously in postverbal position in existential *there*-sentences. What these NPs have in common is their information status: In each case, the referent of the NP constitutes hearer-new information. That is, postverbal position in existential *there*-insertion may felicitously be occupied by exactly those definite NPs that are construable as hearer-new. Definite PVNPs are similarly found in presentational *there*-sentences; however, due to the looser constraint on the use of presentationals, we find not only the same five types of definite PVNP that were found for existentials, but also hearer-old NPs whose definiteness is licensed by individuation on the basis of prior knowledge. The alleged restriction against definite NPs in *there*-sentences, then, is epiphenomenal; it is simply the result of a close but imperfect correlation between the cognitive status to which definiteness is sensitive and that to which the postverbal position in *there*-sentences is sensitive. Given this, there is no reason to appeal to the so-called 'definiteness effect'.

While existential and presentational *there*-insertion share the property of postposing information which is new in some sense, this property is not shared by right-dislocation, a superficially similar construction. Unlike the postposed NPs of existential and presentational *there*-insertion, the marked NP in a right-dislocation is constrained to represent information that is familiar within the discourse; concomitantly, a pronoun coreferential with the marked constituent appears in this constituent's canonical position. This syntactic difference accounts for the fact that right-dislocation does not serve to keep unfamiliar information out of subject position; the presence of the pronoun in fact rules out such a function.

Indeed, reporting on a crosslinguistic study of postposing constructions (to be discussed in detail in Chapter 5), Birner & Ward 1996 shows that in all cases of subject postposing where no referential element appears in syntactic subject position, the postposed constituent represents unfamiliar information, while in right-dislocation, containing a coreferential pronoun, the marked constituent represents familiar information. We therefore propose that the general function of subject postposing is to place logical subjects representing unfamiliar information in postverbal position. This analysis also accounts for the difference between right-dislocation and *there*-insertion with respect to the noncanonical placement of constituents other than the subject. Right-dislocation allows the marked postverbal placement of not only subjects but other constituents as well, including direct objects, indirect objects, and genitives, while *there*-insertion postposes only subjects. This is unsurprising, given that the function of *there*-insertion is precisely to keep new information out of subject position. As we have seen, right-dislocation does not share this function, and in fact cannot, given the existence of the coreferential pronoun in canonical subject position. It follows naturally, then, that right-dislocation should differ from these constructions in permitting the dislocation of constituents other than subjects, since its discourse function is not specifically one of keeping unfamiliar information out of subject position. The restriction of existential and presentational *there*-insertion to subject position, on the other hand, is entirely consistent with their function of postposing unfamiliar information; the functional difference between them is simply a matter of the type of unfamiliarity in question.

Chapter 4

Argument Reversal

While preposing involves the noncanonical leftward placement of a constituent, and postposing involves the noncanonical rightward placement of a constituent, argument reversal incorporates both; and not surprisingly, the felicity of an argument-reversing construction, we will argue, depends on the discourse-status of the information represented by both of these constituents. The English argument-reversing constructions we consider in this chapter are inversion, exemplified in (197a), and *by*-phrase passives, exemplified in (197b):

(197) a. George, can you do me a favor? *Up in my room, on the night-stand, is a pinkish-reddish envelope that has to go out immediately.* [=(6a)]

b. Connaught said it was advised that the Ciba-Geigy/Chiron offer would be increased to $26.51 a share from $25.23 a share if the company adopted a shareholder-rights plan that facilitated the Swiss and U.S. firms' offer. *That offer was rejected by Connaught, which cited its existing pact with Institut Merieux.* [=(5)]

In each case the logical subject appears in postverbal position while some canonically postverbal argument of the verb appears in preverbal position; the difference is that in the case of passivization, this preverbal constituent is canonically the direct object of the SVO sentence, while in the case of inversion, it is some other argument of the verb.

We will show that inversion and *by*-phrase passivization are subject to the same discourse constraint, i.e., that the information represented by the preverbal constituent be at least as familiar within the discourse as that represented by the postverbal constituent. Syntactically, the two constructions are in complementary distribution, in that there exists no sentence for which passivization and inversion constitute equally grammatical alternatives; passivization applies to transitives, while inversion applies to intransitives and copular clauses. Thus, inversion and passivization will be shown to represent distinct means for satisfying a single discourse constraint in distinct syntactic environments.

Inversion

The term 'inversion' as applied to English denotes a clause in which the logical subject appears in postverbal position while some other, canonically postverbal, constituent appears in preverbal position (see Birner 1994, 1996c). Along with (197a), the examples in (198) are instances of inversion:

(198) a. There are huge cartons and tins of nuts, vanilla, honey, peanut butter. Varieties of herb tea are visible. *On the counter are loaves — whole wheat, cinnamon raisin, oatmeal, rye, soy sunflower, corn meal.*
[Terkel 1974:607]

b. *Immediately recognizable here is the basic, profoundly false tenet of Movie Philosophy 101, as it has been handed down from "Auntie Mame" and "Harold and Maude"*: Nonconformism, the more radical the better, is the only sure route to human happiness and self-fulfillment. [=(6b)]

c. She's a nice woman, isn't she? *Also a nice woman is our next guest...* [=(6c)]

d. Arrested were Nathan Thomas, 23, of New York, and his brother, WO Victor Thomas, 32, a 13-year Army veteran. [=(6d)]

As with preposing, any phrasal constituent can be fronted via inversion. Along with the familiar PP inversion (so-called 'locative inversion') in (198a), AdjP inversion, NP inversion, and VP inversion are all possible, as illustrated in (198b)-(198d), respectively. What all of the inversions in (198) have in common is that some canonically postverbal, lexically governed constituent appears in preverbal position, while the logical subject appears in postverbal position. For convenience, we will refer to these as the 'preposed' and 'postposed' constituents, respectively; however, the syntax of inversion remains controversial (see Kuno 1971, Green 1985, Safir 1985, Bresnan & Kanerva 1989, Coopmans 1989, Hoekstra & Mulder 1990, Rochemont & Culicover 1990, Bresnan 1994, and Levine in prep., inter alia), and the use of these terms is not meant to be taken as an endorsement of any particular syntactic account.

This characterization of inversion excludes such superficially similar but distinct constructions as subject-auxiliary inversion, *there*-insertion, and quotation inversion, with which inversion has sometimes been confused in the literature. Consider first subject-auxiliary inversion (henceforth SAI), as exemplified in (199):

(199) Rarely did I hear such overtones of gratitude as went into the utterance of this compound noun.
[=Green 1980, ex. 32e]

Although SAI and inversion have sometimes been classified together under the common rubric of 'inversion' (e.g., McCawley 1977; Green 1980, 1982), in SAI only the first auxiliary verb appears before the subject, whereas in inversion as it is defined here, all auxiliaries plus the main verb appear before the subject, as illustrated in (200):

(200) [Performer] offers to cause the card to penetrate the deck and the handkerchief and come out on the table. But when he lifts the bundle, nothing has happened. He tries again and this time, *on top of the folded hanky is seen the imprint of the selected card!*
[Magic Inc. Trick Catalog #25, p. 71]

Moreover, the range of discourse functions served by SAI is quite distinct from those served by inversion as defined here (see Hartvigson & Jakobsen 1974, Lakoff & Brugman 1987, and Birner 1996c).

Similarly, although inversion and *there*-insertion have sometimes been treated essentially as variants of a single construction (see, e.g., Erdmann 1976, Breivik 1981, Penhallurick 1984, and Freeze 1992), the two are not only formally but also functionally distinct, requiring distinct discourse contexts for felicity (Birner & Ward 1993; see also Green 1985, Levine 1989, and Bresnan 1994). Consider (201):

(201) a. To the left of the altar one of the big wall panels with rounded tops opens, it is a secret door like in a horror movie, and *out of it steps Archie Campbell in a black cassock and white surplice and stole.* [Updike 1981:242]

b. # [...] *out of it there steps Archie Campbell in a black cassock and white surplice and stole.*

In this context, the inversion is felicitous, but the presentational *there*-sentence is not. (See Chapter 5 for a detailed discussion of the functional differences between the two constructions.) Thus, the formal difference between the two corresponds to a functional difference, and they may consequently be considered distinct constructions.

Finally, we exclude what has been called 'quotation inversion', exemplified in (202):

(202) "I think the hyper-cars are more hype than anything," said Larry Carlat, editor of Toy And Hobby World.
[*Chicago Tribune*, 11/21/89]

Although some researchers (e.g., Hartvigson & Jakobsen (1974), Green (1980), and Penhallurick (1984)) have grouped such examples together with other inversions, they differ significantly in a variety of respects. Unlike other inversions, quotation inversion occurs with transitive verbs; moreover, it permits a wide variety of constituent orderings, including not only subject-verb-quotation (SVQ) and the 'inverted' QVS, but also VSQ, QSV, and either SV or VS embedded within the quotation (QSVQ or QVSQ). Quotation inversion is of course semantically distinct by virtue of appearing only with direct or indirect quotes and requiring a verb of saying, and it is intonationally distinct in that its postverbal NP is typically produced with a low pitch accent (L*, in Pierrehumbert's (1980) system of intonational notation), whereas other inversions are produced with a high pitch accent (H*) on the postverbal NP. Finally, it is functionally distinct in that the preposed quotation may represent newer information in the discourse than does the postposed NP, which we will argue below is impossible for inversion proper. Since quotation inversion differs from other inversions at virtually every level of the grammar, it may be considered a distinct phenomenon, and will be excluded from consideration here.

General constraints

Previous accounts have posited a wide range of functional constraints on inversion. For example, inversion with a preposed directional adverb has been claimed to be limited to 'exclamatory' or 'emphatic' statements (Emonds 1976, Hooper & Thompson 1973), or to signal 'counter-expectation' (Gary 1976). However, these proposals do not account for the felicity of the examples in (203):

(203) a. Loud-speakers had been erected along the garden; *through them emerged the bland informal voice of Commander Stephen King-Hall describing the scene as he saw it from St. Paul's Cathedral.* [Holtby 1936:489]

b. Grandma and Grampa raced each other to get across the broad yard. They fought over everything, and loved and needed the fighting.

Behind them, moving slowly and evenly, but keeping up, came Pa and Noah — Noah the first-born, tall and strange, walking always with a wondering look on his face, calm and puzzled. [Steinbeck 1939:72]

These inversions clearly do not convey any special emphasis, nor do they convey information that is counter to expectation in any obvious way.

Inversion has also been said to mark 'focus', but what is meant by this term varies from one account to the next. Prince (1986) refers to the tonically stressed constituent (representing the new information) of an OP-marking construction as the focus of the utterance, and includes 'locative/directional preposing' (PP inversion) in her list of constructions marking an OP as salient shared knowledge in the discourse, whereas it is argued in Birner & Ward 1989 that only *non*-locative inversion serves to mark an OP as salient in the discourse. (See Chapter 5 for a detailed discussion of OPs as they relate to inversion.) Rochemont 1986 and Rochemont & Culicover 1990 also apply the notion of focus to inversion. Rochemont (1986) identifies two types of focus, presentational and contrastive; an expression P is a presentational focus if the sentence containing it is not 'c-construable' (defined as either 'under discussion' or indexical) but the result of extracting P from the sentence is c-construable. In Rochemont's view, the postposed NP in an inversion is syntactically identified as a presentational focus and therefore must represent information that is not c-construable. Rochemont & Culicover (1990) likewise argue that inversion identifies the postposed NP as a structural focus, and, moreover, that a c-construable element can be a focus if it is contrastive. However, the postposed NP in (204) is c-construable yet not contrastive:

(204) Nusseibeh's unusual predicament causes concern all around. His friends fear that Arab hard-liners will turn on Nusseibeh, thinking he is an Israeli ally.

The Israelis, who certainly want to squelch the 17-month-old uprising in the West Bank and Gaza Strip, are under intense pressure from the United States not to jail moderates who may figure in their election proposal for the territories occupied since the 1967 war.

Most immediately affected is Nusseibeh himself.

[*Chicago Tribune*, 5/21/89]

Here, the postposed NP *Nusseibeh himself* represents information that is c-construable under Rochemont's definition, yet the inversion is felicitous. Bresnan

(1994) similarly argues that locative inversion "has a special discourse function of PRESENTATIONAL FOCUS..., in which the referent of the inverted subject is introduced or reintroduced on the (part of the) scene referred to by the preposed locative" (1994:85); however, the inversion in (204) cannot be said to be either introducing or reintroducing Nusseibeh on the scene, given that he is explicitly evoked in the immediately prior discourse.

Green (1980) proposes a variety of distinct discourse functions for inversion, including practical, connective, emphatic, and introductory functions. The necessity for such a wide range of functions arises in part from the inclusion of SAI and quotation inversion in the class of constructions that Green considers; indeed, the array of functions that she attributes to quotation inversion are entirely distinct from those attributed to the other inversion types. If quotation inversion and SAI are eliminated from the class of inversions under discussion, the remaining functions Green lists are readily subsumed under the connective function.

For example, Green argues that the following inversions, taken from sports broadcasts, serve a 'practical function':

(205) a. Underneath the basket is Barbian.
[=Green 1980, ex. 2b]

b. At the line for Lanphier will be Shelly Tunson.
[=Green 1980, ex. 2h]

Here, Green argues that inversion is a type of stalling device, allowing the announcer to begin to describe what is observable while "remembering or figuring out who [e.g.] 'number 30, blond guard' is" (1980:585). However, such an ordering can also be seen as placing more familiar information before less familiar information — i.e., connecting the postposed new information to the prior discourse by means of the preposed locative.

The inversions in (206) exemplify Green's 'emphatic function':

(206) a. Through the revolving doors swept Tom Pulsifer.

b. Springing from its catacomb with a hoard of Kate Greenaway prints he had unearthed came Spitalny, hair as tumultuous as ever but powdered with silver.

c. There before her eyes was the red button she had been looking for.

[=Green 1980, ex. 27a-c]

In each of these cases, the postposed NP represents previously evoked information which however has not been evoked in the current stretch of discourse and is therefore less familiar than the salient information mentioned in the preposed constituent; thus, the inversion again serves to connect the postposed constituent to the prior context.

Green specifically observes that the examples in (207) do not serve a connective function in that "they do not locate the Postposed Subject Phrases with respect to anything referred to before the adverbial. Rather, they locate the referents of the subject NPs 'absolutely' " (1980:590), serving, she argues, an 'introductory' function:

(207) a. In a little white house lived two rabbits.

b. Into the consulting room of a fairly mad physician, whose name I somehow remember as Lucas Membrane, hurtled a haggard middle-aged woman, towing her husband, a psychotic larrikin about seven feet tall.

c. Down the dusty Chisholm Trail into Abilene rode taciturn Spit Weaver, his lean brown face an enigma, his six-gun swinging idly from the pommel of Moisshe, the wonder horse.

[=Green 1980, ex. 15a-c]

Since each of these sentences begins a narrative, it is true that they do not locate the postposed NP with respect to anything referred to previously in the narrative; however, entities may become familiar by a variety of mechanisms, including but not limited to explicit mention in the discourse. For example, in (207c) the author may reasonably assume that the Chisholm Trail and/or Abilene are familiar to the hearer. Similarly, the 'fairly mad physician' in (207b) is anchored (in the sense of Prince 1981a) to the speaker; for this reason, removing the relative clause results in an inversion that is less acceptable discourse-initially (*#Into the consulting room of a fairly mad physician hurtled a haggard middle-aged woman...*).

In (207a) the postposed NP represents a brand-new entity; interestingly, however, in the story from which (207a) is taken, this entity is referred to again immediately following the inversion. An examination of a corpus of 1778 inversions reveals that only 20 cases contain exclusively brand-new information in both the preposed and postposed constituents. In 12 of these cases, the information represented by the postposed constituent (or some portion thereof) constitutes the topic of the following clause; in 4 cases, the topic of the following clause does not appear in the inversion, and in the remaining four cases there is insufficient context to make a determination. However, in none of the 20 tokens does the preposed constituent provide the topic for the next clause. Thus, (207a) is much less acceptable as the first sentence of a story about a little white house than as the first sentence of a story about two rabbits:

(208) a. *In a little white house lived two rabbits.* #It/#The house was the oldest one in the forest, and it was in disrepair. All the animals in the forest worried that someday the house would come crashing down.

b. *In a little white house lived two rabbits.* They/The rabbits were named Flopsy and Mopsy, and they spent their days merrily invading neighborhood gardens.

The inversion in (207a) allows the writer to begin with a relatively uninformative locative element to which he or she can then relate the postposed constituent by way of introducing it in order to say more about it in the succeeding discourse.[1] We will discuss such inversions in detail below and show how they can be accounted for within our framework.

A rather different, taxonomic study of inversion is presented by Hartvigson & Jakobsen (1974), who argue that the felicity of inversion is determined by the relative weight of the subject and verb, where 'weight' refers to either

[1] Notice that the canonical-word-order variant — *Two rabbits lived in a little white house* — would be an acceptable first sentence in either of the contexts in (208).

'formal weight' (number of syllables/syntactic complexity) or 'notional weight' (information content/'news value'), with the weightier element appearing last. However, by their own admission, Hartvigson & Jakobsen have no rigorous mechanism for quantifying weight, and their notion of 'syntactic complexity' remains essentially undefined (cf. Wasow 1997). Furthermore, their requirement that subjects be postposed when they are formally heavier than the verb is too strong, as illustrated in (209):

(209) In the grass little jeweled lizards darted.
[L'Engle 1978:56]

Here the subject is formally heavier than the verb, yet it remains in preverbal position.

Penhallurick (1984) argues that the postposing of the subject is licensed by virtue of its representing new information — that is, "information which the speaker assumes not to be in the consciousness of the hearer at the time of the utterance" (1984:40; cf. Chafe 1976). Penhallurick views inversion as a 'defocussing' device, claiming that subject position is reserved for elements that are 'in focus', where 'focus' is defined as "what the speaker's attention is centred on in relation to the event specified by the verb" (1984:47). Notice that this use of the term 'focus' is quite different from those surveyed above. Moreover, Penhallurick argues that elements that continue to be the focus of the subsequent discourse tend not to be postposed by means of inversion; however, as was demonstrated above in (208), quite the opposite is true. In fact, in over half of the tokens in the corpus for which a determination could be made (659 of 1193), the information represented by the postposed constituent, or some portion thereof, constitutes the topic of the following clause.

Finally, it is simply not the case that the postposed constituent must represent new information. For example, consider (210):

(210) Yes, this is no ordinary general election.
'Evans is a Democrat; Daley is a Democrat. Different Democrats have different points of view about the city of Chicago and its politics,' Jackson

noted. 'The war between forces within the party continues, and within our coalition.'

Standing in the middle of it all is Jesse Jackson. [=(18)]

This inversion is the final sentence of an article about Jesse Jackson; indeed, Jackson himself is quoted just prior to the inversion. Therefore, Jackson cannot be considered new information. However, although he is undeniably salient, Jackson is less salient than the referent of *it*, i.e., the war between forces within the party and within the coalition, which has been referred to even more recently than Jackson. A comprehensive account of the function of inversion therefore requires more than a binary given/new distinction; it must in fact distinguish among types and degrees of familiarity.

Following Birner 1994, we will show that inversion serves an information-packaging function (Chafe 1976), allowing the presentation of relatively familiar information before a comparatively unfamiliar logical subject. In particular, felicitous inversion in English is crucially dependent on the 'discourse-familiarity' of the information represented by the preposed and postposed constituents, where the degree of discourse-familiarity is determined by the presence or absence of a link to the prior discourse and recency of mention within the discourse. The first factor determines whether information is discourse-old or discourse-new, while among discourse-old information, that which has been mentioned more recently in general is treated as more familiar, in the sense of being more salient, than that which has been mentioned less recently.

Birner 1994 shows that inversion is subject to a pragmatic constraint on the information represented by its preposed and postposed constituents: Specifically, the preposed constituent in an inversion must not represent less familiar information in the discourse than does the postposed constituent. This result is based on an examination of a corpus of 1778 naturally occurring tokens of English inversion, taken from a wide variety of sources. Of these, 1661 tokens are from written sources, 107 from spoken sources, and 10 from indeterminate sources. The vast majority of the tokens are intransitive; the only two that appear to contain a transitive verb involve the complex predicates *take place* and *take root*. Of these 1778 tokens, 654 (37%) are instances of inversion around *be*. In 1162 cases

(65%) the sentence is in the past tense, in 603 cases (34%) it is in the present tense, and in 13 cases (1%) it is in the infinitive. Of the preposed constituents, there are 1286 PPs, 282 VPs, 112 AdjPs, 34 NPs, 16 AdvPs, and 48 other (in the case of, e.g., multiple constituents or incomplete tokens). Of the postposed constituents, 1735 are NPs (of which 12 are clauses), and 30 are some other (or indeterminate) constituent.

The results of the corpus study show that discourse-familiarity is crucial to the felicity of inversion: In no case does the preposed constituent represent discourse-new information while the postposed constituent (the PVNP) represents discourse-old information, although all other possible combinations are represented. Moreover, in more than three-quarters (78%) of the tokens, the preposed constituent represents discourse-old information, while the postposed constituent represents discourse-new information, as illustrated in (211):

(211) a. We have complimentary soft drinks, coffee, Sanka, tea, and milk. *Also complimentary is red and white wine.*
[flight attendant on Midway Airlines, 12/30/83]

b. Such corporate voyeurism enables corporations to tailor advertising messages to specific individuals on a mass scale. For example, "What's Hot," a magazine published by General Foods for children aged 4 to 14, is sent to households that are known to be responsive to ad promotions. The "message from the sponsor" is subtle, with brand names worked into activities such as games and quizzes. *Accompanying the magazine are cents-off coupons.*
[*Consumer Reports*, 6/89]

c. They have a great big tank in the kitchen, and *in the tank are sitting all of these pots.*
[Jeff Smith, Frugal Gourmet, 6/17/89]

In (211a), the preposed *complimentary* has been explicitly evoked in the prior utterance and therefore represents discourse-old information, while the PVNP *red and white wine* represents information that is new to the discourse. Likewise, in (211b), *the magazine* represents discourse-old information, while the cents-off coupons are discourse-new. Finally, in (211c) the preposed *tank* represents information that has been previously evoked and is thus discourse-old, while the PVNP *all of these pots* represents discourse-new information. There are no tokens in the corpus in which the situation is reversed; that is, in no case does a preposed discourse-new element appear in combination with a postposed discourse-old element. Indeed, such an ordering of information renders the inversion infelicitous:

(212) a. They have all of these pots in the kitchen, and *#in a great big tank are sitting all of the pots.*

b. A: Hey, Bill, where's the coffee grinder? Our guests will probably want some cappuccino after dinner.
B: *#On the kitchen counter is the coffee grinder.*

The preposed *a great big tank* in (212a) represents discourse-new information while the postposed *all of the pots* represents discourse-old information, and the inversion is infelicitous; similarly, in (212b), *the kitchen counter* represents discourse-new information, while the PVNP *the coffee grinder* represents discourse-old information, and the inversion is correspondingly infelicitous.

On the other hand, combining a preposed *hearer*-new element with a postposed hearer-old element need not result in infelicity, as demonstrated in (213):

(213) a. Napkin notes: *Reopened after a summer siesta is the SMC Club*, only it's not the SMC Club anymore. With renovations and an expansion of the old Videotech concept came a new name–the Kennel Club.
[*Au Courant*, 10/4/83]

b. I had lunch at Marshall Field's yesterday, and you wouldn't believe who was there. *Behind a cluster of microphones was Hillary Clinton, holding yet another press conference.*

In (213a), the preposed constituent *reopened after a summer siesta* represents hearer-new information, while the PVNP *the SMC Club* may be assumed to be hearer-old in context, and the inversion is fully felicitous. The same point is illustrated in (213b). In both examples, the postposed NP represents information that is hearer-old but discourse-new. This category of information status — hearer-old yet discourse-new — corresponds to what Prince 1981a calls 'unused' information. Unused discourse entities are often represented by proper names, as in (213); however, definite descriptions may also have this information status, as in (214):

(214) I wonder what's going on. A police car is parked in front of the Williams' house. *In the back seat is the mayor.*

Here, *the mayor* represents information that is new to the discourse but presumably familiar to the hearer. Hence, it is not the (assumed) hearer-familiarity of the preposed and postposed constituents that is relevant for felicitous inversion, but but rather their discourse-familiarity.

Thus, our proposed pragmatic constraint on the felicitous use of inversion — that the preverbal element in an inversion must not be newer within the discourse than the postverbal element — accounts for all of the data in a unified way. Not only does the corpus contain no inversion tokens containing a preposed discourse-new constituent and a postposed discourse-old constituent, but in postposed position, constituents representing discourse-new information outnumber those representing discourse-old information by more than eight to one (89.3% vs. 10.7%), while preposed constituents representing discourse-old information outnumber those representing discourse-new information by a similar margin (88.9% vs. 11.1%). And in fact, as noted above, in 78% of the tokens the preposed constituent represents discourse-old information while the postposed constituent represents discourse-new information, as in (211). The results, for the 1290 applicable tokens in the corpus (excluding incomplete tokens and those lacking sufficient contextual information to make a determination of discourse-status), are as shown in Table 4.1. Notice that this is not equivalent to saying that the preverbal constituent in an inversion always represents discourse-old information while the postverbal constituent always represents discourse-new information: In 281 tokens (21.8%), the preposed and postposed constituents either both represent discourse-old information (as in (210)) or both represent discourse-new information (as in (207a)). However, in such cases other factors

Table 4.1: *Discourse-Familiarity of Preposed and Postposed Constituents*

		Preposed		
		D-Old	D-New	Total
Postposed	D-Old	138	0	138
	D-New	1009	143	1152
	Total	1147	143	1290

(including, e.g., relative salience and topichood) determine the felicity of the inversion.

For example, it is shown in Birner 1998 that when both the preposed and postposed constituents represent information that has been explicitly evoked in the prior discourse, it is consistently the more recently evoked, hence more salient (and thus arguably more familiar), information that appears in preposed position, as illustrated in (215):

(215) a. Tich made tea in a blackened billy and McPherson filled a telescopic cup he took from a pocket. Seated on a form, he helped himself to sugar and then proceeded to cut chips from a tobacco plug, the cold and empty pipe dangling from his lips against the full grey moustache. *Seated opposite him was Tich, waiting for gossip, wondering, hoping.*
[Upfield 1940]

b. Each of the characters is the centerpiece of a book, doll and clothing collection. The story of each character is told in a series of six slim books, each $12.95 hardcover and $5.95 in paperback, and in bookstores and libraries across the country. More than 1 million copies have been sold; and in late 1989 a series of activity kits was introduced for retail sale. *Complementing the relatively affordable books are the dolls, one for each fictional heroine and each with a comparably pricey historically accurate wardrobe and accessories...* [=(19a)]

In (215a), both Tich and McPherson are evoked previously in the discourse; however, McPherson, as the referent of *he* in the second sentence, has been mentioned more recently and is therefore more familiar (in this restricted sense) than Tich. In (215b), although the dolls have been evoked in the prior discourse, they have been evoked less recently, and therefore are less familiar within the discourse, than the books. For this reason, changing the ordering of these elements in the same context results in infelicity:

(216) Each of the characters is the centerpiece of a book, doll and clothing collection. The story of each character is told in a series of six slim books... *#Complementing the relatively affordable dolls are the books, one for each fictional heroine...*

The infelicity in (216) is due to the fact that the preposed constituent represents less familiar information than does the postposed constituent.

Now consider (217a)-(217b), in which the order of the relevant elements in (215a) is reversed:

(217) a. Tich made tea in a blackened billy and McPherson filled a telescopic cup he took from a pocket. Seated on a form, he helped himself to sugar and then proceeded to cut chips from a tobacco plug, the cold and empty pipe dangling from his lips against the full grey moustache. *#Seated opposite Tich was McPherson, waiting for gossip, wondering, hoping.*

b. [...] *Seated opposite him was McPherson, waiting for gossip, wondering, hoping.*

In (217a), assuming that *he* in the second sentence is taken to denote McPherson, the inversion is infelicitous with *Tich* in preposed position. The inversion in (217b) is likewise acceptable only on the assumption that *he* in the second sentence denotes Tich. Thus, in all cases felicitous inversion requires that the more recently mentioned element appear in preposed rather than postposed position.

It should be noted that the constraint on the relative discourse-status of the preposed and postposed constituents is not the only constraint on the felicitous use of inversion; for example, we will discuss below an additional constraint on the status of the verb. Moreover, a subset of inversions additionally involve a salient or inferrable open proposition of the type discussed in Chapter 2 for preposing. For example, consider (218):

(218) Two CBS crewmen were wounded by shrapnel yesterday in Souk el Gharb during a Druse rocket attack on Lebanese troops.

They were the 5th and 6th television-news crewmen to be wounded in Lebanon this month. One television reporter, Clark Todd of Canada, was killed earlier this month.

Wounded yesterday were cameraman Alain Debos, 45, and soundman Nick Follows, 24.

[*Philadelphia Inquirer*, 9/24/83]

Here, the OP 'X was wounded at {times}' is clearly salient in the context. Not all inversions involve such an OP, however; as we will see in Chapter 5, inversions whose preposed constituent is semantically locative needn't involve an OP.

In sum, then, the results from the corpus study indicate that the postposed constituent in an inversion tends to represent, but need not always represent, discourse-new information; moreover, when it represents discourse-old information, this information is still less familiar within the discourse than that represented by the preposed constituent. That is, even in cases where both constituents have been previously evoked in the discourse, the postposed constituent nonetheless represents less familiar information. Hence, we see once again that the relative discourse-familiarity of the preposed and postposed constituents determines the felicity of the inversion, and that the more familiar information must appear in preposed position in the inversion. Thus, inversion serves an information-packaging function, allowing the relatively new information to be processed in terms of its relationship to relatively familiar information.

Linking relations

If, as we have argued, inversion functions to place relatively familiar information in preposed position in order to facilitate the processing of the newer information in terms of the older information, inversion can be seen as performing a linking function essentially similar to that of preposing. Indeed, given that inversion incorporates a preposing (as well as a postposing), it is not entirely surprising that the two constructions should share a general functional constraint.

That is not to say, however, that inversion or any subtype thereof is triggered by, or otherwise preceded by and dependent on, preposing (see Aissen & Hankamer 1972, Hartvigson & Jakobsen 1974, Emonds 1976, Green 1980, Coopmans 1989, and Rochemont & Culicover 1990). Some analyses have proposed that, given a preposed constituent, inversion of the subject and verb will occur in some circumstances and not others, which in turn determines whether the resulting sentence will be an inversion or (merely) a preposing. However, if inversion were dependent on and triggered by preposing in this way, it follows that the function of inversion should subsume the function of preposing; that is, if an inversion were composed of a preposing plus a secondary reversal of the subject and verb, it should follow that its function would comprise the function of preposing plus (perhaps) some additional function served by the reversal of subject and verb. However, as we have seen, the preposed constituent in a ('pure') preposing is constrained to represent discourse-old information, while the preposed constituent in an inversion may felicitously represent discourse-new information (as in, for example, (207a)), just as long as that information is no less familiar than that represented by the postposed constituent.

Thus, inversion does not, in fact, incorporate the function of (or functional constraints on) preposing, and we may conclude that, from a functional perspective, inversion is not simply the sum of preposing plus an additional reversal of the subject and verb; rather, it is a unitary construction subject to a distinct functional constraint. Nonetheless, as we will argue at length in Chapter 5, all constructions that involve a preposed constituent, i.e. both preposing and inversion, do share the general function of linking the current utterance to the prior discourse by means of the fronted element. We thus distinguish between 'preposing', which involves the fronting of only a single constituent, and 'preposing constructions', which involve *any* fronting, with or without concomitant postposing.[2] Given that inversion constitutes a preposing construction by virtue of involving a preposed constituent (just as it likewise constitutes a postposing construction by virtue of involving a postposed constituent), it is subject to this general constraint on preposing constructions. However, since inversion is at the same time an individual construction distinct from preposing, their specific functions are likewise distinct. That is, the constraints on preposing and inversion represent distinct instantiations of, or ways of satisfying, the more general constraint on the class of preposing constructions as a whole.

Although inversion shares with preposing the constraint that the preposed constituent represent a link to the prior discourse, it is rarely the case that the preposed constituent in an inversion presents only previously evoked information, as in (219a); it generally also contains some new information, as in (219b):

(219) a. G: What's against it?
B: *Against it is the fact that I could just do nothing this summer.*
[G. Ward to B. Birner in conversation]

b. Parents assume that children are being socialized through language into their particular shared cultural group. This process includes explicit teaching and correcting and the creation of social contexts in which learning will naturally take place. *Critical also to this process is the assumption that, whatever the day-to-day frustrations and irritations in communicating with a child, negative*

[2]The terminological similarity between 'preposing' and 'preposing construction' is unfortunate, but necessitated by our desire to retain consistency with the prior literature. With this in mind, we have attempted to make it clear throughout this book which sense of 'preposing' is intended in any given use; in general, we will use the term 'preposing construction' to refer to the more inclusive class (including argument-reversing constructions), and 'preposing' to refer to the set of preposings defined in Chapter 2.

evaluations will be suspended when a matter of real importance to a child arises.
[Jupp et al. 1982:246-7]

In (219a), the preposed constituent *against it* is a verbatim repetition of prior discourse, providing no further information. In most cases, however, additional information is provided in the preposed constituent. Thus, in (219b), the link *this process*, which represents evoked information, is supplemented by the new information that something is critical to it. Although the notion of something being critical has not yet been evoked in the discourse, the constituent *critical also to this process* nonetheless links the inversion to the prior discourse by virtue of the discourse-old *this process*. Therefore, the presence of the link within the preposed constituent does not preclude the possibility of new information appearing there as well.

Similarly, although the discourse entity represented by the entire PVNP represents relatively unfamiliar information in context, there may nonetheless be some smaller constituent within this NP that represents familiar information, as illustrated in (220):

(220) Greetings from Apple Computer,
Enclosed is a publication I think you will find interesting.
[letter, 5/1/89]

Here, both *I* and *you* represent familiar, situationally evoked entities (Prince 1981a), yet the entire NP *a publication I think you will find interesting* represents new information in the discourse (specifically, what Prince (1981a) calls 'brand-new anchored' information, anchored to the discourse by the situationally evoked 'I' and 'you'). Thus, the information represented within each constituent may vary in information status; nevertheless, in every case the preposed constituent contains a link representing information that is more familiar in the discourse than the entity represented by the postposed constituent.

In the case of a preposed constituent representing information previously evoked in the discourse, the mechanism by which the link is connected to the prior discourse is relatively straightforward; consider for example (211c), repeated here as (221):

(221) They have a great big tank in the kitchen, and *in the tank are sitting all of these pots.* [=(211c)]

Here, *the tank* in the preposed constituent constitutes the link. Recall from Chapter 1 that the link represents information that stands in a contextually licensed poset relationship with previously evoked or inferrable information, and serves as a point of connection between the information presented in the current utterance and the prior context. Recall also that identity is a poset relation. Thus, the information represented by *the tank* in (221) stands in a poset relation (i.e., the identity relation) with the tank evoked in the prior sentence; moreover, by virtue of this poset relationship, it serves as the point of connection between the inversion and the prior sentence. Thus, *the tank* in (221) constitutes the link, with the linking relation being one of identity.

This raises the question of how to deal with inversions whose preverbal constituent represents discourse-new information, as in (207a), repeated below:

(222) In a little white house lived two rabbits. [=(207a)]

We have argued above that this type of inversion allows the writer to begin with a relatively uninformative locative element to which he or she can then relate the PVNP by way of introducing it in order to say more about it in the succeeding discourse. In support of this analysis, we have shown that the information presented in the preposed constituent of such an inversion never represents the topic of the next sentence; instead, the preposed constituent provides a (presumably less informative) setting within which the postposed material may be situated. Notice also that this type of inversion has a strongly literary flavor; that is, outside of a storytelling context it is much less acceptable to use an inversion whose preposed and postposed constituents both represent discourse-new information:

(223) a. Hey, Sam — Did you hear the weird report on the evening news? *#In the basement of a department store are living a bunch of alligators.*

b. Hey, Sam — Did you hear the weird report on the evening news? A bunch of alligators are living in the basement of a department store.

Here, the clearly colloquial context disallows the use of the inversion in (223a), despite the fact that the information status of the preposed and postposed constituents as equally discourse-new does not violate the constraint on their relative status. We would argue that the oddness of (223a) is due to the fact that the discourse-new preposed constituent does not provide the necessary link to the prior context. In literary contexts, however, such preposed constituents are acceptable because of the expectation of the hearer/reader that stories have spatiotemporal settings. Thus, in the context of the beginning of a story, the notion of a setting may be assumed to be situationally evoked (Prince 1981a), providing the trigger for the inference to a poset of settings, to which the preposed constituent (e.g., *the little white house* in (222)) is related via a set/subset relation. In contrast, the context in (223a) provides no such expectation, and therefore no situationally evoked poset, and the inversion is correctly predicted to be infelicitous. In this way, inversion in literary contexts may be used to introduce the entity represented by the postposed constituent by providing a minimal setting in the preposed constituent.[3]

We have argued, then, that inversion is sensitive to the relative discourse-status of the preposed and postposed constituents, and moreover that the preposed constituent contains a link to the prior context. We have furthermore followed Prince 1992 in distinguishing between hearer- and discourse-status. Prince, however, leaves unresolved the status of what she calls 'inferrable' elements, i.e., those that have not been explicitly evoked in the prior discourse but which the speaker believes the hearer can plausibly infer from the context (cf. Clark's (1977) 'bridging inferences'). According to Prince (1992), for an entity to count as inferrable, the speaker must believe a) that the hearer believes it to be 'plausibly related' to some other discourse-old entity, and b) that the hearer will be able to infer its existence. Consider for example (224):

[3]See Green 1982 for a detailed discussion of 'colloquial' and 'literary' uses of inversion.

(224) a. She got married recently, and *at the wedding was the mother, the stepmother and Debbie.* [=(16b)]

b. Labor savings are achieved because the crew is put to better use than cleaning belts manually; *also eliminated is the expense of buying costly chemicals.*
[*WOODEXTRA*, August 1988]

The wedding in (224a) is inferrable, given the mention of somebody getting married; similarly in (224b), *eliminated* represents inferrable information, since mention of labor savings renders inferrable the notion that something is being eliminated (i.e., labor). Birner 1994 shows that inferrable information is treated as discourse-old with respect to inversion; that is, inferrable information may not follow discourse-new information, though it may either precede or follow discourse-old information, as shown in (225):

(225) a. It is especially so with a story as extraordinary as this week's cover story by Marc Schogol. Last spring, I invited Marc, a former ace rewrite man who is now an assistant sports editor of The Inquirer, to write something for the magazine. A few days later, he submitted a list of ideas, and *at the top was the article in this week's issue.*
[*Philadelphia Inquirer*, 9/25/83]

b. She's a nice woman, isn't she? *Also a nice woman is our next guest...* [=(6c)]

Here, both the preposed *the top* in (225a) and the postposed *our next guest* in (225b) count as inferrable information by Prince's definition; that is, given a list one may infer that it has a top, and given a talk show one may infer that there will be guests on it. As seen in these examples, the inferrable information is treated as neither more nor less familiar than the explicitly evoked information in the inversions; both relative orderings are possible. However, the corpus contains no instances of a discourse-new preposed element preceding an inferrable postposed element. Thus, just as we don't find evoked information in postposed position when new information is preposed, we also don't find inferrable information in postposed position when new information is preposed, although all other possible combinations are instantiated. Inferrables, then, are treated as neither more nor less familiar within the discourse than explicitly evoked information; hence, we may conclude that inferrable elements and explicitly evoked elements behave as a single class of discourse-old information for the purposes of word order in inversion.

While this result may initially seem surprising, it follows quite naturally from our account. As noted in Birner 1995a, if the purpose of the link is to establish a connection between the current utterance and the prior discourse context, then what is relevant for felicity is simply whether this connection can be established. Given that the relation between the link and the anchor is always a poset relation, and that the set of poset relations includes the identity relation, it follows that a link representing explicitly evoked information and one representing information that is merely implicit in the prior discourse are both related to the anchor via a poset relation and both serve to establish a similar point of connection to the prior context (see also Strand 1996a). Moreover, in both cases an inference is in fact involved. Although in the case of an implicit link the need for an inference is more obvious, in the case of a link that is coreferential with the trigger an inference is nonetheless necessary to relate the two. Consider the examples in (226):

(226) a. The BMOC is Garson McKellar (Tim Quill), the handsome scion of a Kennedy-esque political family who is the star of the varsity debate team. No quarterback ever had half of Garson's problems, fighting as he must each day to clear a path through the hordes of beautiful co-eds begging for his favors. *Into this heady atmosphere strides Tucker Muldowney (Kirk Cameron), a maddeningly self-confident, gee-shucks freshman from Oklahoma who has entered Kenmont on a debating scholarship.*
[*Chicago Tribune*, 5/8/89]

b. With 87% of the vote reported, Councilman Francis Rafferty and former Councilman Al Pearlman — former Rizzo supporters — were leading the pack. *Following them were the three Democratic at-large candidates who were on Goode's slate during the primary:*

Councilwoman Augusta A. Clark, Councilman David Cohen, and Ed Schwartz, a community organizer.
[*Philadelphia Inquirer*, 11/9/83]

c. The small menu lacks pretense and offers English descriptions under French titles. *Included on the menu are traditional choices such as French onion soup, smoked salmon with caviar, beef with three mustard sauces and salmon with herbs.* The waiter recites a long list of intriguing daily specials, which are thankfully printed as well.
[*Chicago Tribune*, 7/7/89]

In (226a), *this heady atmosphere* stands in an identity relationship with the atmosphere described in the preceding two sentences. This is a case of a 'characterizational' identity relationship, in that the link is not a verbatim repetition of the previous evocation of this entity; i.e., it has not been characterized in precisely these terms in the prior context (see Ward 1988, Takami 1992). Although the heady atmosphere has clearly been explicitly evoked in the prior context, it is being referred to here with a new characterizing phrase in the preposed constituent of the inversion.[4] Thus, the reader must make the inference that the atmosphere described in the preceding sentences constitutes the same heady atmosphere mentioned in the preposed constituent of the inversion. Similarly, in (226b), the reader must infer that *Councilman Francis Rafferty and former Councilman Al Pearlman* is the antecedent of *them* in the preposed constituent. Finally, in (226c) the reader makes the (trivial) inference relating *the menu* in the preposed constituent with the coreferential *the small menu* in the prior sentence. In each case, although the apparent complexity of the required inference varies, an inference is as fully necessary as with the non-identity relationships involved in Prince's class of 'inferrables'. Thus, links involving identity and non-identity relations (corresponding to explicitly evoked information and implicit information, respectively) are alike in being constrained to be in a poset relationship with the anchor, and in requiring the hearer to infer the relationship in question.

[4]The characterizational linking relation is discussed in more detail in Chapter 5.

'Discourse-old' information, then, includes not only explicitly evoked information (i.e., information related to the prior context via an identity relation) but also implicit information related to the prior context via a non-identity poset relation.[5]

Inversion and definiteness

The inversion corpus shows a significant asymmetry in the distribution of definites in preposed position; of the 1485 tokens containing an NP within the preposed constituent (i.e., those tokens which could be assessed for definiteness), 1332 (89.7%) contain a preposed definite, as in (227a), while only 153 (10.3%) contain a preposed indefinite, as in (227b):

(227) a. After the duck came a salad of watercress and chicory in a faint mist of chives.
[Waugh 1945:176]

b. In a tiny office here, buried under shelves filled with dictionaries, sits Dr. Jeffery Triggs, the director of the first North America Reading Program for the Oxford English Dictionary.
[*New York Times* News Service, 1990]

The results for the postposed constituent are much more symmetrical, with 763 (51.4%) postposed definites, as in (200) (repeated here as (228a)), and 722 (48.6%) postposed indefinites, as in (228b):

(228) a. [Performer] offers to cause the card to penetrate the deck and the handkerchief and come out on the table. But when he lifts the bundle, nothing has happened. He tries again and this time, *on top of the folded hanky is seen the imprint of the selected card!*
[=(200)]

[5] This is not to deny the importance of the distinction between the identity relation and other poset relations with respect to other phenomena; for instance, it is certainly the case that pronominalization is sensitive to precisely this distinction. That is, we would say that pronominalization is sensitive not (merely) to discourse-old status, but more particularly to information that not only is discourse-old but also stands in an identity relation to previously evoked information.

b. The products come complete with bags for the microwave cooking. Both popped up nicely enough, with an ear producing about five cups of popped corn. *In there with the popcorn, of course, is a dessicated-looking cob, with quite a few unpopped and semi-popped kernels clinging to it.*
[*Consumer Reports*, 6/89]

Given the discourse-based constraint on inversion presented above, the facts regarding definiteness are easily accounted for: While inversion is sensitive to relative discourse-familiarity, definiteness is sensitive to individuability within the discourse context (see Chapter 3). Since the preposed constituent in an inversion typically (though not always) represents discourse-old information, and since discourse-old status typically (though not always) gives rise to individuability within the discourse model, thus satisfying the constraint on definiteness, we would predict that this position would indeed favor definites.

There is, however, no corresponding tendency for the postposed constituent to be indefinite. The reason is that the class of discourse-new information, which typically appears in this position, includes not only the brand-new, unindividuated entities that would be represented by indefinites, but also discourse-new entities that are individuable by virtue of being hearer-old, as well as entities falling into one of the classes of hearer-new yet individuable information listed in Chapter 3. All of these may be realized by a definite NP despite their discourse-new status. For example, in (228a) *the imprint of the selected card* is discourse-new, since it has not been evoked in, and is not inferrable from, the prior discourse; nonetheless, it is definite because this NP fully individuates the imprint in question (see Chapter 3 for discussion).

Thus, a consideration of the discourse constraints on the use of inversion accounts for the distribution of definites in this construction as well. That is, the preponderance of discourse-old (and therefore individuable) links accounts for the corresponding preponderance of definites in preverbal position, while the more balanced distribution of definites in postposed position is due to the greater variety of information statuses subsumed by the discourse-new status typical of postposed information.

'Locative inversion' and verb choice

It has long been argued that not all verbs may appear in central position in inversion.[6] That is, many researchers have argued that the verbs appearing in English inversion can be characterized as belonging to a particular syntactic or semantic class. Past attempts to characterize this class have focused on a subset of inversions, typically referred to as 'locative inversions', in which the preposed constituent is a semantically locative PP and the verb is something other than *be*. Yet attempting to delimit such a subclass of locative inversions is problematic. For example, there certainly exist semantically locative inversions around *be* as well, as in (229); the corpus contains 430 such tokens.

(229) He was making tea and warming his deeply lined, cracked hands on the pot — *under his ragged nails was the mechanic's permanent, oil-black grime.*
[Irving 1985:291]

Nor do all inversions around verbs other than *be* contain preverbal PPs. While it is true that PPs constitute the vast majority of preposed constituents in such inversions (1096/1124, or 98%), other constituent types are also found. Consider the VP inversions in (230a) and the AdvP inversions in (230b):[7]

---

[6]By 'central position' we mean the position between the preposed and postposed constituents, disregarding other verbs that may appear within these constituents. Henceforth, we will refer to the verb that appears in this central position (along with its auxiliaries, if any) simply as 'the verb', despite the possible presence of other verbs within the sentence.

[7]As noted in Birner & Ward 1992, there exists an interesting asymmetry that holds in the interpretation of certain VP inversions and their corresponding canonical-word-order variants. Consider the sentences in (i):

(i)a. Senator Jones was voting for the President's proposal.
b. Voting for the President's proposal was Senator Jones.
c. Senator Jones voted for the President's proposal.

From the canonical-word-order variant (ia), one could plausibly infer that the completed, or perfective, interpretation in (ic) does not hold. From the VP inversion in (ib), on the other hand, one could reasonably infer that the perfective interpretation does in fact hold. This asymmetry can be attributed to an interaction between Gricean principles and a grammatical constraint on VP inversion. See Birner & Ward 1992 for discussion.

(230) a. You can drive as fast as you like in the outside lane on a West German highway and may feel like the king of the road — until you look in the rear mirror. *Zooming in on you like a guided missile comes a rival contender, bullying you to get out of the way.* [*Chicago Tribune*, 8/8/89]

b. Upali was going to turn 45 in two days. A gala party was planned at his palatial mansion, with his cousin, the nation's president, among the guests. Upali never made it... *Thus was born one of southern Asia's best real-life mysteries.* [*Philadelphia Inquirer*, 8/21/83]

And, as noted above, just as non-*be* verbs can appear in non-PP inversions, *be* can also appear in PP inversions, as in (229) above; of 1309 PP inversions in the corpus, 213 (16%) have *be* as their central verb. Finally, while discussions of locative inversion are often restricted to inversions with a preverbal PP, there are 251 non-PP inversions in the corpus whose preposed constituents nonetheless denote location or direction, as in (231):

(231) Weeds had taken over the path, showing no sign of damage from the movement of the gate or the tramp of feet. *Flanking the gates were low walls topped with railings.* [Grant-Adamson 1986:11]

Thus, there is no perfect correlation between verb class in this sense (i.e., *be* vs. non-*be*) and either the semantic locativity or the syntactic category of the preposed constituent. For this reason, we avoid the term 'locative inversion' as a catch-all term for inversion, and instead shall restrict our use of the term to just those instances of inversion that involve a preposed semantically locative element (see Chapter 5).

Instead, we find that inversions can be grouped into two major categories: those in which the verb is *be* (henceforth '*be* inversion') and those in which it is some other verb (henceforth 'non-*be* inversion'). An examination of the corpus shows that non-*be* inversion is by far the more constrained of the two types both syntactically and semantically. The preposed constituent is a locative PP in 97% of the tokens of non-*be* inversion, as in the examples in (232), but in only 29% of the inversions around *be*.[8]

(232) a. From the lips of a cab driver came an enlightened expression that I thought should be shared.
[*Chicago Tribune*, 3/1/90]

b. East of Cape Kenneth, the tourist trap, lies Heart's Haven; inland from the small, pretty harbor town that's called a haven squats the town of Heart's Rock.
[Irving 1985]

In only 2% of the non-*be* inversion tokens, as opposed to 67% of the *be* tokens, is the preposed constituent a non-PP constituent. Moreover, in all of the tokens of non-*be* inversion, the preposed constituent is either a PP or a semantically locative element;[9] on the other hand, the corpus contains 194 tokens of *be* inversion that fall into neither of these categories (30%). In fact, inversion around *be* permits a wide variety of preposed constituent types, including VPs, PPs, AdjPs, and NPs, as shown in (233a)-(233d), respectively:

(233) a. The most visually enticing selection is the chocolate "delice": a hatbox-shaped dessert made of dark chocolate and filled with berries and white chocolate mousse. *Surrounding the creation is a mosaic of four fruit sauces.*
[*Chicago Tribune*, 7/7/89]

b. Donald Wallace, 28, who faces murder charges in Cook County, has told Hammond police he would be willing to help them find the body. But his court-appointed attorneys have filed a motion with the Illinois Supreme Court to keep him from doing so. *At issue is whether an Illinois judge can allow a man accused of murder to*

[8]The difference between the 97% figure given here for non-*be* inversion with preposed locative PPs and the 98% figure given above for non-*be* inversion with preposed PPs is due to a small number of cases of non-*be* inversion with non-locative PPs in preposed position.

[9]The only exceptions are 16 tokens with *thus*, *so*, or *as* in preposed position, as in (i):

(i) [...] Thus was born one of southern Asia's best real-life mysteries. [=(230b)]

cooperate with authorities in another state without going through criminal extradition proceedings.
[*Chicago Tribune*, 4/14/89]

c. The minimal syntactic theory introduced relies on phrase structure... *Much more prominent than theory is methodology — i.e., argumentation and syntactic reasoning* — because an important goal of the book is guiding readers to think of grammatical analyses as empirically motivated.
[Kaplan 1989:x]

d. An excellent appetizer is the squab ravioli with garlic sauce.
[*Chicago Tribune*, 7/7/89]

Thus, there are significant differences both syntactically and semantically between the two types of inversion, with *be* inversion being by far the less constrained of the two. Within the class of *be* inversion we can further distinguish two types: those containing main-verb *be*, as in (234a), and those containing auxiliary *be* with a preposed VP, as in (234b):

(234) a. *Immediately recognizable here is the basic, profoundly false tenet of Movie Philosophy 101, as it has been handed down from "Auntie Mame" and "Harold and Maude"*: Nonconformism, the more radical the better, is the only sure route to human happiness and self-fulfillment. [=(198b)]

b. The man who thought exercise was a waste of time, who "lived on cholesterol," who routinely worked 14-hour days even on Sundays, no longer exists. Instead, *sitting in the hotel dining room is a trim, tanned Californian who exudes good health.*
[*Chicago Tribune*, 2/14/90]

The data show that auxiliary *be* inversion, as in (234b), patterns with inversion around *be* rather than non-*be* inversion. See Birner 1994 for details.

Auxiliaries other than *be*, though perhaps less common, appear felicitously in both types of inversion. Although Emonds (1976) and Coopmans (1989), inter alia, claim that auxiliaries are categorically disallowed in locative PP inversion, such examples appear in the corpus with some regularity, as in (235):

(235) a. Placed at a disadvantage in that he could not follow tracks in the blackness of night, whereas the night would not prevent the quarry from travelling so long as Dot could see the stars, Bony determined to cover as much ground as possible before the daylight waned and vanished. Arrived at the northern boundary of this run he saw where a deep fire-break had been burned along the east west fence. Ahead of him, to north and west, all the vast region of "open country", unsettled, unfenced, uninhabited. *Into it had gone Dot and Dash in the middle of summer, when there had been no rain for four months, when even the seemingly permanent water-holes might, when reached, be dust-dry.*
[Upfield 1931:202]

b. The West was still a region of great wildness, a fact that had earned it the nickname "the Great Plains." *In this rough, untamed environment had emerged the cowboy, a hard-ridin', cow-punchin' breed of hombre who was to become the stuff of several major cigarette promotions.*
[*Chicago Tribune*, 6/89]

In fact, we have found no restriction on the occurrence of auxiliaries in any type of inversion; in all cases, felicity is determined by the information status and not the semantic category of its constituents.

Other authors have proposed more sweeping restrictions on the semantic category of the verb in inversion. For example, it has been argued that inversion is restricted to locative or directional verbs (e.g., Bresnan 1994), or to verbs of existence and appearance (e.g., Penhallurick 1984; see also Bolinger 1977). Such restrictions have been attributed to inversion's proposed function of 'presentational focus' (Guéron 1980, Penhallurick 1984, Bresnan & Kanerva 1989, and Bresnan 1994, inter alia). However, as we have shown above, inversion in fact does not serve to introduce a new entity onto the scene; given appropriate discourse conditions, the PVNP may represent quite familiar information.

Bresnan argues, moreover, that "verbs in English permit locative inversion if they predicate location or direction of their subjects" (1994:83) and that without this locative/directional predication, inversion around a verb other than *be* is impossible. However, while non-*be* inversion is admittedly less common in non-locative contexts, it is certainly possible, not only in non-PP inversions such as in (230b) above, but also in non-locative PP inversions such as those in (236):

(236) a. Against the greatest odds will surface the greatest story of survival. [voice-over introducing TV movie]

b. Second, to this structure would apply, optionally, a rule we may call Verb Second...
[Langendoen 1973:30]

c. By syntax (the technical term for sentence structure) is meant, for example: Grouping...
[Kaplan 1989:29]

Nor is inversion restricted to verbs of existence or appearance. The corpus contains verbs such as *apply, bubble, decay, die, doze, flap, labour, shriek, war, work,* and *yawn,* which are clearly not verbs of existence or appearance. As we will see below, however, these verbs share with other verbs the property of appearing in inversion only when their lexical content has already been evoked or is inferrable from the context; thus, it is not the semantic class of the verb that determines its felicity in inversion, but rather an interaction of verb meaning and discourse context.

It has also been claimed (Levin 1983, Coopmans 1989, Hoekstra & Mulder 1990, Bresnan 1994, and Watanabe 1994, inter alia) that inversion permits only unaccusative verbs.[10] And indeed, in each of the examples of non-*be* inversion in (232) above, the postposed constituent represents a semantic theme — i.e., a nonagentive, inanimate entity of which some location or direction is being

[10]The class of unaccusative verbs was posited in Perlmutter 1978, and corresponds to the 'ergative' class of Burzio 1986. Simply put, an unaccusative verb takes a D-structure object typically representing a theme or patient, while an unergative verb takes a D-structure subject typically representing an agent.

predicated — and the verbs are prototypical unaccusative verbs. However, there are a number of difficulties with the claim that inversion is limited to unaccusatives. As Levin & Rappaport Hovav (1995) point out, the set of verbs found in naturally occurring inversions is both too large and too small to map comfortably onto the class of unaccusatives. That is, there are on the one hand unaccusative verbs that do not seem to occur in inversions, and there are on the other hand unergative verbs that do.

First, as Levin & Rappaport Hovav observe, certain subclasses of unaccusative verbs are not typically found in inversion, including verbs of externally-controlled change of state, as exemplified in (237):

(237) a. *On the top floor of the skyscraper broke many windows.

b. *On the streets of Chicago melted a lot of snow.

c. *On backyard clotheslines dried the weekly washing.

[=Levin & Rappaport Hovav 1995, Ch. 6, ex. 18 (judgments theirs)]

Here, the verbs *break, melt,* and *dry* are all uncontroversially unaccusative, yet they seem unacceptable in inversion.[11]

Moreover, as noted by Rochemont and Culicover (1990), Levine (in prep.), Levin & Rappaport Hovav (1995), and others, inversion may in fact occur with unergative verbs. Examples are shown in (238):

(238) a. As Daley passed, thousands of onlookers cheered along the 1 1/2-mile parade route down Broadway to Diversey Parkway. "Thank you, thank you," one man said to Daley as he shook the mayor's hand. *Several groups behind the mayor's car marched police officers from Sheriff James O'Grady's parade unit.*
[*Chicago Tribune*, 6/26/89]

b. I sat alone in an office while across the hall the sound engineer, the pop-eyed, silent but hyper James Hill, worked behind a heavy wooden door lined with what looked like foam-rubber waffles.

[11]Although Levin & Rappaport Hovav (1995) star these sentences, we would argue that the unacceptability of such examples is pragmatic rather than syntactic.

On the third floor worked two young women called Maryanne Thomson and Ava Brent, who ran the audio library and print room.
[Colwin 1990:54]

c. From this pulpit preached no less a person than Cotton Mather.
[=Levine (in prep.), ex. 3d; originally cited in Bolinger 1977:103]

The verbs *march*, *work*, and *preach* are uncontroversially unergative, yet these inversions are felicitous. Since, as we have seen, the set of verbs found in naturally occurring inversions seems to include certain unergatives and to exclude certain unaccusatives, inversion is clearly not restricted to unaccusative verbs.

Instead, following Birner 1995a, we would argue that what has been presented as a constraint on the syntactic or semantic class of verbs appearing in inversion is in fact a pragmatic constraint on the information status of the verb in context: namely, that it must not represent new information in the discourse. We will show that, while *be* inversion and non-*be* inversion have different syntactic and semantic profiles in some respects, the discourse-level constraints they observe are identical, not only for the preposed and postposed constituents but also for the verb. To state it more generally, all inversions share identical constraints on the discourse-status of their constituents.

Consider, first, inversion around *be*, as illustrated in (233), repeated below:

(239) a. The most visually enticing selection is the chocolate "delice": a hatbox-shaped dessert made of dark chocolate and filled with berries and white chocolate mousse. *Surrounding the creation is a mosaic of four fruit sauces.*

b. Donald Wallace, 28, who faces murder charges in Cook County, has told Hammond police he would be willing to help them find the body. But his court-appointed attorneys have filed a motion with the Illinois Supreme Court to keep him from doing so. *At issue is whether an Illinois judge can allow a man accused of murder to cooperate with authorities in another state without going through criminal extradition proceedings.*

c. The minimal syntactic theory introduced relies on phrase structure... *Much more prominent than theory is methodology — i.e., argumentation and syntactic reasoning* — because an important goal of the book is guiding readers to think of grammatical analyses as empirically motivated.

d. An excellent appetizer is the squab ravioli with garlic sauce.

[=(233)]

As Hartvigson & Jakobsen (1974) note, *be* is 'notionally light'; i.e., it generally contributes no new information to the discourse. Thus, in each of the inversions in (239), the verb *be* provides no more information than would, say, a colon in the same context:

(240) a. Surrounding the creation: a mosaic of four fruit sauces.

b. At issue: whether an Illinois judge can allow a man accused of murder to cooperate with authorities in another state without going through criminal extradition proceedings.

c. Much more prominent than theory: methodology.

d. An excellent appetizer: the squab ravioli with garlic sauce.

Thus, in inversion around *be*, the verb is inherently light.

Although other verbs appearing in inversion are not inherently light in this way, Birner 1995a shows that when they appear in inversion, they consistently represent information that is either evoked or inferrable in context, and therefore contribute no new information to the discourse. Thus these verbs, like *be*, are 'informationally light' in the context of inversion, contributing no more information to the discourse than would a copula. Moreover, this evocation or inferrability may be due to information appearing in the prior context (as in (241a)), the preposed constituent of the inversion itself (as in (241b)), and/or the postposed constituent of the inversion (as in (241c)):

(241) a. Later that night she made 59 harassing calls between the hours of 11 p.m. and 1 a.m. *Three nights later came another 28 calls*

between 1:52 and 2:30 a.m.
[*Chicago Tribune*, 5/14/89]

b. He opened the door and took a folded canvas bucket from behind the seat. *Coiled on the floor lay a one-hundred-and-fifty-foot length of braided nylon climbing rope three-eighths of an inch thick.* [=Birner & Ward 1992, ex. 17]

c. The giant leader roared and shouted and cheered on the guests. *Beneath the chin lap of the helmet sprouted black whiskers.* [Upfield 1960:178]

In (241a), the notion of calls coming has been evoked in the prior discourse, even though the verb *come* has not appeared explicitly. Similarly, in (241b), the semantic content of the verb *lay* can be inferred from *coiled on the floor*; that is, *lay* contributes no element of meaning that is not already inferrable given *coiled on the floor*. For this reason, replacing *lay* in (241b) with *was* results in no discernible loss of information conveyed:

(242) Coiled on the floor was a one-hundred-and-fifty-foot length of braided nylon climbing rope three-eighths of an inch thick.

Finally, the verb may also be rendered informationally light by the information presented in the postposed constituent of the inversion, as in (241c). Here, the verb describes a state that is characteristic of the entity denoted by the PVNP (see Firbas 1966, Bolinger 1977, Babby 1980, Ljung 1980, Lumsden 1988, and Levin & Rappaport Hovav 1995); that is, sprouting represents a characteristic state of whiskers, rendering *sprout* inferrable in context.

The proposed constraint on the verb in an inversion can help to explain the intuitions motivating prior claims that inversion is limited to unaccusative verbs, or to verbs of existence and appearance. Levin & Rappaport Hovav (1995) note that verbs of existence and appearance are typically informationally light in context, "since they add no information to that provided by the pre-verbal PP, which by setting a scene suggests that something will exist on that scene." Thus it is unsurprising that these verbs are commonly found in inversion. In fact, verbs that are not inherently verbs of existence or appearance can in effect serve as such verbs when they represent a characteristic and therefore inferrable state or activity of the entity in question, and hence contribute no information to the discourse beyond the existence or appearance of that entity. For example, *sprout* in (241c) above represents a characteristic state of whiskers; thus, given mention of whiskers, the verb *sprout* conveys nothing more than their existence. Note also that active, visible sprouting is not inferred, as this would render the verb informative and therefore infelicitous in the inversion.

The requirement that the verb be informationally light also accounts for both the ability of unergative verbs to appear and the apparent (but only apparent) inability of certain unaccusative verbs to appear. As noted by Levin & Rappaport Hovav (1995), the ease with which unaccusative verbs appear felicitously in inversion corresponds to the ease with which they satisfy inversion's discourse constraint; in the right context, however, unergative verbs may also satisfy this constraint and felicitously appear in inversion. Thus, consider again the examples in (238), repeated here as (243):

(243) a. As Daley passed, thousands of onlookers cheered along the 1 1/2-mile parade route down Broadway to Diversey Parkway. "Thank you, thank you," one man said to Daley as he shook the mayor's hand. *Several groups behind the mayor's car marched police officers from Sheriff James O'Grady's parade unit.*

b. I sat alone in an office while across the hall the sound engineer, the pop-eyed, silent but hyper James Hill, worked behind a heavy wooden door lined with what looked like foam-rubber waffles. *On the third floor worked two young women called Maryanne Thomson and Ava Brent, who ran the audio library and print room.*

c. From this pulpit preached no less a person than Cotton Mather.

[=(238)]

In (243a), the unergative verb *march* represents information that is rendered inferrable by the mention of a parade; similarly, in (243b) the verb *work* represents information explicitly evoked in the previous sentence. Finally, in (243c), the verb *preach* represents information that may be inferred from the prior mention of a pulpit. Such cases show that unergative verbs may in fact appear in inversion, as long as they can be rendered informationally light in context; that is, it is their pragmatic information status, rather than their semantic status, that determines their felicity in inversion.

On the other hand, certain classes of unaccusative verbs do not commonly appear in inversion, simply because they characteristically contribute new and unpredictable information to the discourse. Verbs of externally-controlled change of state (Levin 1993) are one such class, as evidenced in (237), repeated here as (244):

(244) a. *On the top floor of the skyscraper broke many windows.

b. *On the streets of Chicago melted a lot of snow.

c. *On backyard clotheslines dried the weekly washing.

[=(237)]

Here, *broke*, *melted* and *dried* all represent new information, and therefore fail to meet inversion's requirement that they be informationally light. However, even these verbs can appear felicitously in inversion when the context renders them sufficiently inferrable. Consider the examples in (245), in which the verb *melt* is inferrable in context:

(245) a. The hot August sun beat down on the children as they walked down the street. Johnny was spooning up soggy sherbet out of a cardboard cup; *in Maria's sticky hand melted a chocolate-chip ice cream cone.*

b. The news of the accident had brought the banquet to a halt. The banquet hall was now deserted, with tables of uneaten food left to spoil. The lettuce on the buffet was beginning to wilt; *in the center of the buffet table melted the once-impressive ice-sculpture swan.*[12]

---

[12]We thank Bill Ladusaw (p.c.) for suggesting such a context.

Thus, the distribution of verbs in inversion cannot be characterized by reference to a single syntactic or semantic class, but instead requires reference to the information status of the verb in its discourse context. In particular, the verb in a felicitous inversion may not add new information to the discourse.[13]

Passivization

Like inversion, English *by*-phrase passives reverse the canonical order of two constituents, and we will argue that such passives, like inversion, are also constrained pragmatically in that the syntactic subject must not represent newer information within the discourse than does the NP in the *by*-phrase (Birner 1996a). We will argue on the basis of these facts that passivization and inversion represent distinct syntactic means for performing the same information-packaging function in different syntactic environments.

For the purposes of this discussion, we will restrict ourselves to a consideration of passives with *by*-phrases containing the logical subject, as exemplified in (246):

(246) The mayor's present term of office expires Jan. 1. *He will be succeeded by Ivan Allen Jr....*
[Brown Corpus]

This restriction excludes such passives as that in (247):

(247) A lamp was stolen yesterday.

We will refer to the preverbal NP in a *by*-phrase passive (e.g., the pronoun *he* in (246)) as the syntactic subject, and to the postverbal NP (e.g., *Ivan Allen*

[13]This constraint does not apply to topicalization, in which the main verb may in fact constitute new information as the focused instantiation of the OP. Consider the topicalization in (i):

(i) G: Why are there two different types of pages?
S: Some of it [S's dissertation] we got for free, *some of it we had to pay for.*
[S. Pintzuk to G. Ward in conversation]

Here, the OP is, roughly, 'We X'd S's dissertation, where X is a member of the poset {means of obtaining a dissertation}'.Thus, the verb represents the instantiation of the OP and constitutes new information.

Jr. in (246)) as the *by*-phrase NP. Breaking with traditional terminology (e.g., Siewierska 1984), we will not refer to the *by*-phrase NP as the agent, nor to these clauses as agentive passives, because an examination of natural language data shows that in many cases the *by*-phrase NP does not act as a semantic agent (in the sense of Fillmore 1968). In (246), for example, *Ivan Allen Jr.* is not an agent, nor are the *by*-phrase NPs in (248) semantically agentive:

(248) a. "This was the coolest, calmest election I ever saw," Colquitt Policeman Tom Williams said. "Being at the polls was just like being at church. I didn't smell a drop of liquor, and we didn't have a bit of trouble." The campaign leading to the election was not so quiet, however. *It was marked by controversy, anonymous midnight phone calls and veiled threats of violence.*
[Brown Corpus]

b. If the Cardinals heed Manager Gene Mauch of the Phillies, *they won't be misled by the Pirates' slower start this season.*
[Brown Corpus]

Here, neither the controversy, phone calls and threats in (248a) nor the slow start in (248b) are acting agentively — i.e., willfully or volitionally. Nonetheless, by virtue of their syntactic form and the existence of an active counterpart, it is clear that the examples in (246) and (248) are all passives (see also Beedham 1982). On the other hand, notice that there exist other sentence-types that superficially resemble *by*-phrase passives but have no corresponding active variant, such as in (249):

(249) The books are carried around by truck in canvas bags from headquarters to the other libraries.
[Brown Corpus]

This cannot be a true *by*-phrase passive since it has no corresponding active variant (**Truck carries the books around*); notice, moreover, that the same type of *by*-phrase that is seen in (249) is equally permissible in active clauses, unlike a true passive *by*-phrase:

(250) In an apparent effort to head off such a rival primary slate, Mr. Wagner talked by telephone yesterday with Representative Charles A. Buckley... [Brown Corpus]

Therefore, tokens such as that in (249) do not constitute instances of *by*-phrase passives.

We restrict this discussion, then, to clear passives containing a syntactic subject, auxiliary *be*, a passive verb form, and a *by*-phrase, and for which there exists a grammatical active variant.[14]

General constraints

Previous functional studies have linked passivization with thematicity. For example, Tomlin (1985) argues that the function of syntactic subjecthood in English is primarily to encode thematic information, and secondarily to encode agentivity, with passivization serving to place the most thematic (or, secondarily, agentive) material in subject position. 'Thematic information' for Tomlin is "that knowledge which the speaker assumes is relevant to the goal of the communicative event" (1985:64). Recognizing, however, that this definition does not provide an objective measure of thematicity, he goes on to link thematicity with attention or salience. Thus, for example, in a game of ice hockey the players are all salient and therefore thematic, the puck is even more so, and the player with the puck is the most salient and thematic of all. Examining videotaped play-by-play descriptions of instances of a single ice-hockey situation — bringing the puck down the ice — Tomlin finds that in 98% of the clauses appearing in the play-by-plays, the subject encodes the most thematic information in the clause.

There are problems with this account, however. First, Tomlin doesn't say how many of these clauses contain only one NP and therefore satisfy his constraint by default. Second, his database represents an artificially narrow range of language data: Since the play-by-play announcer describes the action at the same time that the viewer is seeing it, all of the NPs under consideration represent what Prince

[14]We will not consider here *get*-passives; see, however, Givón 1993 and Givón & Yang (1994), inter alia, for discussion of this type of passive.

(1981a) calls 'situationally evoked' information, leaving open the question of how passivization functions with respect to other information statuses. Even more problematic is Tomlin's evidence for his second claim — that when two NPs in a clause represent equally thematic information, the NP representing the agent appears in subject position. This claim arises from his observation that in a second ice-hockey situation, in which a shot is stopped by the goalie, the corresponding clause is active 50% of the time (i.e., with the goalie realized in subject position), as in (251a), and passive 50% of the time (i.e., with the goalie realized in the *by*-phrase), as in (251b):

(251) a. Palmateer knocked that into the corner.
[=Tomlin 1985, ex. 17]

b. That's blocked by Resch.
[=Tomlin 1985, ex. 14]

That is, only half of the cases display the passivization that Tomlin would predict based on his assumption that the puck is more thematic than a player without the puck. Tomlin accounts for the active cases by suggesting that in this situation the relative thematicity of the puck and the goalie is 'neutralized', and that because the two are now thematically equal, the subject takes the agent — that is, the goalie. Thus, he argues, subject secondarily encodes agent, in precisely those situations in which two competing NPs are equally thematic. However, if that were the case, we would expect all such examples to be active — that is, with the goalie realized in subject position.

In more recent work, Tomlin (1995) recasts the notion of thematicity in terms of focal attention, such that 'theme' may be redefined as "the referent which is focally attended at the moment of utterance formulation" (1995:545). Within this framework, he postulates a revised analysis of the choice between active and passive sentences, arguing that "at the time of utterance formulation, the speaker codes the referent currently in FOCAL ATTENTION as the SYNTACTIC SUBJECT of the utterance" (1995:527, emphasis in the original). Thus, the clause is active when the focally attended referent is the agent, and passive when the focally attended referent is the patient (but see above regarding agentivity in passives).

Tomlin's revised analysis, however, does not account for examples such as the following:

(252) a. It was the season's first night game and an obvious refocusing of the lights are in order. The infield was well flooded but the expanded outfield was much too dark. Mary Dobbs Tuttle was back at the organ. Among the spectators was the noted exotic dancer, Patti Waggin who is Mrs. Don Rudolph when off the stage. Lefty Wyman Carey, another Denver rookie, will be on the mound against veteran John Tsitouris at 8 o'clock Tuesday night. *Ed Donnelly is still bothered by a side injury* and will miss his starting turn.
[Brown Corpus]

b. *An old man is kicked to death by muggers.* The medical examiner states that death was due to 'natural causes'. I once heard a comedian say that *if you are killed by a taxicab in New York*, it is listed as 'death due to natural causes'.
[Brown Corpus]

In (252a), it does not seem that the subject NP *Ed Donnelly* denotes a referent in focal attention at the time of utterance, nor do the subjects of the two passives in (252b) — *an old man* and *you* — appear to denote focally attended referents.

Thompson (1987) likewise appeals to thematicity in her account of the passive, maintaining that *by*-phrase passives are used when the syntactic subject is more closely related than the *by*-phrase NP either to the theme of the paragraph (i.e., 'what the paragraph is 'about' ') or to a participant in the immediately preceding clause. In taking this dual approach, Thompson combines a theme-based account with a familiarity-based account. She notes that both strategies illustrate "the same cohesive principle of thematic unity" (1987:501), with the theme-based strategy simply operating across a larger domain. However, because thematicity is defined in terms of 'aboutness', the two are in fact qualitatively different, with one reflecting the presence or absence of information in the prior clause and the other reflecting a more abstract notion of discourse topic. Moreover, there remain examples that are not accounted for by either strategy, as in (252) above. That is, in (252a), *Ed Donnelly* represents neither the theme of the paragraph nor previously mentioned information; the same holds for both *an old man* and *you* in the two passives in (252b). Such examples are similarly problematic for the theme-based account in Kilby 1984.

While Thompson is correct in her basic insight that passives are used to establish connections between the current subject and the prior discourse, Birner 1996a shows that her disjunctive strategies may be replaced by a single unified constraint on the relative status of the information represented by the subject and that represented by the NP within the *by*-phrase. That is, like inversions, *by*-phrase passives allow the speaker to present information that is relatively familiar within the discourse before information that is relatively unfamiliar within the discourse. This analysis is similar in spirit to that of Givón (1993), who argues that "the pragmatics of voice involves the RELATIVE TOPICALITY of the agent and patient participants of the event" (1993:47; emphasis in the original); that is, for Givón, the entity represented by the *by*-phrase NP in a passive clause (the agent, in Givón's terms) is less topical than the entity represented by the syntactic subject. (See Siewierska 1984 for a similarly topic-based account.) However, based on the data presented below, we would argue that relative topicality accounts for the distribution of passives only to the extent that topicality is defined in terms of information status — specifically, familiarity within the discourse, i.e., precisely the principle that we are proposing.[15]

Based on an examination of the first 200 *by*-phrase passives appearing in the Brown Corpus, Birner 1996a shows that the syntactic subject of such passives consistently represents information that is at least as familiar within the discourse as that represented by the *by*-phrase NP. Moreover, when the information status of the relevant NPs is reversed, infelicity results. Consider again example (246), repeated here as (253a), as compared with (253b):

[15]See also Bernardo 1980, where it is argued that the passive voice of certain verbs is used only when the *by*-phrase NP has "much less prior activation" than does the subject NP. However, Bernardo argues that, in addition to activation, 'salience' plays a role in affecting subjecthood, where salience is determined by semantic, not discourse, factors.

(253) a. The mayor's present term of office expires Jan. 1. *He will be succeeded by Ivan Allen Jr....* [=(246)]

b. Ivan Allen Jr. will take office Jan. 1. *#The mayor will be succeeded by him.*

The subject *he* in (253a) represents discourse-old information, while the *by*-phrase NP, *Ivan Allen Jr.*, represents discourse-new information, and the token is felicitous. In (253b), on the other hand, the syntactic subject, *the mayor*, represents discourse-new information while the NP in the *by*-phrase, *him*, represents discourse-old information, and the passive is infelicitous. Thus, the subject NP in a *by*-phrase passive must not represent less familiar information within the discourse than does the NP within the *by*-phrase.

Again, one might argue that it is hearer-status, rather than discourse-status, that is relevant for the felicity of the passive; however, consider (254):

(254) A formula to supply players for the new Minneapolis Vikings and the problem of increasing the 1961 schedule to fourteen games will be discussed by National Football League owners at a meeting at the Hotel Warwick today.
[Brown Corpus]

In this utterance, which is discourse-initial, the information in the subject NP is hearer-new, while the National Football League owners mentioned in the *by*-phrase are hearer-old. Thus, this token presents hearer-new information in the subject and hearer-old information in the *by*-phrase; nonetheless, the utterance is felicitous because both constituents represent information that is discourse-new.

For the 200 tokens in the corpus, the information statuses of the entities represented by the subject and the *by*-phrase NP break down as shown in Table 4.2. Here we see that there are no tokens in which the subject of the passive represents newer information than does the *by*-phrase NP, although all other combinations are represented.

Table 4.2: *Discourse-Status and Passivization*

		Subject NP		
		D-Old	D-New	Total
By-phrase NP	D-Old	75	0	75
	D-New	88	37	125
	Total	163	37	200

Linking relations

Given that passivization, like inversion, places relatively familiar information before relatively unfamiliar information, it too can be viewed as performing a linking function. That is, in passivization as in inversion, the information represented by the preverbal constituent generally stands in a poset relationship with a previously evoked or inferrable anchor.[16] Consider first the identity relation, exemplified in the passives in (255):

(255) a. The plan does not cover doctor bills. *They would still be paid by the patient.*
[Brown Corpus]

b. Vincent Sorrentino, founder and board chairman of the Uncas Mfg. Co., has been designated a Cavaliere of the Order of Merit of the Republic of Italy.
The decoration will be presented by A. Trichieri, Italian consul

[16]The one exception to this generalization is the case of passives whose subject and *by*-phrase NPs both represent discourse-new information, as discussed in the next section.

general in Boston, at a ceremony at 3:00 p.m. on Dec. 7 at the plant, which this year is celebrating its golden anniversary.
[Brown Corpus]

In (255a), the subject of the passive (*they*) is coreferential with *doctor bills* in the preceding sentence; similarly, in (255b) the subject *the decoration* is coreferential with the previously mentioned designation (*Cavaliere of the Order of Merit of the Republic of Italy*). In both cases, the subject represents a link to the prior context; the only difference is that in (255b), the identity relation is a characterizational one, in that *the decoration* provides a new description of the designation in question.

As with preposing and inversion, the link in a passive utterance may also be related to the anchor via a relation other than identity. Such a link would again constitute what Prince has termed 'inferrable' information; however, we have argued above that in fact all links require the use of inference to establish the proper connection to the prior discourse, and moreover that identity is simply one among a wide range of poset relations that may serve as linking relations in these constructions. Consider (256):

(256) a. After being closed for seven months, the Garden of the Gods Club will have its gala summer opening Saturday, June 3. *Music for dancing will be furnished by Allen Uhles and his orchestra, who will play each Saturday during June.*
[Brown Corpus]

b. California Democrats this weekend will take the wraps off a 1962 model statewide campaign vehicle which they have been quietly assembling in a thousand district headquarters, party clubrooms and workers' backyards. They seem darned proud of it. *And they're confident that the GOP, currently assailed by dissensions within the ranks, will be impressed by the purring power beneath the hood of this grassroots-fueled machine.*
[Brown Corpus]

Mention of the gala opening of a club in (256a) gives rise to a set of typical components of such an event, including drinks, food, dancing, and music for dancing; this is the anchoring set to which *music for dancing* is related via a set/subset relation. Likewise, in (256b), *Democrats* and *the GOP* represent members of the anchoring set {U.S. political parties}; thus, the link *the GOP* represents information that stands in a poset relation with information evoked in the prior discourse. In this way, the linking theory we have presented here eliminates the need for additional machinery to handle 'inferrable' elements in discourse.[17]

A comparison of passivization and inversion

We have shown that inversion serves an information-packaging function, preposing information that is more familiar within the discourse while postposing information that is less familiar within the discourse. Moreover, this same distribution of information is seen in passivization, which similarly places more familiar before less familiar information. Thus, inversion and passivization share a pragmatic constraint to the effect that the preverbal constituent must not represent information that is less familiar within the discourse than that represented by the postverbal constituent.

Notice also that, syntactically, the two constructions are in complementary distribution, in that there exists no canonical-word-order clause for which inversion and passivization represent equally grammatical variants. Passivization applies to transitives, while inversion does not; conversely, inversion occurs with intransitives and copular clauses, which do not passivize.[18] Moreover, both constructions effectively reverse the linear order of the logical subject and some other argument of the verb, and both constrain the relative information status of these two constituents in identical ways. Recall that in neither construction

[17]In Chapter 5, the linking relations involved in both preposing and argument reversal will be examined in more detail.

[18]Although certain passives may undergo inversion (e.g., *On the stairs had been left a pair of shoes*), notice that *by*-phrase passives are typically infelicitous as inversions: *#On the stairs had been left a pair of shoes by Mary.*

is discourse-new information disallowed in preverbal position, nor is discourse-old information disallowed in postverbal position; what is disallowed in these constructions is the placement of newer information in preposed position than in postposed position. That is, in passivization as in inversion, argument reversal results in the presentation of relatively familiar information before relatively unfamiliar information. This suggests that passivization and inversion represent distinct mechanisms for performing a single information-packaging function in different syntactic environments.

Notice, however, that although passivization, like inversion, requires that its initial marked constituent represent information that is at least as familiar as that represented by the final marked constituent, passivization permits cases in which the subject NP does not in fact represent a link to the prior discourse. Consider (257):

(257) *An alert 10-year-old safety patrol boy was congratulated by police today for his part in obtaining a reckless driving conviction against a youthful motorist.*

Patrolman George Kimmell, of McClellan Station, said he would recommend a special safety citation for Ralph Sisk, 9230 Vernor East, a third grader at the Scripps School, for his assistance in the case.
[Brown Corpus]

In this discourse-initial passivization, *an alert 10-year-old safety patrol boy* represents information that is not only discourse-new, but also (unlike the discourse-new scene-setting PPs of inversion) does not stand in a poset relationship with information evoked in or inferrable from the prior discourse. Such discourse-new subjects appear in 37 out of the 200 tokens in the corpus (18.5%); in every case, however, the *by*-phrase NP also represents discourse-new information. Thus, in every token in the corpus, the subject NP represents information that is at least as familiar in the discourse as is the *by*-phrase NP; moreover, in all passives other than those presenting only discourse-new information in their marked constituents, the subject NP constitutes a discourse-old link to the prior discourse.

To summarize, then, we have seen that both inversion and passivization serve to present relatively familiar information before relatively unfamiliar information, and therefore serve the same information-packaging function in different syntactic environments.

PP Preposing with 'There'-Insertion

As noted above, inversion as it is defined here is distinct from *there*-insertion; more particularly, it is to be distinguished from PP preposing with *there*-insertion, as illustrated in (258):

(258) a. There are two O-rings around the seal, and on about five, perhaps half a dozen STS flights, *on each flight there are six seal areas, three segments, three breaks in each of two solids.* [=(7a)]

b. The Government of Canada has declared a world heritage site and this particular administration has put the finishing touch on a national park at that location. *In this land that received the first settlers to the new world, today, centuries later, there exist small communities of people who are close to the land and sea.* [=(7b)]

Such sentences are formally distinct from inversion by virtue of containing expletive *there* in subject position, and not surprisingly, they are functionally distinct as well.

For example, while felicitous use of inversion requires that the information represented by the preposed constituent be at least as familiar within the discourse as that represented by the postposed constituent, this constraint is inadequate to account for the distribution of sentences combining PP preposing and *there*-insertion. For example, *there*-sentences do not become felicitous in the presence of a preposed PP containing more recently evoked information:

(259) a. Jill and John sat eating pizza. Jill took a slice and carefully picked off all the mushrooms, then took a big bite. *#Across from her there sat John, working on his fourth or fifth slice.*

b. [...] Across from her sat John, working on his fourth or fifth slice.

c. [...] John sat across from her, working on his fourth or fifth slice.

Here we see that when the preposed PP represents more recently mentioned information than does the postposed NP, the inversion in (259b) is felicitous but the corresponding presentational *there*-insertion in (259a) is not. (Notice that the canonical-word-order variant in (259c) is fully felicitous.) That is, the presence of a discourse-old PVNP in a presentational *there*-sentence (which has been shown above to require a discourse-new PVNP) is not rendered felicitous by the existence of a preposed PP representing more recently mentioned information. At the same time, we see that inversion does not require the postposed constituent to represent discourse-new information in an absolute sense, as long as the preposed constituent represents more recently evoked and therefore more familiar information. Reversing the order of information, of course, results in infelicity for both the inversion and the *there*-sentence:

(260) a. Jill and John sat eating pizza. John took a slice and carefully picked off all the mushrooms, then took a big bite. *#Across from Jill sat John, working on his fourth or fifth slice.*

b. Jill and John sat eating pizza. John took a slice and carefully picked off all the mushrooms, then took a big bite. *#Across from Jill there sat John, working on his fourth or fifth slice.*

In (260a), the preposed *Jill* represents less recently evoked information than does the postposed *John*, so the constraint on inversion is not satisfied and the utterance is infelicitous. Likewise, in (260b) the discourse-old status of *John* renders it unacceptable as a PVNP in a presentational *there*-sentence, and the utterance is correspondingly infelicitous.

We find similar results when we consider inversion vs. existential *there*-insertion. Recall that for existentials, the PVNP must represent hearer-new information. Again, simply ensuring that the information represented by the PVNP is less recently mentioned than that represented by the preposed PP is insufficient:

(261) a. Jill and John sat eating pizza. Jill took a slice and carefully picked off all the mushrooms, then took a big bite. *#Across from her there was John, working on his fourth or fifth slice.*

b. [...] Across from her was John, working on his fourth or fifth slice.

Again, the more recent mention of Jill in (261a) does not render the postverbal mention of the hearer-old John felicitous; in contrast, the felicity of (261b) demonstrates once again that inversion does not require either discourse- or hearer-new information in postposed position, as long as the preposed constituent represents information that is more recently evoked.

The reason for the discrepancy between the felicity of the inversions and the corresponding *there*-sentences lies in the formal and functional differences between the two sentence-types. Whereas inversion is a single construction performing an argument-reversing function, a *there*-sentence with a preposed PP, as in (258), is a combination of two distinct constructions, each of which places distinct constraints on one of the noncanonically placed constituents (Birner, in prep.). The italicized sentence in (259a), for example, incorporates both a topicalization and a presentational *there*-sentence, and requires that both the constraint on topicalization and the constraint on the use of presentational *there* be satisfied. The constraint on topicalization is satisfied in that the entity represented by the preposed *her* stands in a salient poset relationship with the prior evocation of Jill; however, the constraint on the use of presentational *there* is not satisfied, since *John* represents discourse-old information. Similarly, the italicized sentence in (261a) incorporates a topicalization and an existential *there*-sentence, and correspondingly requires that both the constraint on topicalization and the constraint on the use of existential *there* be satisfied. Again, the constraint on topicalization is satisfied by virtue of the fact that Jill has been previously evoked, but the constraint on the use of existential *there* is not satisfied, because John is hearer-old. Such sentences, then, are subject to the constraints on both constructions. Thus, while inversion is a single argument-reversing construction subject to a single functional constraint, sentences such as those in (258) combine two distinct constructions and are correspondingly subject to two distinct constraints simultaneously.

In a sense, then, inversion is less constrained than the dual-construction phenomena exemplified by the two types of 'PP + *there*' sentences shown above. First, inversion has only one constraint to satisfy, as opposed to the two constraints on the use of PP + *there*; second, inversion is constrained only with respect to the relative status of the two noncanonically positioned constituents, whereas PP + *there* is constrained with respect to the absolute status of its noncanonically positioned constituents.

Moreover, since PP topicalization constrains the preposed PP to represent discourse-old information while presentational *there* constrains its PVNP to represent discourse-new information, we would expect a felicitous instance of a topicalized PP in conjunction with presentational *there* to correspond to an equally felicitous inversion (providing inversion's additional constraints on, e.g., the status of the verb are met). That is, satisfaction of the constraints on topicalization and presentational *there* would entail satisfaction of inversion's constraint that the preposed PP represent information that is at least as familiar in the discourse as that represented by the postposed NP. This prediction is indeed borne out, as illustrated in (262):

(262) a. The most illustrious aspect of the Old Regime was the work and influence of its philosophers of the Enlightenment. *From the essays, tracts, encyclopedias, novels, plays, and letters of such intellectual giants as Denis Diderot, Montesquieu, Voltaire, Caron de Beaumarchais, and Jean Jacques Rousseau, there flowed a penetrating critique of man and society.*
[token provided by D. Yarowsky, AT&T Bell Laboratories]

b. The most illustrious aspect of the Old Regime was the work and influence of its philosophers of the Enlightenment. *From the essays, tracts, encyclopedias, novels, plays, and letters of such intellectual giants as Denis Diderot, Montesquieu, Voltaire, Caron de Beaumarchais, and Jean Jacques Rousseau flowed a penetrating critique of man and society.*

Here, the poset relationship between the work of the philosophers mentioned in the previous sentence and the essays, tracts, etc. mentioned in the preposed PP renders this PP discourse-old, while the penetrating critique evoked in the postposed NP is discourse-new; thus, the constraints on both PP + presentational *there* and inversion are satisfied, and both variants are felicitous. Thus, the relationship between felicity in inversion and felicity in PP + presentational *there* is unidirectional: Satisfaction of the constraints on the preposed and postposed constituents of the latter entails satisfaction of the constraints on these same constituents in the former, but it is not the case that satisfying the constraints on these constituents in inversion entails satisfying them for PP + presentational *there* (as evidenced above in (259)). Similarly, since hearer-new information is necessarily discourse-new, the same point can be made for PP + existential *there*. That is, because the topicalized PP necessarily represents discourse-old information and the PVNP necessarily represents discourse-new information (by virtue of being hearer-new), satisfaction of the constraints on the preposed and postposed constituents of this type of PP + *there* will also entail satisfaction of the constraints on the preposed and postposed constituents of the corresponding inversion.[19] Again, however, it is important to note that this holds only for true PP topicalizations (i.e., where the PP is lexically governed); thus, we would not expect a felicitous instance of PP + *there* such as that in (263a) to correspond to the inversion in (263b), whereas we would expect the topicalization in (264a) to correspond to the felicitous inversion in (264b):

(263) a. After the flood, there were a number of devastated families.

b. #After the flood were a number of devastated families.

(264) a. In the town there were a number of devastated families.

b. In the town were a number of devastated families.

That *after the flood* is not a true topicalized PP is evidenced by the infelicity of placing the constituents of (263a) in S-V-PP word order:

(265) #A number of devastated families were after the flood.

Compare (265) with the result of placing the constituents of (264a) in canonical S-V-PP word order:

[19] This parallel does not hold, however, for *there*-sentences and passivization because of their very different argument structures; that is, passivization involves a transitive relation, while *there*-sentences involve an intransitive relation.

(266) A number of devastated families were in the town.

Here, *in the town* is clearly a predicate complement in a way that *after the flood* in (265) is not. This difference in argument status gives rise to the difference in the status of the preposed PPs in (263a) and (264a) (i.e., as topicalized or not), which is in turn reflected in the difference in acceptability of the corresponding inversions.

To summarize, we have seen that inversion and PP + *there* are subject to distinct sets of constraints. Whereas inversion constrains its preposed constituent to represent information that is at least as familiar within the discourse as the postposed constituent, PP + *there* requires its topicalized PP to satisfy the constraint on topicalization (i.e., to represent discourse-old information) and also requires its postposed NP to satisfy the constraint on *there*-insertion (i.e., to represent either discourse-new or hearer-new information, depending on whether the sentence is an instance of presentational or existential *there*-insertion, respectively). Thus, despite previous treatments of inversion and *there*-insertion as essentially variants of a single construction (e.g., Erdmann 1976, Breivik 1981, Penhallurick 1984, and Freeze 1992), their functional behavior argues strongly against such a treatment. Not only do the two constitute distinct constructions with distinct functions, but PP + *there* in fact combines two distinct constructions in a single sentence, whose use is constrained to satisfy the constraints on each of its component constructions.

We have seen above that argument-reversing constructions in English require that the postposed constituent not represent more familiar information than does the preposed constituent. We have also seen that PP + *there* is subject to a different set of constraints. On the assumption that PP + *there* constitutes a case of argument reversal (since a canonically postverbal constituent is preposed while a canonically preverbal constituent is postposed), this would appear to present a counterexample to our claim regarding functional constraints on argument reversal. However, we have shown that in fact, PP + *there* does not constitute a single argument-reversing construction, but rather arises from a complex of two distinct constructions combined in a single utterance. Thus, a true argument-reversing construction places a single constraint on the relative status of the two reversed arguments, while PP + *there* places two absolute constraints on the status of the two noncanonically positioned constituents involved in its two component constructions. The constraints on PP + *there*, then, can be seen as the sum of the constraints on the two component constructions. In this way, we see that PP + *there* is not an argument-reversing construction, and our generalization regarding functional constraints on argument-reversing constructions is preserved.

Summary

It has long been recognized that there exists a general tendency in many languages for 'given' information to precede 'new' information in an utterance; in light of the results presented here, it appears that the use of argument-reversing constructions in English serves to preserve this ordering of information in cases where canonical word order would result in discourse-new information preceding discourse-old information. We have argued in earlier chapters that preposing in general applies to information that is 'old' in some sense, whereas postposing in general applies to information that is 'new' in some sense. The details of the constraints vary from construction to construction, but in each case the constraint makes reference to *absolute* information status, whereas for the argument-reversing constructions discussed here, the constraint makes reference to the *relative* status of the reversed constituents. Moreover, argument reversal is consistently sensitive to the discourse-status, rather than the hearer-status, of its constituents. Thus, argument-reversing constructions in English require that the information represented by the initial marked constituent be at least as familiar within the discourse as that represented by the final marked constituent (while for inversion the preposed constituent must also represent a link to the discourse context). In the case of PP + *there*, which on the surface would appear to involve a similar reversal of arguments, this constraint does not account for the data; however, we have argued that this is because PP + *there* in fact comprises two distinct constructions used simultaneously rather than a single construction with a single function, and is correspondingly subject to the constraints on its two component constructions rather than the unitary constraint to which argument reversal is subject.

Chapter 5

Noncanonical Word Order and Discourse Structure

Having presented the discourse functions of particular constructions in previous chapters, we are now in a position to develop a number of significant generalizations that hold *across* classes of syntactic constructions. For example, we have seen that preposed position is reserved for information that is related to the prior discourse by one of a small number of linking relations, while postposed position is reserved for new information. Argument-reversing constructions support both generalizations in that they require the information represented by the preverbal constituent to be at least as familiar within the discourse as that represented by the postverbal constituent. Thus, an investigation of a broad range of English constructions demonstrates strong correlations between sentence position (preverbal/postverbal) and familiarity, and between the number of constituents involved and whether it is relative or absolute information status that is constrained. Within each of the three classes of constructions, however, individual constructions may be sensitive to either familiarity within the discourse or (assumed) familiarity within the hearer's knowledge store.

Corresponding to the posited functional correlations among the constructions, we would expect to find a number of related correlations in such areas as distribution, intonation, and the like; similarly, corresponding to the posited functional differences, we might expect to find differences in these areas. Below we investigate these correlations and differences. First we compare the distribution of preposing, postposing, and argument reversal in discourse, showing how their distribution is predicted by our account. Next, we examine properties shared by preposing and argument reversal, i.e. those constructions that involve a preposed constituent. We compare the types of linking relations and anchoring sets that license the use of preposing and argument reversal; we then examine another commonality between the two with respect to the presence or absence of a presupposed open proposition in the discourse model. Finally, we consider correlations between information structure and intonation, and conclude by summarizing our findings thus far.

Commonalities and Differences Across Constructions

Previous accounts of preposing and postposing constructions have grouped together disparate constructions that are in fact functionally distinct, while other accounts have failed to consider a sufficiently broad range of constructions, thus failing to capture significant generalizations. While we have alluded briefly to such accounts in other chapters, here we will consider them in more detail and show how the taxonomy of constructions that we have laid out, together with the discourse-functional properties that we have argued for, can account for data that other analyses leave unexplained. For example, a number of previous studies (e.g. Hartvigson & Jakobsen 1974, Erdmann 1976, Breivik 1981, and Penhallurick 1984) have claimed or assumed that existential *there*-sentences and locative PP inversions are functionally equivalent with respect to the information status of the PVNP. Indeed, some have gone so far as to assume that these two sentence-types are variants of a single construction. Consider, for example, the existential *there*-sentence in (267a) and the PP inversion in (267b):

(267) a. In the garden there was a parrot.

b. In the garden was a parrot.

Previous studies have attributed the same general discourse function to both constructions: that of presenting new information in postverbal position. For example, Hartvigson & Jakobsen 1974 and Erdmann 1976 claim that the function of both inversion and *there*-sentences is to preserve the basic distribution of thematic information preceding rhematic information (Firbas 1964); that is, both constructions serve as devices for presenting rhematic, or new, information in sentence-final position. In a similar vein, Breivik (1981) argues that *there* can be 'dispensed with' (under certain conditions) if the locative adverbial is preposed; for example, according to Breivik's 'Visual Impact Constraint', *there* appears if the sentence fails to convey visual impact (cf. Bolinger 1977). Likewise, Penhallurick (1984) considers *there*-sentences to be 'non-paradigm' cases of inversion, with *there* simply serving to fulfill the requirement that some expression must precede the verb; for cases where *there* is preceded by a PP, he appeals to Breivik's Visual Impact Constraint. Nonetheless, for Penhallurick, both sentence types serve to present new information in postverbal position.

Given the constraints we have presented in Chapters 3 and 4, on the other hand, we would expect *there*-sentences and inversions to have very different distributions in naturally occurring discourse, with inversion placing a single, relative constraint on the discourse-status of its noncanonically placed constituents and existential *there*-insertion placing an absolute constraint on the hearer-status of the postposed constituent. For example, we would expect that in contexts where the information represented by the PVNP is familiar to the hearer but nonetheless new to the discourse, inversion would be felicitous while the corresponding existential *there*-sentence would not be. An examination of the corpus bears out this prediction. Consider the examples in (268)-(269):

(268) a. I wonder what's going on. A police car is parked in front of the Williams' house. *In the back seat is the mayor.* [=(214)]

b. I wonder what's going on. A police car is parked in front of the Williams' house. *#In the back seat there's the mayor.* [cf. The mayor is in the back seat.]

(269) a. Now way out front with the ball is Brenner. [=Green 1980, ex. 5d]

b. #Now way out front with the ball there is Brenner.

In both of these examples, the PVNP represents information that is at once hearer-old and discourse-new. The felicity of the inversions in (268a) and (269a) is due to the discourse-new status of the PVNP, while the infelicity of the corresponding existential *there*-sentences in (268b) and (269b) is due to the hearer-old status of the PVNP.

If an NP represents information that is both hearer-new and discourse-new, on the other hand, it will be felicitous as the PVNP in both inversion and the corresponding *there*-sentence, as in (270):

(270) a. George, can you do me a favor? *Up in my room, on the nightstand, is a pinkish-reddish envelope that has to go out immediately.* [=(197a)]

b. George, can you do me a favor? *Up in my room, on the nightstand, there's a pinkish-reddish envelope that has to go out immediately.*

Likewise, if a PVNP represents information that is both hearer-old and discourse-old, then it will be infelicitous in a *there*-sentence, and also infelicitous in an inversion (unless the preverbal constituent represents more recently evoked, and hence more familiar, information in the discourse, as discussed in Chapter 4). We have already seen an infelicitous inversion of this type ((212b), repeated below as (271a)); in (271b) we see that the corresponding *there*-sentence is equally infelicitous:

(271) a. A: Hey, Bill, where's the coffee grinder? Our guests will probably want some cappuccino after dinner.
B: *#On the kitchen counter is the coffee grinder.* [=(212b)]

b. A: Hey, Bill, where's the coffee grinder? Our guests will probably want some cappuccino after dinner.
B: *#On the kitchen counter there's the coffee grinder.*

Thus, the constraints on inversion and *there*-insertion result in a partial — but only partial — overlap of contexts in which the two may felicitously appear.

Another pair of constructions whose functions have been conflated in the literature are inversion and topicalization, which a number of previous authors have claimed are both syntactically and functionally related. As noted in Chapter 4, many researchers (e.g., Aissen & Hankamer 1972, Emonds 1976, Green 1980, Coopmans 1989, and Rochemont & Culicover 1990) have assumed that at least certain types of inversions are triggered by, or otherwise preceded by and dependent on, topicalization (or preposing in general). Hartvigson & Jakobsen (1974) go so far as to argue that there is no syntactic or functional difference between the fronting that constitutes a topicalization and that which is incorporated in inversion; that is, they argue that inversion and topicalization share the same syntactic fronting process, with inversion involving an additional subject-postposing operation.[1] Such analyses make the claim, either implicitly or explicitly, that the shared fronting correlates with a shared function — that is, that fronting serves exactly the same function in both topicalization and inversion, while inversion serves an additional function related to the noncanonical ordering of the subject and verb.

Although inversion and topicalization do have much in common, we have taken great pains to show that there are clear differences between them. Syntactically, of course, they differ in the relative placement of the subject and verb. Pragmatically, they differ in the status of the discourse elements represented by the constituents of the sentence. In a felicitous topicalization the preposed constituent must represent discourse-old information; similarly, the preposed constituent in a felicitous inversion tends to represent discourse-old information. Importantly, however, in inversion this requirement is not absolute; discourse-new information may in fact appear in this position, but only if the information represented by the postposed constituent is also discourse-new. Thus, compare (272) and (273):

(272) a. In a little white house lived two rabbits. [=(222)]

b. #In a little white house two rabbits lived. [discourse-initially]

(273) a. Once upon a time there was a little white house. In the house lived two rabbits.

[1]Huffman 1993 argues for a similarly componential, though less sequential, account.

b. Once upon a time there was a little white house. In the house two rabbits lived.

The inversion in (272a) is the first sentence of a children's story; hence, the preposed and postposed elements are both discourse-new, and the inversion is felicitous. The PP topicalization in (272b), however, is not felicitous discourse-initially, since the preposed constituent does not represent discourse-old information. If the house represents previously evoked information, however, both variants are felicitous, as illustrated in (273).

Thus, inversion and topicalization differ in that for topicalization the requirement that the preposed constituent represent discourse-old information is absolute, while for inversion it is relative. From this, we can conclude that the function of topicalization does not apply consistently to inversion, and that inversion cannot, therefore, be considered to be simply the sum of topicalization and subsequent subject-verb inversion. On the other hand, we have argued that the functions of topicalization and inversion are not unrelated; on the contrary, we have shown that, while the two constructions differ in terms of the way in which they relate to the preceding discourse, they nonetheless share the general property of preposing information that is (either relatively or absolutely) familiar within the discourse, in the sense of Prince 1992. Thus, we maintain that preposing itself consistently serves to situate a link to the prior discourse in preverbal position (cf. Horn 1986), although this general function is manifested differently in different preposing constructions.

Linking Relations and Noncanonical Word Order

We have argued that preposing constructions in English are sensitive to a very general discourse constraint: The preposed constituent must represent a link standing in an inferrable linking relation to the 'anchoring poset', a contextually licensed, partially ordered set of items ordered by one of a small number of linking relations. We have found that the same types of links and linking relations apply to the entire class of preposing constructions, including argument reversal.

In addition, the information status of the preposed constituent is strikingly uniform across these constructions: Both preposing and argument reversal favor the preposing of discourse-old information. Although the two constructions differ as to whether this information must be relatively or absolutely familiar within the discourse, it is in both cases the discourse-familiarity of the preposed information that is relevant for the felicity of the marked expression. Thus, we have proposed that the function of preposing constructions in general is to front discourse-old information (Horn 1986).

However, we have also found that the information represented by the preposed constituent is often not explicitly evoked in the prior discourse; indeed, in our combined corpora, almost half (971/2153, or 45%) of the preposed constituents contain non-evoked elements that are nonetheless inferrable from information that *is* evoked in the prior context. Thus, whether the link represents information that is explicitly evoked in the prior discourse or is merely inferentially related to previously evoked information is irrelevant: Both are treated alike with respect to preposing constructions. In fact, as we have already seen for inversion, even when the preposed constituent contains explicitly evoked information, it is rarely the case that this information is presented verbatim as in its prior evocation. It is far more common for the two evocations to differ in some way, with the preposed constituent presenting additional information while still representing the link between the current utterance and the prior discourse. In this section we examine in more detail the nature of the linking relations licensing preposing and inversion.

Preposing

As shown in Chapter 2, preposing relates the link within the preposed constituent to the prior discourse via a contextually licensed linking relation that holds between the link within the preposed constituent and the anchoring poset.[2] The

[2]For ease of exposition, we restrict our attention here to cases where the preposed constituent is not the focus of the utterance. Preposed foci are also links, and are related to the prior discourse in an analogous way. See page 83ff for discussion.

first linking relation we will consider is the set/subset relation, as illustrated in (274):

(274) a. The exam can be either next Thursday or a week from next Thursday. *I think a week from Thursday you'll all feel more comfortable with.*
[T. Kroch in class lecture]

b. We don't get involved in *all* murders, *but this one we thought we'd take a look at.*
["ABC World News Tonight"]

In both (274a) and (274b), the link is related to the anchor via a set/subset relation. The only difference between them is that in (274a), the relevant poset {possible exam times} must be inferred on the basis of the individual poset members, whereas in (274b) the entire anchoring poset itself ({murders}) has been evoked in the discourse.

One subtype of topicalization, distinguishable on the basis of its syntactic form, involves a slightly different type of set/subset linking relation. This type involves the topicalization of an indirect question, as illustrated in (275):

(275) a. Two U.S. Secret Service officers witnessed the "cold-blooded" shooting of a doorman at an elegant condominium yesterday, but made no effort to arrest or stop the suspect, authorities said. *"Why they didn't intervene I don't know,"* said a police officer at the scene.
[*Philadelphia Inquirer*, 10/28/83]

b. There are other areas, *but what those areas are, we don't know.*
[Nixon 1974:669]

c. Al was away last week. *Where he went I have no idea.*
[conversation]

In these examples, the topicalized indirect question queries some aspect of a proposition already salient in the discourse. In (275a), it has been established that the Secret Service officers made no effort to intervene on the victim's behalf; what is being questioned with the topicalization is the reason. In (275b), the existence of 'other areas' is being asserted while their exact identity is being questioned. Finally, in (275c), Al's absence is asserted while his actual whereabouts are questioned.

In all cases of indirect-question topicalization, the link represents a member of a contextually licensed set of propositions ordered via a set/subset relation. The poset can be inferred on the basis of a trigger proposition previously evoked in the discourse. For example, the proposition 'Chris lives in New York' may trigger a set of related propositions such as 'Chris lives in New York at some time', 'Chris lives in New York for some reason', 'Chris lives in New York on some street', and so on. These related propositions constitute an inferrable anchoring poset that forms the basis for indirect question topicalization. While the anchoring poset of associated propositions is typically inferred, the member propositions can, of course, be explicitly evoked, as in (276):

(276) A: Can you please tell us when she left? And why?
B: We don't know *why* she left, *but* when *she left we* do *know*.

Although felicitous, no such examples appear in the corpus; all 28 tokens of indirect question topicalization involve an inferred set of propositions.

Although the set/subset relation is perhaps the most common for preposing, other linking relations are frequently encountered as well. Consider first the greater-than relation in (277):

(277) R: If there're fewer than five students [waiting in line] then I guess we can start. How many are there?
T: Five.
R: *Five students we don't have to wait for. More than that we would.* [=(38c)]

The link in B's second preposing in (277), *more than that*, represents a value on the number scale that is greater than the mentioned value *five students* in the preceding sentence. Numeric values are related to one another via the linking relation greater-than, a partial ordering relation.

Another example of a greater-than linking relation is provided in (278):

(278) This is not a role we sought. We preach no Manifest Destiny. But like Americans who began this country and brought forth this last, best hope of mankind, history has asked much of the Americans of our own time. Much we have already given. *Much more we must be prepared to give.* [former president Ronald Reagan in televised address]

Here, the link *much more* represents a higher value in the inferred poset {amounts} than the aforementioned *much.*

Next, consider the part/whole relation, illustrated in (279):

(279) a. At bottom, things just are the way they are, a heterogeneous reality. Yet parts of this reality have a capacity for perception, for acquiring information from other parts, and an accompanying capacity for acting on still others. *Those parts having the capacity for perception and action we call organisms.*
[Barwise & Perry 1983:14]

b. G: How could you take an exam with all those students pestering you?
M: It wasn't easy, but they were all done by three-thirty, and I had until five. *The hard part I left for the end.*
[M. Schultz to G. Ward in conversation]

c. G: So, how'd it go?
S: *The historical question I had some problems with,* but I think it's ok. The descriptive I just wrote a whole lot. We'll see.
[S. Pintzuk to G. Ward in conversation about Ph.D. exam]

In (279a), the link *those parts having the capacity for perception and action* is a member of the poset {parts of reality}, ordered by the part/whole relation. The relevant poset in both (279b) and (279c), defined by the same relation, is {parts of an exam}.

Examples of the type/subtype relation are provided in (280):

(280) a. Alexis: What about me? I'm his mother. I have love for him too.
Blake: *Your brand of love, Alexis, he can do very well without.*
["Dynasty"]

b. [Grandpa and Herman Munster are trying to find a buried treasure in their backyard by means of a map, which makes reference to an oak tree.]
Persimmon trees we got. Cypress trees we got. Oak trees we haven't got. [=(90c)]

c. [discussion of A's partner]
A: It's amazing. I never dreamed it would last. We met purely by accident.
B: *Friendships you develop. Lovers you fall into.*
[conversation]

In (280a), the relevant poset {types of love} is defined by the ordering relation type/subtype; in (280b), the poset is {types of trees}; and in (280c), the poset is {types of relationships}. Although these additional types of linking relations can also be seen in terms of simple set relations (since posets are defined as sets of values partially ordered by some relation), there are many instances of topicalization (as seen in refrellen-(280)) for which a simple set-inclusion relation would underspecify the connection between the link and anchor. The notion of poset provides a more explicit characterization of the types of linking relations that can hold in discourse, as well as providing more unified and complete coverage of the data.

A final type of linking relation found to hold between the link and anchor is that of simple identity.[3] Consider the example in (281):

(281) I have a recurring dream in which... I can't remember what I say. I usually wake up crying. *This dream I've had maybe three, four times.*
[Terkel 1974:118; (ellipsis in the original)]

Here, the link *this dream* is related via an identity relation to the anchoring poset, consisting of a singleton dream; there is no mention of any other dream in the prior or subsequent context. Such topicalizations are problematic for Chafe

[3]Although fully felicitous, NP topicalizations whose link stands in an identity relation to the anchoring poset are nonetheless relatively rare. Of the 409 tokens of NP topicalization in the corpus, only 17 (4%) involve the identity relation.

(1976), who argues that *all* preposing is 'contrastive'. Similarly, Creider (1979) claims that "for many speakers of English, a sentence derived with Topicalization is grammatical only with contrastive topics" (1979:5). Yet there is no sense of contrast in (281) or in the other examples of identity discussed below.

Alternatively, and more commonly, the preposed constituent in a topicalization may represent an evoked entity in new terms; consider the characterizational links in (282):

(282) a. The only time the guy isn't considered a failure is when he resigns and announces his new job. That's the tipoff, "John Smith resigned, future plans unknown" means he was fired. "John Smith resigned to accept the position of president of X company" — then you know he resigned. *This little nuance you recognize immediately when you're in corporate life.* [=(35)]

b. Facts about the world thus come in twice on the road from meaning to truth: once to determine the interpretation, given the meaning, and then again to determine the truth value, given the interpretation. *This insight we owe to David Kaplan's important work on indexicals and demonstratives*, and we believe it is absolutely crucial to semantics. [=(24)]

In these examples, the poset relation is again one of identity, in that the links represent information that has already been evoked in the discourse; however, the link itself contains additional characterizational information that describes the evoked entity in new terms (Ward 1988, Takami 1992). In (282a), a nuance is introduced into the discourse without initially being described as such. The preposed link (*this little nuance*), then, stands in a relation of identity with the anchoring poset, which consists of a single member (the nuance). Note also that the demonstrative in these examples is not being used contrastively; that is, in (282a), there are no other nuances being contrasted with the one represented by the link. Similarly, in (282b), the insight represented by the link is unique in the discourse. Therefore, if these tokens were produced orally, we would expect neither the demonstrative nor the noun to receive a contrastive accent.[4]

Interestingly, in every case of NP topicalization in the corpus involving the characterizational identity relation, the preposed NP contains the demonstrative determiner *this*. According to Gundelet al.'s (1993) givenness hierarchy, such NPs are used to identify discourse entities that are 'activated', i.e. evoked in the discourse (either linguistically or extralinguistically) and represented in current short-term memory. Although activated, such entities have not been previously introduced into the discourse in the same terms, and are therefore insufficiently salient to be represented by a pronoun. Indeed, consider attempting to refer to the nuance and insight of (282a) and (282b), respectively, with a pronoun:

(283) a. Facts about the world thus come in twice on the road from meaning to truth: once to determine the interpretation, given the meaning, and then again to determine the truth value, given the interpretation. *#We owe it to Dave Kaplan's important work on indexicals and demonstratives...*

b. The only time the guy isn't considered a failure is when he resigns and announces his new job. That's the tipoff, "John Smith resigned, future plans unknown" means he was fired. "John Smith resigned to accept the position of president of X company" — then you know he resigned. *#You recognize it immediately when you're in corporate life.*

Here, the relevant discourse entities are insufficiently given to permit pronominal reference.

In (281), on the other hand, the link *this dream* is not characterizational in this way, given that the dream has been explicitly introduced into the discourse qua dream. However, the demonstrative is nonetheless required; notice that the definite article in the same context is infelicitous:[5]

[4]Such an accent, while felicitous, would force the link to be interpreted as a non-singleton member of the anchoring poset.

[5]These observations hold only for relations of identity; when the contextually licensed relation between link and anchor is other than identity, e.g. set/subset, the definite article *is* felicitous, as in (i):

(284) a. I have a recurring dream in which... I can't remember what I say. I usually wake up crying. *#The dream I've had maybe three, four times.*

b. I have a recurring dream in which... I can't remember what I say. I usually wake up crying. I've had the dream maybe three, four times.

In (284a), where the dream has been explicitly evoked in the prior discourse, the definite article is markedly less felicitous than the demonstrative. Notice that this difference applies only to the preposed variant; the canonical-word-order variant in (284b) is felicitous. However, with the addition of a deictic adjective, the preposed definite becomes equally felicitous:

(285) I have a recurring dream in which... I can't remember what I say. I usually wake up crying. *The aforementioned dream I've had maybe three, four times.*

Thus, it is not the demonstrative per se that accounts for the difference; the addition of the deictic adjective in the link of (285) is sufficient to render the preposing felicitous.

Argument reversal

As with the link of preposing, the link of argument reversal is related to the prior discourse via a contextually licensed linking relation. Indeed, many of the same types of linking relations are found for preposing and argument reversal; however, their distributions are somewhat different. In the case of inversion, for example, there are fewer set/subset relations and far more identity relations, as illustrated in (286):

(286) a. They have a great big tank in the kitchen, and *in the tank are sitting all of these pots.* [=(211c)]

(i) I've been having panic attacks and a recurring dream lately. *The dream I've had maybe three, four times.*

b. The supply of inmate clothing was recently supplemented by the acquisition of a batch of secondhand gas-station uniforms. Inmates say they run out of toilet paper and soap occasionally. *Also scarce are the tools to appeal their recent court convictions — legal forms, books and even paper — and telephones to call their attorneys or families.*
[*Philadelphia Inquirer*, 5/6/84]

c. The BMOC is Garson McKellar (Tim Quill), the handsome scion of a Kennedy-esque political family who is the star of the varsity debate team. No quarterback ever had half of Garson's problems, fighting as he must each day to clear a path through the hordes of beautiful co-eds begging for his favors. *Into this heady atmosphere strides Tucker Muldowney (Kirk Cameron), a maddeningly self-confident, gee-shucks freshman from Oklahoma who has entered Kenmont on a debating scholarship.* [=(226a)]

In these examples, the link in the preposed constituent represents information that stands in a contextually licensed poset relation of identity with previously evoked information; however, the way in which the identity relation is realized differs. In (286a), the (singleton) poset member has been explicitly evoked in the prior discourse, whereas in (286b) and (286c), the link stands in a characterizational relation of identity to the anchor. In (286b), the reader must infer that running out of toilet paper and soap constitutes a scarcity, while in (286c), the situation in question has been evoked but not as a 'heady atmosphere'.

Examples of inversions illustrating other types of linking relations are provided in (287):

(287) a. On the left was a voracious creature in red, white, and blue with its mouth open to reveal the teeth of Pershing 2s. And to the right, an equally hungry figure in red, with a yellow hammer and sickle and claws that were missiles, too. *In between, tiny and helpless, was the flag of West Germany, about to be gnawed from both sides.*
[*Philadelphia Inquirer*, 10/23/83]

b. First came the man and the two children from the contortionist act. They passed close to the pair in the doorway without noticing them. *Then came a couple who might have been the trainer of the animal act and his girl assistant.*
[Thane 1943:151]

c. Though certainly relevant, the criterion based on the principle of relevance, like any criterion based on the intent or purpose of an utterance, is somewhat vague. *More illuminating is Strawson's second criterion of truth-assessment.* He argues that "assessments of statements as true or false are commonly though not only topic-centered."
[Reinhart 1982:6]

In (287a), the link *in between* is a member of the poset {locations}, inferrable on the basis of the triggers *on the left* and *to the right* in the prior context; it is related to that set by the linking relation set/subset. In (287b), the link *then* is related via temporal precedence to the other members of the inferrable poset {times}. Finally, in (287c), the link *more illuminating* is a member of the poset {amounts}, defined by a greater-than relation. Note that this poset must be inferred; from the trigger *somewhat vague* the reader can infer 'not illuminating', thus licensing an inference to the relevant poset.

As for passives, the vast majority of linking relations are simple identity, as illustrated in (288):

(288) Mrs. Huntley was held on $20,000 bond in Phoenix. *She was arrested by Phoenix Police after they received the indictment papers from Portland detectives.*

Here, the pronominal link *she* represents explicitly evoked information and is related to the anchoring poset via the identity relation. As with the other constructions we have examined, a link standing in an identity relation in a passive may include additional characterizational information, as in (289):

(289) James P. Mitchell and Sen. Walter H. Jones (R–Bergen) last night disagreed on the value of using as a campaign issue a remark by Richard

J. Hughes, Democratic gubernatorial candidate, that the GOP is "campaigning on the carcass of Eisenhower Republicanism". Mitchell was for using it, Jones against, and Sen. Wayne Dumont Jr. (R–Warren) did not mention it when the three Republican gubernatorial candidates spoke at staggered intervals before 100 persons at the Park Hotel. *The controversial remark was first made Sunday by Hughes at a Westfield Young Democratic Club cocktail party at the Scotch Plains Country Club.* It was greeted with a chorus of boos by 500 women in Trenton Monday at a forum of the State Federation of Women's Clubs.
[Brown corpus]

Here, the link *remark* stands in an identity relation to the anchoring poset, yet is described with the additional characterization *controversial*, which is inferrable from the prior context.

Finally, the link in each of the following examples is related to the anchor via a set/subset relation:

(290) a. The Georgia Constitution gives the Legislature the power to exempt colleges from property taxation if, among other criteria, "all endowments to institutions established for white people shall be limited to white people, and all endowments to institutions established for colored people shall be limited to colored people." At least two private colleges in the Atlanta area now or in the past have had integrated student bodies, but *their tax-exempt status never has been challenged by the state.*
[Brown corpus]

b. The fire fighters association here offered a \$5,000 reward for information leading to the arrest of the person or persons responsible for the bombing. *A \$500 reward was offered by the association's local in Kansas City.*
[Brown corpus]

In (290a), the link *at least two private colleges* constitutes a subset of the poset {colleges} evoked in the prior discourse. In (290b), the poset {rewards} must be inferred on the basis of the trigger *a $5,000 reward* and the link *a $500 reward*, but again the linking relation is a set/subset relation. Thus, for both inversion and passivization we observe the same kinds of linking relations that were found for preposing.[6]

The anchoring poset

We have argued that felicitous use of preposing constructions requires the establishment of a contextually licensed poset in the discourse model. However, given the infinitely many posets of which any given discourse entity may be a member, we might ask ourselves what renders one poset contextually licensed and not some other.

First, it is clear that certain posets can be inferred on the basis of very little contextual information. These posets are defined independently of the particular context in which they are evoked, e.g. the cardinal number scale or the quantifier scale. In addition, certain posets defined on the basis of world knowledge are 'predefined' as well; consider the topicalizations in (291) and the inversions in (292):

(291) a. "I wish I were [fond of wine]. It is such a bond with other men. At Magdalen I tried to get drunk more than once, but I did not enjoy it. *Beer and whiskey I find even less appetising...*" [Waugh 1945:91]

b. I'm getting a new terminal tomorrow. *The modem I won't get till next week.*

(292) a. She got married recently, and *at the wedding was the mother, the stepmother and Debbie.* [=(16b)]

[6]See also recent work by Strand (1996a, 1996b), who presents a set-based analysis of the range of relations linking a felicitous definite NP to elements in the prior context. This approach follows in the tradition of Christophersen (1939), who suggests that a definite is possible when there is an unambiguous relation between the entity denoted and some other, familiar entity. Although we have elsewhere taken issue with the 'familiarity' approach to definiteness (see Birner & Ward 1994), the notion of (in our terms) an anchoring set does seem necessary to account for preposing constructions in English.

b. I set up my new terminal yesterday. *With the modem came a pile of manuals I'll never read.*

The coherence of these discourses depends on the hearer's ability to construct the relevant poset on the basis of world knowledge. For example, the interpretation of the preposing in (291a) requires the hearer to draw on his presumed knowledge that wine, beer, and whiskey are related to one another in a certain way. Similarly, the inversion in (292a) assumes that the hearer knows that getting married involves a wedding. Finally, for both the preposing in (291b) and the inversion in (292b), the hearer is being called upon to draw a connection between terminals and modems. In each case, the relation in question exists independent of the particular example.

Other links that readily lend themselves to the construction of posets involve lexical items with set-inducing meanings. Examples of such lexical items are the preposition *like* and the adjectives *such* and *similar*; all three mean something like 'having the relevant attributes of'. Despite their syntactic differences, they all share the function of evoking a poset ordered by a type/subtype relation. These posets relate entities in the discourse model that share some relevant property or attribute.

The set-inducing function performed by *like* is illustrated by the preposing in (293):

(293) KYW-TV's amiable Dick Sheeran, who usually covers New Jersey, is sure that his one-on-one with Mondale provided a rare moment of insight for him and the Channel 3 viewers. "There are 3 or 4 standard questions everybody asks, you know? But I like to people-ize my questions. So, I asked him something different. I said, 'Mr. Vice President, campaigning is grueling, with all the stops from one place to another, all the speeches, all the debates and the questions. It's gotta be tough to just bear up under it all. So what I want to know, Mr. Vice President, is... what do you eat?' And, you know what? He was stumped for an answer. He was programmed to handle political questions, *but a simple question like this he had trouble answering.*"
[*Philadelphia Inquirer*, 6/3/83]

Here, the link *a simple question like this* stands in a type/subtype poset relation with the higher value *questions*. This higher value is inferrable from an alternate value, the evoked set of {political questions}. The phrase *like this* serves to restrict the set {simple questions} to those that are simple in the same way as the actual question that was put to Mondale. If, instead of *a simple question like this*, the reporter had used *this simple question*, topicalization would still be felicitous given the salient poset {questions}. Had this been the case, *political questions* and the link *this simple question* would then have been alternate members of this poset. However, in doing so, the reporter would have then limited his statement about Mondale's question-answering abilities to that *particular* simple question. Of course, we would still be free to infer that Mondale might have had difficulty answering other simple questions as well. However, through his use of *a simple question like this*, the reporter invokes a poset of simple questions, strongly implicating that the set is not a singleton and therefore that Mondale would indeed have also had trouble answering other simple questions.

Sometimes it is necessary to infer the relevant attribute in order to construct the appropriate poset. Consider (294):

(294) a. People are really stupid. When I was on surveillance, during this hijacking case, we were working for a newspaper. The guys delivering were selling papers on the side. The newspaper was earning a fortune. These guys knew they were being tailed and they still continued the same shit. *People like that you have no sympathy for*, they're stupid. They deserve everything they get. There were 52 indictments and 22 convictions.
[Terkel 1974:212]

b. So a bit of self-deception is demanded by the situation. The interesting cases are those which arise when one's *conatus* becomes intensely focused on some external object, which gathers it up as in a lens, producing a dazzling display of special effects. *From such optical tricks arise all the varieties of romantic hallucination, from the relatively innocent delusions of sexual love to the full thrashing*

horrors of the false hero, the awaited savior, the frenzied masses shouting as one voice.
[Goldstein 1989:167]

As with (293), the link in each of these cases is related to the anchoring poset via a linking relation of type/subtype. The use of the PP *like that* within the link in (294a), for example, evokes a subtype of people with some identifiable property or attribute; similarly, the use of the link *such optical tricks* in (294b) evokes a subtype of optical tricks. However, unlike (293), the attribute characterizing the relevant subtype in each of these cases must be inferred. The attribute in (293) could also have been left to inference with equal felicity, as illustrated in (295):

(295) But a question like this he had trouble answering.

Here, as in (294a), the reader must infer the relevant attribute — 'simple' — in order to construct the appropriate poset. Several other possibilities also suggest themselves: 'personal', 'unexpected', 'non-political', etc. Usually, the relevant attribute is clear from the context; however, the more instructions a speaker can provide the hearer about how to construct the intended poset, the less chance there is of miscommunication. To reduce the possibility of misunderstanding, one might be tempted to employ the strategy of specifying the relevant attribute as explicitly as possible to ensure that the intended poset is inferred. However, there are powerful and well-known forces working against such a strategy (Grice 1975, Horn 1984).[7]

Nonetheless, more often than not the relevant poset is entirely context-specific.[8] Consider the following examples:

---

[7]In Horn's (1984) theory of conversational implicature, a 'division of pragmatic labor' is proposed in which the Gricean maxims of Quantity, Relation, and Manner (Grice 1975) are reduced to two competing principles. Briefly, the hearer-based 'Q Principle' requires the speaker to say as much as possible (thus, *John ate two apples* can be used to Q-implicate 'John did not eat four apples'), while the speaker-based 'R Principle' enjoins the speaker to say no more than is necessary (thus, *John ate the brownies* can be used to R-implicate 'John ate all the brownies'). In this way, the speaker may R-implicate that he is leaving it to the hearer to draw the intended inference; to be unduly explicit would violate the R Principle. Thus, a hearer may rely on R to convey information implicitly.

[8]See Cumming & Ono 1996 for a discussion of how hearers use information from a variety

(296) a. There are five unrelated objects on the table. I want you to pick up one of them and hold it. *The other four I want you to place on the floor.*

b. There are five unrelated objects on the table. Each of them has something different under it. *Under the object in the middle is a dollar bill.*

Here, the five items in question comprise an entirely ad hoc poset. Nonetheless, the poset is sufficiently salient in this context to support both the preposing in (296a) and the inversion in (296b).

While in all cases the relevant poset must be inferred, some posets are more readily construed than others. Consider the difference between the preposings in (297a) and (297b):

(297) a. It is nearly 8 and Ellerbee, back from dinner, tidies up some details in her narrow, windowless third-floor office before moving down the hall to the studio. Her son and his friend pore over computer workbooks in a small area outside her office. Joshua and his 14-year-old sister, Vanessa, take turns spending Friday nights at the studio. *"Sleep they can catch up on,"* Ellerbee says, *"Mom they can't."*
[*Philadelphia Inquirer*, 8/31/83]

b. Half of them I liked; half I didn't.

In (297a), the hearer must construct a nonce poset in which sleep and Mom cooccur as members, i.e. {things children need}. Contrast this with the constructed example in (297b), in which little is left to inference in constructing the relevant poset. The meaning of *half* suffices in itself to render salient a poset containing the other half as an alternate value. Thus, irrespective of the contexts in which they occur, certain posets are more naturally constructed than others (recall the examples in (291) and (292) discussed earlier). On the other hand, the entities

of sources — general world knowledge, knowledge of taxonomic relations (e.g. part/whole), knowledge of grammatical/lexical constructions, inter alia — to form ad hoc hierarchies and set relationships.

'sleep' and 'Mom' cannot be assumed to stand in a poset relation with each other independent of the particular context in which they occur; thus the poset in (297a) would presumably be more difficult to infer than, say, that in (297b).

Open Propositions and Locative Constituents

We argued in Chapter 2 that preposing involves not only a link but also a salient or inferrable open proposition. Here we will extend this discussion to include inversion and to distinguish between two broad categories of preposing constructions: (1) presuppositional — those that require a salient or inferrable open proposition in discourse (see Prince 1981b, 1986); and (2) locative — those that contain a locative constituent in preposed position.[9] We begin with a discussion of presuppositional preposing.

Presuppositional preposing

Recall that an open proposition is a sentence that contains an unbound variable, which is instantiated with the focus of the utterance. The focus constitutes the 'new information' of the utterance, and, like the link, represents a member of a contextually licensed poset. This division of information within a sentence into an OP and focus corresponds closely to the 'focus/presupposition' distinction of Jackendoff 1972, Rochemont 1978, Prince 1981b, Lambrecht 1994, inter alia.

We have shown that the felicitous use of many types of preposing constructions requires that an OP be salient or inferrable in discourse, as in (298):

(298) G: Do you watch football?
E: Yeah. *Baseball I like a lot better.* [=(29)]

Here, *baseball* serves as the link to the inferred poset {sports}. This poset constitutes the anchor and can be inferred on the basis of the link *baseball* and the trigger *football*. To identify the OP, the link is first replaced with the

[9]As will be explained below, these two categories are not mutually exclusive; that is, the preposed constituent of presuppositional preposing may also be locative.

anchoring poset of which it is a member; the focused item is then replaced with a variable, which also represents a member of a contextually licensed poset. This process is illustrated in (299):

(299) a. OP = I like-to-X-degree {sports}, where X is a member of the poset {amounts}.

b. Focus = a lot better

In (299), the OP includes the variable corresponding to the focus, but note that the link *baseball* has been replaced by its anchor {sports}, i.e. the poset that includes both the trigger and the link. In other words, the OP that is salient in (298) is not that the speaker likes baseball per se, but rather that he likes (certain) sports to various degrees, as indicated in (299a).[10] As noted earlier, this OP is salient given the prior context in which E is asked if he watches football, from which it can inferred that G is asking for E's interest in and evaluation of the sport in question.

Now recall the inversion in (218), reproduced below:

(300) Two CBS crewmen were wounded by shrapnel yesterday in Souk el Gharb during a Druse rocket attack on Lebanese troops.

They were the 5th and 6th television-news crewmen to be wounded in Lebanon this month. One television reporter, Clark Todd of Canada, was killed earlier this month.

Wounded yesterday were cameraman Alain Debos, 45, and soundman Nick Follows, 24. [=(218)]

Here, the link *wounded yesterday* is related to the poset {injury times}, ordered by a relation of temporal precedence. This poset is inferrable on the basis of the triggers *wounded by shrapnel yesterday*, *wounded in Lebanon this month*, and *killed earlier this month* in the preceding discourse, from which the reader can infer the relevant poset. Associated with this inversion is an OP formed in exactly the same way as with the preposing in (298). The link is replaced with

[10]Recall from Chapter 2 that the link in a preposing typically represents a proper subset of the anchoring poset.

the anchoring poset and the focused item (the postposed NP) is replaced with a variable, as illustrated in (301):

(301) a. OP = X was wounded at {injury times}, where X is a member of the poset {television-new crewmen}.

b. Focus = cameraman Alain Debos, 45, and soundman Nick Follows, 24

Once again, we see that the OP includes the anchoring poset of which the link is a member. Thus, the OP is not simply that X was wounded yesterday, but rather the more abstract fact that X was wounded at some time. It is this OP that must be salient or inferrable in context for the inversion to be felicitous. Consider the same utterance in a context where the OP is not so licensed:

(302) Several CBS crewmen arrived in Souk el Gharb last week to cover the latest peace talks. *#Wounded yesterday were cameraman Alain Debos, 45, and soundman Nick Follows, 24.*

Here, without an appropriate trigger to license the necessary poset, the relevant OP is neither salient nor inferrable, and the inversion is consequently ill-formed. Thus, it appears that at least some types of inversion involve the same sorts of OPs that have been shown to be relevant for preposing.

A slightly more abstract type of OP involves affirmation or negation as the focus.[11] Consider the preposing in (303):

(303) The plan is to purchase the quaint fishing village of Ferness and replace it with a giant new refinery. The villagers — who've been farming, fishing, raising families and pub crawling in splendid isolation for generations — offer amazingly little resistance. *Humble they may be. But daft they ain't.* If the Americans are all that eager to turn a few industrious Scotsmen into instant millionaires, they should not be denied the privilege. [=(40d)]

The relevant OP and focus for the second preposing in example (303) are provided in (304):

[11]Notice that this type of focus does not occur in inversion, as inversion does not permit main verb negation and, as we have seen in Chapter 4, its main verb never constitutes new information.

(304) a. OP = They X (be) {attributes of villagers}, where X is a member of the poset {affirmation/negation}.

b. They are/aren't daft, humble, etc.

c. Focus = negation (*ain't*)

The OP in (304a) can be paraphrased as in (304b); what the speaker takes to be salient is the proposition that the villagers either do or do not possess certain attributes.

Finally, consider the proposition assessment in (305), where the focus is affirmation rather than negation:

(305) At the end of the term I took my first schools; it was necessary to pass, if I was to stay at Oxford, *and pass I did*... [=(45)]

To obtain the relevant OP, the element bearing nuclear accent (*did*) is replaced by a variable, resulting in the OP in (306a).

(306) a. OP = I X {pass}, where X is a member of the poset {affirmation/negation}.

b. Focus = affirmation (*did*)

Given the trigger *it was necessary to pass* in (305), the speaker is clearly in a position to assume that the OP in (306a) is salient at the time of the preposing. The new information of the utterance is simply that the relevant proposition is true with respect to some past time. This new information, conveyed by the tense-bearing element *did*, constitutes the focus of the utterance.

Locative preposing constructions

Up to this point, we have been discussing preposing constructions that require both a link and a salient or inferrable OP. However, for a distinct subclass of preposing constructions, no salient OP is required. This subclass is restricted to links that are semantically locative. Consider the following examples of locative preposing constructions, in (307) and (308):

(307) a. In the VIP section of the commissary at 20th Century-Fox, the studio's elite gather for lunch and gossip. The prized table is reserved for Mel Brooks, *and from it he dispenses advice, jokes and invitations to passers-by.*
[*Philadelphia Inquirer*, 2/19/84]

b. OP = He dispenses X from {places}, where X is a member of the poset {types of banter}.

(308) a. There are three ways to look at East State Street Village, a low-income apartment complex in Camden. None of them are pretty views. *To the west of the 23 brightly colored buildings flows the Cooper River, a fetid waterway considered one of the most polluted in New Jersey.*
[*Philadelphia Inquirer*, 5/7/84]

b. OP = X flows to {locations}, where X is a member of the poset {waterways}.

In each of these examples, the preposing construction is felicitous despite the absence of the relevant OP. In the preposing in (307), for example, the proposition that Mel Brooks dispenses something from some location (307b) is not salient, yet the preposing is felicitous. Similarly, for the inversion in (308), the mention of a Camden apartment complex does not, in itself, evoke the proposition that something flows somewhere; thus, the OP in (308b) seems unlikely to be salient on the basis of the prior discourse.

Notice, however, that the other constraint on preposing constructions, that the preposed constituent represent a discourse-old link, is clearly satisfied by these examples. Moreover, in both the preposing in (307) and the inversion in (308), the link in the preposed constituent occurs within a semantically locative constituent. Note that it is not the entire preposed constituent that constitutes the link; rather, it is typically an NP complement within the PP that stands in a poset relation with a member of the anchoring set (in these cases, a singleton). The locative PP, then, functions as a 'bridge' between the link in the preposed constituent and the rest of the matrix clause (cf. Haviland & Clark 1974, Creider

1979, Davison 1984). In the preposing in (307), for example, the PP *from it* serves as a locative bridge from the referent of the link (the table) to the referent of the direct object of the verb, i.e. those items dispensed to passers-by. Similarly, in the inversion in (308), the PP *to the west of the 23 brightly colored buildings* serves to bridge the referent of the link (the 23 buildings) and the river (represented by the postposed NP). Thus, we can say that the function of this type of preposing construction is to serve as a bridge between discourse entities within a sentence, one of which stands in a poset relation to the prior discourse (cf. Kuno 1975).[12]

Again, when the preposed locative constituent in a preposing construction does not contain a link standing in a contextually licensed poset relation to other discourse entities, the use of that construction is correspondingly infelicitous.[13] Consider the following examples of preposing constructions with a completely discourse-new, hearer-new NP within the preposed PP:

(309) a. During my tour of the 20th Century-Fox studios last week, I saw Mel Brooks. *#From a table, he was dispensing advice, jokes and invitations to passers-by.* [cf. (307)]

b. Camden has fallen on hard times. *#To the west of a brightly colored building flows the Cooper River, a fetid waterway considered one*

[12]While both locative and temporal adverbials can perform this function, the present discussion will be confined to locative PPs. Since verbs do not generally subcategorize for temporal adverbials, they fail to satisfy the formal definition of preposing that we have adopted in this study. Functionally, however, it is clear that the two behave alike in this regard.

[13]A potential counterexample to this generalization, brought to our attention by Joyce Kleckner-Gatto (p.c.), appears in (i), where the preposed constituent constitutes discourse-new (and, for that matter, hearer-new) information:

(i) In the biggest brownest muddiest river in Africa, two crocodiles lay with their heads just above the water.
[Dahl 1978:1]

However, it seems here that the subcategorized argument of *lay* is not the preposed PP but rather the postverbal PP *with their heads just above the water*. Thus, it appears that the locative PP is simply an initial adverbial not subject to the constraints on preposing as outlined here. Compare (i) with (ii), where the preposed PP is clearly the subcategorized argument of *lay*, and the preposing is correspondingly infelicitous:

(ii) *#In a big pool, a crocodile lay.*

of the most polluted in New Jersey. [cf. (308a)]

In both the preposing in (309a) and the inversion in (309b), the link in the preposed constituent represents discourse-new, hearer-new information that does not stand in any readily identifiable poset relation with information in the prior context, and as a result the tokens are infelicitous.

Thus, all preposing constructions are alike in requiring the preposed constituent to represent familiar information; nonetheless, locative preposing is less constrained than presuppositional preposing in not requiring a salient or inferrable OP for felicity. Instead, what is required for locative preposing is that the preposed constituent be semantically locative. In fact, an examination of both the preposing and inversion corpora reveals that, in every instance, the absence of a salient or inferrable OP correlates with a semantically locative preposed constituent.

The difference between locative preposing and presuppositional preposing can be brought more sharply into focus by comparing the locative inversion in (308a) with the presuppositional inversion in (310):

(310) The Chief of Police has developed a sore throat and is concerned about the prospect of an extended sick leave. *In even worse condition is the mayor himself, who has been out for the past several days with a raging fever.*

While the preposed constituent in (308a) is clearly locative vs. presuppositional. Preposings and inversions with a, that in (310) is not. However, the requisite OP of presuppositional inversion is clearly salient in (310); the context here licenses the OP 'X is {degrees of fitness}'. Thus, in the case of presuppositional preposing constructions, but not locative preposing constructions, an OP must be salient or inferrable in the discourse. Nonetheless, for both construction types, a poset relation must hold between the link and the anchor.[14]

However, while most bridges in locative preposing are realized by PPs, not all PPs can serve as bridges in this construction. First, prepositions that are

[14]The two construction types can also be distinguished intonationally, as will be seen below.

part of verb-preposition compounds (discussed above in section 2 on Yiddish-movement) cannot undergo locative preposing:[15]

(311) a. John needs Mary so much. *#On her he relies for everything.*

b. I was supposed to meet your sister at work. *#For her I waited over an hour.*

Second, as noted above, only semantically locative constituents can be preposed in the absence of an OP. Consider, for example, the preposed instrumentals in (312), the preposed goals in (313), and the preposed benefactives in (314):

(312) a. Ah, there's a knife. *#With it, I'll cut the bread.*[16] [cf. I'll cut the bread with it.]

b. *#With the razor shaved Joe.* [cf. Joe shaved with the razor.]

(313) a. This homeless person accosted me at the 7-11. *#To the poor guy, I gave a dime.* [cf. I gave a dime to the poor guy.]

b. *#To many charities gives John.* [cf. John gives to many charities.]

(314) a. Our next-door neighbors bought a cat last week. *#For it, they bought a diamond-studded collar.* [cf. They bought a diamond-studded collar for it.]

b. *#For Johnny is the next gift.* [cf. The next gift is for Johnny.]

In fact, for both preposing and inversion, only those preposed PPs that denote static locations are possible in the absence of the relevant OP. Preposed directional PPs, for example, are infelicitous in both constructions, as shown in (315) and (316):

(315) a. A: Did you get tickets to the Degas exhibit?
B: Yeah. *#To it we're going tomorrow.* [cf. Yeah. We're going to it tomorrow.]

[15]Given that main verbs in inversions are necessarily intransitive or copular, this restriction does not apply to that construction.

[16]But cf. the archaic preposing 'With this ring I thee wed'.

b. We have a new mail carrier. *#To him runs the dog every day.* [cf. The dog runs to him every day.]

(316) a. A: Did you see the accident on the Schuylkill?
B: Yeah. *#Past it I drove on my way to work.* [cf. Yeah. I drove past it on my way to work.]

b. A: Have you seen the new Bloomingdale's?
B: Not yet. *#Past it goes Andy every day on his way to work.* [cf. Not yet. Andy goes past it every day on his way to work.]

Instead, the bridges involved in locative preposing are just those that spatially situate the link with respect to other discourse entities: e.g. *above*, *after*, *around*, *before*, *below*, *beside*, *between*, *from*, *in*, *into*, *on*, *over*, *through*, and *under*. Thus, for both preposing and inversion, locative preposing is restricted to links that represent static locations.

In fact, we have found that even apparently non-locative links in these constructions take on a static locative sense in the absence of an OP. Consider the examples in (317):

(317) a. From the kitchen came a wonderful aroma.

b. From the kitchen came a blood-curdling scream.

Here, the preposed PP is most naturally interpreted not as a directional, as the preposition *from* might suggest, but as a locative. That is, in the case of (317a), for example, it is the location of the aroma (i.e., its presence), and not its movement, that is being described. Compare (317a) with the inversion in (318), where no such interpretation is possible:

(318) From the kitchen came a proud cook.

Additional examples of locative PPs posing as directionals appear in (319):

(319) a. "But you, Eva: how did your travels go?"
She was about to tell me when *in again rolled the trolley, now with afternoon tea on it.*
[Bowen 1968:167]

b. Bony's eyes were never still. All physical and mental powers had become concentrated on the effort to probe the gloom. *Across his skyline ran a shapeless form, so grotesque, so indistinct, that to name it was impossible.*
[Upfield 1953:28]

c. He squatted this early evening on the hotel veranda beside the solitary chair occupied by D.I. Napoleon Bonaparte, unaware of the guest's profession and rank and his reputation in every police department of the Commonwealth. *Along the stone street passed a flock of goats in the charge of a small white boy and an aborigine of the same age and size...*
[Upfield 1954:14-5]

In (319a), the OP 'X rolled somewhere' does not seem to be salient or inferrable in context; similarly for the OPs 'X ran somewhere' and 'X passed somewhere' in (319b) and (319c), respectively. Upon closer examination, however, these apparently directional PPs can be seen to have a locative interpretation. For example, in (319a), it is the appearance of the trolley on the scene that is relevant to the narrative, rather than its movement into the room. Similarly, in (319b), the preposed PP *across his skyline* describes a static scene — i.e. the position of the shapeless form — rather than the form's movement. Likewise, *along the stone street* in (319c) does not denote the goats' movement from one point to another, but rather their presence along the street in question.

To draw this distinction more clearly, consider (320a), in which an apparently directional PP receives a locative interpretation.

(320) a. My neighbors have a huge back yard. *Across it runs a string of beautiful Japanese lanterns.*

b. My neighbors have a huge back yard. *#Across it runs their German shepherd all the time.*

In (320a), what is being described is the location of the lanterns, not their movement. Notice that *run across* is ambiguous: It can receive either a static (locative) interpretation, as in (320a), or a dynamic (directional) interpretation. When a truly directional reading is forced, as in (320b), the inversion is infelicitous.

Precisely the same state of affairs holds for preposing. Consider the examples in (321):

(321) a. My neighbors have a huge back yard. *Through it they've run a string of beautiful Japanese lanterns.*

b. My neighbors have a huge back yard. *#Through it my kids like to run.*

Again, there are two interpretations of *run through*. One, the static interpretation, is associated with the preposing in (321a). Under this interpretation, it is the location of the string of lanterns that is being described. The other interpretation, associated with the preposing in (321b), has a strictly directional interpretation: It describes movement across a path. Only the former, locative, interpretation is felicitous with locative preposing in the absence of the relevant OP. Therefore, it is the class of locative elements alone that permits felicitous preposing in the absence of the OP.

Thus, we posit two distinct classes of preposing constructions in English — presuppositional and locative — each of which is subject to distinct discourse constraints. Presuppositional preposing is constrained in two ways: The link must be related to the prior discourse via a contextually licensed poset relation, and the relevant OP must be salient or inferrable in the current discourse segment. Locative preposing, on the other hand, requires only a semantically locative link but no salient OP.

Intonation

Although, as we have seen, explicitly evoked information and implicit information behave as a single class with respect to word order in preposing and argument reversal, they do not behave similarly with respect to whether they may be felicitously deaccented. An examination of the prosody of preposing constructions reveals that in order to be deaccentable, the link within the preposed constituent must not only represent discourse-old information, but must in fact represent information that has been explicitly evoked in the prior discourse. Links representing information that is merely implicit in the discourse may not be felicitously deaccented. In this way, the constraints on deaccentability are stronger than those on occurrence in preposed position in preposing constructions.[17]

Inversion

A corpus-based study of 80 naturally occurring inversions reported in Birner 1995b reveals that there is an imperfect correspondence between intonation and the discourse-familiarity of an element. That study demonstrates that in order to be deaccentable, the link must represent information that is not only discourse-old, but in fact explicitly evoked in the prior discourse. For example, consider (322):[18]

(322) a. Such corporate voyeurism enables corporations to tailor advertising messages to specific individuals on a mass scale. For example, "What's Hot," a magazine published by General Foods for children aged 4 to 14, is sent to households that are known to be responsive to ad promotions. The "message from the sponsor" is subtle, with brand names worked into activities such as games and quizzes. *ACCOMPANYING the magazine are CENTS-off COUPONS.* [=(211b)]

[17]Recall that we are limiting our discussion to the intonation of noncanonical word orders; space does not permit a full discussion of canonical-word-order intonation. See Bolinger 1972, 1989; Schmerling 1976; Zacharski 1993; Terken & Hirschberg 1994; inter alia, for discussion of some of the factors that influence deaccentability in canonical word order.

[18]Capitalization in the following examples indicates words in the relevant sentence that are likely to receive a pitch accent in an oral utterance, not simply the nuclear accent. It should be kept in mind that most of the examples could felicitously be uttered with more than one intonation pattern; what is of interest here is what information would require an accent in an oral rendering, and what may felicitously be deaccented. Finally, although for ease of reading the entire word has been marked as accented, obviously the accent is associated with a single syllable within the word.

b. We have 160 acres here. *AROUND us are INDUSTRIAL PARKS.* [Terkel 1974:656]

c. The issue is whether this city of 95,000 should ban all research and development of nuclear weapons within its borders. It was to be decided in balloting yesterday, although results will not be known for several days because the city uses paper ballots that are counted by hand. *ALSO at issue is whether this CITY, the HOME of HARVARD and MIT, should impose FINES and JAIL sentences on ANYONE — such as the 1,800 EMPLOYEES of DRAPER LABORATORY here — who CONTINUES to DO such work after OCT. 1, 1985.*
[*Philadelphia Inquirer*, 11/9/83]

Here, *the magazine* in (322a), *us* in (322b), and *at issue* in (322c) all represent information that has been explicitly evoked in the prior discourse, and each of them may be felicitously deaccented. This is not meant to suggest that they must be deaccented; for example, in (322a), *magazine* could be uttered with 'contrastive stress' in order to contrast the magazine with the coupons. Note also that the portion of the preposed constituent that represents discourse-new information — *accompanying* in (322a), *around* in (322b), and *also* in (322c) — must receive a pitch accent for felicity. However, the link within the preposed constituent in each of these examples, as evoked information, may be deaccented.

Contrast such examples with those in (323), in which the link constitutes information that is merely implicit in the discourse:

(323) a. By the time he got to Kendall's Lobster Pound, Ray was home. He was making tea and warming his deeply lined, cracked hands on the pot — *UNDER his RAGGED NAILS was the MECHANIC'S PERMANENT, OIL-BLACK GRIME.*
[Irving 1985:291]

b. Donald Wallace, 28, who faces murder charges in Cook County, has told Hammond police he would be willing to help them find the body. But his court-appointed attorneys have filed a motion with the Illinois Supreme Court to keep him from doing so. *At ISSUE is whether an ILLINOIS JUDGE can ALLOW a MAN ACCUSED of MURDER to COOPERATE with AUTHORITIES in ANOTHER STATE without going through CRIMINAL EXTRADITION PROCEEDINGS.* [=(233b)]

c. Bony was taken into a small room furnished with a writing desk, a lounge, stiff-backed chairs and bookcases crowded with volumes. *On the WALLS hung FRAMED ORIGINAL DRAWINGS of ILLUSTRATIONS of the man's STORIES.*
[Upfield 1946:185]

The mention of hands in (323a) renders nails inferrable; similarly, in (323b), the mention of the attorneys' motion renders inferrable that something is at issue; and finally, the mention of a room in (323c) renders walls inferrable. Thus, all three of these links count as discourse-old; nonetheless, all three require pitch accents due to their representing implicit rather than explicitly evoked information.

An investigation of the corpus reveals that in every one of the 32 tokens in which the link may be felicitously deaccented, it constitutes explicitly evoked information. On the other hand, of 40 tokens in which the link is not deaccentable, in only six cases does it represent explicitly evoked information. (The remaining eight tokens lack sufficient context to judge whether the link has been explicitly evoked.) These results are shown in Table 5.1.

Table 5.1: *Deaccentability and Information Status of the Link*

	Deaccentable?		
	Yes	No	Total
Explicitly evoked	32	6	38
Implicit	0	34	34
Total	32	40	72

As these data show, explicit evocation in the discourse is a necessary but not sufficient condition for deaccentability of the link. Interestingly, of the six non-deaccentable links in the corpus that constitute evoked information, five are either deictic, as in (324a), or contrastive, as in (324b):

(324) a. For his camp Venters chose a shady, grassy plot between the silver spruces and the cliff. *HERE, in the STONE WALL, had been WONDERFULLY CARVED by WIND or WASHED by WATER SEVERAL DEEP CAVES above the level of the TERRACE.* [Grey 1912:58]

b. First would apply a fronting rule, perhaps Topicalization, that would apply to (15) 'An elegant fountain stands in the Italian garden' to yield (16) 'In the Italian garden stands an elegant fountain'... *SECOND, to THIS structure would APPLY, OPTIONALLY, a rule we may call VERB SECOND, that places a VERB PHRASE consisting simply of a VERB immediately AFTER the PREPOSED CONSTITUENT to yield (18) 'In the ITALIAN GARDEN stands an ELEGANT FOUNTAIN', whose DERIVED STRUCTURE would be (19).* [Langendoen 1973:30]

The words *here* in (324a) and *this* in (324b), may not be deaccented in these examples, despite representing textually or situationally evoked information. Thus, it appears that prior evocation within the discourse is a necessary, but not sufficient, criterion for the deaccentability of the link in an inversion.

Recall that the preposed constituent of an inversion may also contain phrases representing relatively unfamiliar information, as in (325):

(325) Parents assume that children are being socialized through language into their particular shared cultural group. This process includes explicit teaching and correcting and the creation of social contexts in which learning will naturally take place. *CRITICAL ALSO to this process is the ASSUMPTION that, whatever the DAY-to-DAY FRUSTRATIONS and IRRITATIONS in COMMUNICATING with a CHILD, NEGATIVE EVALUATIONS will be SUSPENDED when a matter of REAL IMPORTANCE to a child ARISES.* [=(219b)]

We would expect that the portion of the preposed constituent that represents unfamiliar information would not be deaccentable, and this prediction is borne out. In (325), *critical* and *also*, neither of which has been explicitly evoked, must each receive a pitch accent; however, the link within the preposed constituent, *this process*, represents explicitly evoked information and may be deaccented.

We would also expect that if the postposed constituent (generally an NP) represents relatively unfamiliar information, then it would not be deaccentable, and this prediction is also borne out. As with preposed constituents, the postposed constituent often has its own internal information structure. As demonstrated in (220) (repeated here as (326)), entities represented within the postposed NP may be familiar; it is the entity represented by the NP itself that must be relatively unfamiliar.

(326) Greetings from Apple Computer,
ENCLOSED is a PUBLICATION I think you will find INTERESTING.
[=(220)]

Here, *a publication I think you will find interesting* represents new information, and its head noun *publication* may not be deaccented. However, the pronouns *I* and *you* within this NP represent situationally evoked information and may therefore be deaccented.

Of the 80 tokens in the corpus, 65 do not permit the head noun in the postposed constituent to be deaccented, while 13 do.[19] Most of the 13 tokens permitting deaccenting of the postposed NP's head noun fell into two classes. First, 9 of these NPs were of the form NP-PP, with *of* as the head of the PP, as in (327):

(327) a. "Glad to meet you, Nat. We like a man with a fast mind. Trust Mike Conway to choose well."
"Yes, Dad, Mike didn't choose too bad, did he?"
BESIDE the man's FACE appeared the OVAL face of his DAUGHTER.
[Upfield 1960:109]

[19]In the remaining two, the postposed constituent was a full clause.

b. They walked carefully across the twins' vegetable garden, picking their way through rows of cabbage, beets, broccoli, pumpkins. *LOOMING on their LEFT were the TALL stalks of CORN.* [L'Engle 1962:49]

The deaccentability of *face* in the postposed NP in (327a) can be straightforwardly accounted for, in that a face has been mentioned in the preposed constituent; nonetheless, the particular face represented by the entire NP — that of the daughter — is new to the discourse, and indeed, *daughter* may not be deaccented. In (327b), on the other hand, *stalks* may be deaccented despite representing discourse-new information. Notice, however, that *corn* may not be deaccented; here, although it is not the head noun of the NP, *corn* denotes the entity being introduced as discourse-new, and of which *stalks* is descriptive. In each of the 9 cases of this type in the corpus, the noun within the PP (e.g., *corn* in (327b)) is not deaccentable.

In another three of the tokens in which the head noun of the postposed NP is deaccentable, the NP contains a relative clause, as in (324b) above, repeated here as (328):

(328) First would apply a fronting rule, perhaps Topicalization, that would apply to (15) 'An elegant fountain stands in the Italian garden' to yield (16) 'In the Italian garden stands an elegant fountain'... *SECOND, to THIS structure would APPLY, OPTIONALLY, a rule we may call VERB SECOND, that places a VERB PHRASE consisting simply of a VERB immediately AFTER the PREPOSED CONSTITUENT to yield (18) 'In the ITALIAN GARDEN stands an ELEGANT FOUNTAIN', whose DERIVED STRUCTURE would be (19).* [=(324b)]

Here, the head noun *rule* may be deaccented, but *Verb Second* may not. Again, notice that the notion 'rule' has already been evoked in the discourse, hence it is not surprising that *rule* in the postposed NP is deaccentable. What is new to the discourse is the particular rule being referred to as *Verb Second*, and predictably, *Verb Second* cannot be deaccented.

The final token whose postposed head noun may be deaccented is provided in (329):

(329) You can drive as fast as you like in the outside lane on a West German highway and may feel like the king of the road — until you look in the rear mirror. *ZOOMING IN on you like a GUIDED MISSILE comes a RIVAL contender, BULLYING you to get OUT of the WAY.* [=(230a)]

Here, *contender* may be deaccented only if *rival* bears a contrastive accent — suggesting that one contender (*you*) is already discourse-old and that what is new is the rival.

Thus, in all cases the postposed constituent in an inversion receives an accent on the discourse-new information. Notice that although the preposed constituent typically also receives an accent, it is possible to have a completely deaccented preposed constituent if the entire constituent represents evoked information, as in (330a), but it is not possible to have a completely deaccented postposed constituent ((330b)-(330c)), given that some portion of it must represent information that is relatively new to the discourse:

(330) [Did you hear that there's a WOLF in the PARK?]

a. No; in the park is a DOG.

b. No; #in the PARK is a dog.

c. No; #in the GARDEN is a wolf.

Where the postposed constituent is less familiar than the preposed constituent, as in (330b), it must receive a pitch accent; where it is more familiar, as in (330c), the inversion itself is infelicitous, regardless of intonation. Thus, even when the entire inversion constitutes a single intonational phrase, the nuclear accent falls on the postposed constituent.

Preposing

With respect to explicitly evoked vs. implicit information, preposing patterns in precisely the same way as does inversion. That is, in order to be deaccentable, the link within the preposed constituent must be not only discourse-old, but in fact explicitly evoked in the prior discourse. Consider (331):

(331) a. John has a very well-stocked kitchen. *In the REFRIGERATOR he keeps a WIDE VARIETY of IMPORTED CHEESES.* [cf. #IN the refrigerator he keeps a wide variety of imported cheeses.]

b. John just bought a new refrigerator, which he paid next to nothing for. *IN the refrigerator he keeps a WIDE VARIETY of IMPORTED CHEESES.* [cf. #In the REFRIGERATOR he keeps a wide variety of imported cheeses.]

In (331a), the link of the topicalization must be accented, despite the inferrable poset relation that holds between refrigerators and kitchens. In (331b), on the other hand, the refrigerator has been explicitly evoked and thus must be deaccented.

When the link represents one member of a *non-singleton* anchoring poset, however, it must be accented even when it represents explicitly evoked information. Consider (332):

(332) How do you make a two-minute parody of Canadian life and Canadian television into a feature-length comedy? Thomas and Moranis (who worked together on the script and share the directing credit) do it by putting together a mixture of Monty Python, the Marx Brothers and Cheech & Chong. Especially Cheech & Chong. *From MONTY PYTHON they borrow a CERTAIN SATIRIC EDGE and an ANARCHIC APPROACH to MOVIES, such as having an "INTERMISSION" CARD appear INEXPLICABLY in the MIDDLE of the PICTURE, then QUICKLY DISAPPEAR. From the MARX BROTHERS, the McKenzies borrow the OLD, SAPPY PLOT LINE about a YOUNG COUPLE in LOVE, KEPT APART by CRUEL FATE... From CHEECH & CHONG, the McKenzies borrow their SOULS.* This is slob comedy at its most unrelenting.
[*Philadelphia Inquirer*, 8/29/83]

In this example, the anchoring poset is the set of comedians evoked in the prior discourse. Each of the three preposings contains a link that represents a different member of that poset; thus, they induce a contrastive interpretation. Hence, the

NP complement of each preposed PP is accented, and in fact must be, despite representing explicitly evoked information.

Now consider again (307a), in which the link represents a singleton poset member:

(333) In the VIP section of the commissary at 20th Century-Fox, the studio's elite gather for lunch and gossip. The prized table is reserved for Mel Brooks, *and FROM it he dispenses ADVICE, JOKES and INVITATIONS to PASSERS-BY.* [=(307a)]

Here, the link *it* represents explicitly evoked information (the table) that constitutes the only member of the anchoring poset. In this case, it is the preposition *from* — and not the NP *it* — that bears the accent. With accent on the NP, as in (334) below, a contrastive interpretation is induced:

(334) a. #and from IT...

b. #and from this TABLE...

c. #and from THIS table...

In the context provided for (333), such an interpretation is unwarranted and the preposings are correspondingly infelicitous. The difference, then, between (332) and (331b) above is that in the latter example the link represents a singleton member of the anchoring poset that has been explicitly introduced into the prior discourse.

However, accent on a preposed preposition does not necessarily indicate that its complement represents a singleton poset member. Another possibility is for the PP itself to represent a member of a contextually licensed poset with multiple members. Consider (335):

(335) A: Aw, look at little Johnny spreading icicles under the Christmas tree.
B: No, Johnny — put the icicles ON the tree. *UNDER the tree we put the PRESENTS.*

In (335), the PPs *on the tree* and *under the tree* represent alternate members within the poset {locations relative to the tree}. However, given that the NP within the preposed constituent represents explicitly evoked information (the tree), this NP may be felicitously deaccented.

In sum, we see that for both inversion and preposing, the constraints on deaccentability are stricter than those on placement in preposed position. Whereas implicit information is treated as discourse-old with respect to constituent order, and may therefore be realized as the link within the preposed constituent, such links may nonetheless not be deaccented; links may be deaccented only when they represent information that has been explicitly evoked in the discourse. This lack of correspondence between preposability and deaccentability makes sense, however, if we consider the role of the link within the discourse. That is, if the purpose of the link is to establish a connection between the current utterance and the prior discourse (presumably for reasons of processing ease), then what is relevant is only whether this connection can be established, regardless of whether the connection is explicit or implicit. Deaccentability, on the other hand, does not depend only on the ability to establish such a link; instead, it additionally requires salience within the discourse.

Toward a Unified Theory of Noncanonical Word Order

Having described individual constructions as well as classes of constructions, we are now in a position to summarize the discourse properties we have found to be common to various noncanonical word orders in English. As we have seen, both preposing and argument reversal favor the preposing of discourse-old information. Although the two construction types differ as to whether this information must be relatively or absolutely familiar, it is in both cases the discourse-familiarity of the preposed constituent that is relevant for the felicity of the marked construction. Thus, we hypothesize that preposing constructions in general serve to place discourse-old information in preverbal position. This property is not shared by left-dislocation, which has been shown to be both formally and functionally distinct. These findings are summarized in Table 5.2.

Table 5.2: *Constraints on the Information Status of the Preverbal Constituent in English Preposing Constructions (vs. Left-Dislocation)*

CONSTRUCTION	INFORMATION STATUS OF PREVERBAL CONSTITUENT
inversion	relatively familiar in the discourse
by-phrase passive	relatively familiar in the discourse
topicalization	discourse-old
focus preposing	discourse-old
left-dislocation	hearer-new or discourse-new

Thus, for the class of preposing constructions, but not left-dislocation, we find that the constituent appearing in a noncanonical preverbal position represents a discourse-old link to the prior discourse. We therefore propose that the general function of preposing in English is to situate familiar information in preverbal position.

Conversely, our analysis of English postposing constructions — inversion, passive, existential *there*-insertion, and presentational *there*-insertion — has revealed that all four postpose information that is unfamiliar, either within the discourse or within the hearer's knowledge store. In the case of argument reversal, the PVNP is required to represent information that is less familiar in the discourse than that represented by the preposed constituent. Presentational *there*-insertion is similarly sensitive to discourse-familiarity, but requires that the PVNP represent information that is absolutely, rather than relatively, new within the discourse. Finally, existential *there*-insertion requires that the PVNP represent information that is not only new to the discourse, but also (presumed to be) new to the hearer. Thus, these four constructions share the property of postposing information that is 'new' in some sense. Moreover, this property is not shared by right-dislocation, a formally and functionally distinct construction. These findings are summarized in Table 5.3.

Table 5.3: *Constraints on the Information Status of the Postverbal Constituent in English Postposing Constructions (vs. Right-Dislocation)*

CONSTRUCTION	INFORMATION STATUS OF THE POSTVERBAL CONSTITUENT
inversion *by-phrase* passive existential *there* presentational *there*	relatively unfamiliar in the discourse relatively unfamiliar in the discourse hearer-new discourse-new
right-dislocation	discourse-old

We find, then, that in all cases where no referential element appears in subject position, the postposed subject represents unfamiliar information, while in right-dislocation, containing a coreferential pronoun, the marked constituent represents familiar information. We therefore propose that the general function of postposing in English is to situate new information in postverbal position.

Chapter 6

Extensions and Implications

Our investigation has focused on three major classes of marked syntactic constructions in English: preposing, postposing, and argument reversal. We have shown that these constructions serve to link preposed material to the prior context (in the case of preposing) or to mark information as being unfamiliar in some sense (in the case of postposing). The constraint on argument-reversing constructions, on the other hand, is relative: They require only that the postposed constituent represent *less* familiar information within the discourse than does the preposed constituent. In this chapter, we will present some crosslinguistic data that suggest that these generalizations are not limited to English.

Crosslinguistic Extensions

In the following sections, we examine constraints on the use of five sentence-types in languages other than English, all of which permit the appearance of one or more constituents in noncanonical position: inversion in Farsi and Italian, presentational *ci*-sentences and subject postposing in Italian, and *es*-sentences in Yiddish. We will show that these sentence-types satisfy the general constraints we have proposed for noncanonically positioned constituents. First, each of these constructions permits the noncanonical appearance of the logical subject in postverbal position, and in each case this NP is required to represent information that is unfamiliar in some sense. Moreover, inversion in both Farsi and Italian satisfies the proposed constraint on argument reversal in that information that is relatively familiar within the discourse is consistently placed before information that is relatively unfamiliar within the discourse. The other three constructions — *ci*-sentences and subject postposing in Italian and *es*-sentences in Yiddish — require that the postposed constituent represent absolutely new information within the discourse.

Farsi inversion

Recall that inversion in English, as an argument-reversing construction, consistently presents relatively familiar information before relatively unfamiliar information, thus linking relatively unfamiliar information to the prior context through the placement of more familiar information in preposed position.

In Birner & Mahootian 1996 it is argued that discourse-functional constraints on inversion in Farsi correspond to those on inversion in English, despite differences in word order. Farsi is a verb-final language that canonically exhibits SXV word order, as in (336):[1]

(336) a. Pir-e maerd doxtaer-o komaek kaerd.
old-EZ man girl-def help did
'The old man helped the girl.'

b. Deraext-e chenar-e kohaen-i yek taeraef-e meydan bud.
tree-EZ sycamore-EZ old-indef one side-EZ square was
'An old sycamore tree was on one side of the square.'

c. Donya-i ru-ye haer qali haest.
world-indef on-EZ every carpet is
'There is a world in every carpet.'

[=Birner & Mahootian 1996, ex. 6]

These examples show not only that Farsi is an SOV language, but also that PPs, like direct objects, canonically follow the subject and precede the verb.

[1]The EZ, or *ezafe*, particle shown in the gloss is essential to the internal structure of Farsi NPs, APs and PPs, but is not relevant to the issues being considered here. See Mahootian 1993 for discussion.

Farsi also permits a marked ordering of XSV, as shown in (337):

(337) a. Chaend dokan-e kuchik-e nanvai, qaesabi, aetari, do qaehvexane vae yek saelmani... taeshkil-e meydan-e vaeramin ra midad...
'A few small bakeries, a butcher's shop, spice shop, two coffee houses and a barber shop... made up the Vaeramin (town) square...'

Yek taeraef-e meydan deraext-e chenar-e kohaen-i bud.
one side-EZ square tree-EZ sycamore-EZ old-indef was

'On one side of the square was an old sycamore tree.'

b. Maen mixahaem qese-i daer bare-ye golha-ye qali baeraye to be-gaem. Ta be hal ba mehr vae mehraebani be golha-ye qali negah kaerdei?
'I want to tell you a story about the designs in carpets. Have you ever looked with affection and caring at the designs in carpets?'

Ru-ye haer qali donya-i haest.
on-EZ every carpet world-indef is

'In every carpet is a world.'

[=Birner & Mahootian 1996, ex. 8]

Although the linear order of the constituents in such sentences corresponds to that of English topicalization (i.e., PP-S-V), the two constructions are functionally distinct. As argued above in Chapter 2, the preposed constituent in an English topicalization must represent discourse-old information, related to the previous discourse via a contextually licensed linking relation; Farsi XSV word order, however, does not share this constraint. Consider (338):

(338) Daer yeki aez rustaha-ye kerman chupan-i zendegi mikaerd.
in one from villages-EZ Kerman shepherd-indef life did
'In one of the villages of Kerman lived a shepherd.'
[=Birner & Mahootian 1996, ex. 11a]

This sentence introduces a story about a shepherd. Here, neither the villages nor Kerman is evoked in or inferrable from the prior discourse; indeed, all of the information presented in this sentence is discourse-new. Therefore, while this example satisfies the constraint on English inversion, in that the subject does not represent more familiar information in the discourse than does the preposed PP, it does not satisfy the constraint on English topicalization.

Instead, Farsi XSV word order corresponds functionally to English inversion. That is, in every instance of PP inversion in the Farsi corpus, the preposed PP represents information that is at least as familiar within the discourse as that represented by the subject NP. For example, in (337a) above, the author is describing the center of a small town. The town square is discourse-old, having been previously mentioned, while the sycamore tree is discourse-new. Similarly, in (337b), the preposed *carpet* represents discourse-old information, while the subject NP *a world* represents discourse-new information.

On the other hand, in no token in the corpus does the reverse order hold; that is, in no case does the subject represent discourse-old information while the PP represents discourse-new information. And in fact, such an ordering of information is infelicitous, as shown in (339):

(339) Ye maerd-e piri dasht ye doxtaeraek-i ra komaek mikaerd. Doxtaeraek gom shode bud. Aez in kuche be un kuche miraeftaend. Belaexaere, vared-e haeyat-i shodaend. Aetrafeshan ra negah kaerdaend.
'An old man was helping a young girl. The girl had gotten lost. They went from one street to another. Finally, they entered a courtyard. They looked around at their surroundings.'

#Paehlu-ye	yek	deraext-e	saerv-i	doxtaeraek	bud.
next-EZ	a	tree-EZ	cedar-indef	girl	was

'Next to a cedar tree was the young girl.'
[=Birner & Mahootian 1996, ex. 9]

Here, a discourse-new PP precedes a discourse-old subject, resulting in infelicity. Thus, felicitous inversion in Farsi requires that the subject not represent more familiar information within the discourse than does the preposed PP; hence the same pragmatic constraint holds for inversion in both Farsi and English.

Moreover, as in English, the link within the preposed constituent of Farsi inversion is not restricted to representing explicitly evoked information. Consider (340):

(340) Naefaes-aem paes miraevaed, aez cheshman-aem aeshk mirizaed.
breath-my short is, from eyes-my tears flow

'My breath is short, from my eyes flow tears.' [=Birner & Mahootian 1996, ex. 16a]

Here, *cheshman-aem* ('my eyes') is implicitly linked to the prior discourse since, given an individual, one may infer that he or she has eyes; *aeshk* ('tears'), on the other hand, is discourse-new. In Farsi inversion, then, as in English inversion, implicit information patterns exactly like explicitly evoked information; both are discourse-old.

Thus, although the XSV word order in Farsi corresponds to the word order of English topicalization, it does not share the function of that construction. Rather, the felicitous use of this word order in Farsi is subject to the same constraint on the relative information status of the preposed PP and the logical subject to which inversion in English is sensitive. Moreover, when independent syntactic factors (concerning the canonical position of the verb) are abstracted away from, the two constructions can be seen to involve the same change in relative order between the subject and the PP, the very constituents whose relative information status determines the constructions' felicitous use. Thus, despite differences in linear word order, Farsi inversion and English inversion both constitute argument-reversing constructions, and both share the same constraint on the relative status of the reversed constituents.

Italian presentational 'ci'-sentences

Like English (and many other languages), Italian also has a so-called 'presentational' construction ('*c'è presentativo*'), consisting of an expletive or dummy surface subject, some form of the verb *essere* ('be'), and a postverbal logical subject.[2] The expletive element is the same morpheme as the locative anaphor *ci* ('there'), from which it is derived. However, as with the *there* of the English existential and presentational constructions, no locative meaning is associated with *ci* in its presentational use.

As argued in Ward 1998, the postposed NP in an Italian *ci*-sentence, like that in an English *there*-sentence, is required to represent discourse-new information, as in (341):

(341) C'è un ponticello dove ogni anno, la notte del 2 aprile
there's a bridge where each year, the night of the 2 april

appare un fantasma.
appears a ghost

'There's a bridge where, each year on the night of April 2nd, a ghost appears.'
[ANSA, 5/91]

Here, the PVNP — *un ponticello* ('a bridge') — represents information that is new both to the discourse and presumably also to the hearer/reader as well (see Berruto 1986). However, postverbal position in *ci*-sentences, like that of English presentational *there*-sentences, admits hearer-old information, as long as that information is discourse-new. Consider the examples in (342):

(342) a. Il quotidiano inglese "Independent" scrive che
the daily newspaper English "Independent" writes that

l'esame di frammenti dei detonatori indicano
the examination of fragments of the detonators indicate

che dietro l'attentato c'è la Libia.
that behind the attempt there's the Libya

[2] Presentational *ci*-sentences require main-verb *essere* ('be'); use of other main verbs requires either canonical word order or subject postposing. See below.

'The English daily "[The] Independent" writes that the examination of the fragments of the detonators indicates that Libya is behind the attempt.'
[ANSA, 9/92]

b. Oggi, c'è il sole.
today, there's the sun
'Today, the sun is out.'
[ANSA, 4/91]

In these examples, the referent of the PVNP is new to the discourse, though it can safely be assumed to be already familiar to the reader.

While hearer-old information may be felicitously represented by a PVNP in a *ci*-sentence, discourse-old information may not. Consider (343):

(343) A: Ho parlato con la Giulia oggi. Sta molto bene.
(I) have spoken with the Julia today. is very well
'I talked to Julia today. She's doing very well.'

B: Mi fa piacere. #A proposito, sai che
to-me makes happy. by the way, you know that

c'era la Giulia alla festa di Paolo ieri sera?
there was the Julia at the party of Paul yesterday evening

'That's good. By the way, did you know that Julia was at Paul's party last night?'

Here, Giulia has been evoked within the same discourse and, as a discourse-old entity, cannot be represented by a PVNP in an Italian *ci*-sentence.

Thus, Italian *ci*-sentences require that the PVNP represent a discourse-new entity, regardless of hearer-status. This is exactly the constraint found for English presentational *there*-sentences, though not for English existential *there*-sentences. Indeed, translating the *ci*-sentences in (342) with the corresponding English existential *there*-sentence would result in infelicity, as illustrated in (344):

(344) a. #The examination of the fragments of the detonators indicates that behind the attempt there's Libya.

b. #Today, there's the sun.

Note that it is the information status and not the definiteness of the Italian PVNP that renders these English translations infelicitous; when a definite PVNP can be interpreted as hearer-new, both the *ci*-sentence and its English equivalent are perfectly appropriate, as shown in (345):

(345) a. Alla festa, c'era quel buffone di cui ti
at the party there was that fool of whom to you

ho parlato ieri.
(I) spoke yesterday

'At the party, there was that fool I talked to you about yesterday.'

b. Alla riunione, c'erano le solite obiezioni da parte
at the meeting, there were the usual objections from

dei docenti.
the faculty

'At the meeting, there were the usual objections from the faculty.'

c. Secondo Agnoletto, c'è il rischio che si tenda
according to Agnoletto, there's the risk that one tends

a limitare il diritto dei bambini sieropositivi a
to limit the right of the children seropositive to

frequentare la scuola insieme agli altri.
frequent the school together with the others

'According to Agnoletto, there's the risk that you might restrict the right of HIV-positive children to go to school with other children.' [ANSA, 5/91]

In fact, the same types of definite hearer-new PVNPs found in English *there*-sentences (see Chapter 3) are found in Italian *ci*-sentences.

However, while they both tolerate definite hearer-new PVNPs, English existential *there*-sentences and Italian *ci*-sentences are nonetheless sensitive to different discourse constraints. Although the two constructions are formally quite similar (both in the presence of the expletive and in the presence of main-verb *be*), we have shown that English existential *there*-sentences are sensitive to hearer-status, while Italian *ci*-sentences are sensitive to discourse-status. In fact, pragmatically speaking, *ci*-sentences have much more in common with English presentational *there*-sentences, which likewise require discourse-new PVNPs. Just as presentational *there*-sentences disallow discourse-old information in postverbal position, so too do *ci*-sentences. In this way, the Italian *ci* construction corresponds pragmatically not to the English existential construction — its syntactic analog — but rather to the English presentational construction.

Italian subject postposing

In addition to *ci*-sentences, Ward 1998 discusses another construction in Italian that shares the pragmatic constraint found for English presentational *there*-sentences, namely subject postposing (Burzio 1986, Belletti 1988, Calabrese 1992, Saccon 1993, Pinto 1994).[3] In this construction — generally restricted to unaccusative verbs other than *essere* ('be') — the subject is postposed, as illustrated (346):[4]

[3]Previous studies use the term 'subject inversion' for this construction; however, that term is misleading in that it is used to refer to pure subject postposing (with no concomitant preposing) as well as argument reversal (involving preposing and postposing). As we shall see, the two are subject to distinct discourse constraints and, we maintain, constitute distinct constructions; thus, we shall use distinct terms to refer to them. It should also be noted that there is a superficially similar construction in Italian in which the logical subject also appears postverbally. This construction, variously termed right-dislocation or 'emargination', requires an intonational boundary between the VP and the postposed subject. As Calabrese (1992) and Saccon (1993) point out, emargination is both formally and functionally distinct from subject postposing, in which the matrix clause and postposed subject occur within a single intonational phrase.

[4]The facts surrounding postposing with other semantic types of verbs (e.g. unergatives and transitives) are complex (see Pinto to appear for discussion); we shall therefore restrict our

(346) È arrivato stamattina una lettera dall'America.
arrived this morning a letter from the America
'A letter from America arrived this morning.'

Here, the indefinite PVNP represents an entity that is new both to the discourse and presumably to the hearer as well. However, as previous studies have pointed out (e.g. Calabrese 1992, Saccon 1993, Pinto 1994, inter alia), what is relevant for felicitous subject postposing is the discourse-status of the PVNP. Postverbal position in subject postposing is restricted to those NPs representing entities new to the discourse — or, equivalently, NPs that are 'non-anaphoric' (Calabrese 1992), 'non-presupposed' (Saccon 1993), or '–d-linked' (Pinto 1994). Consider the examples of discourse-new, hearer-old PVNPs in (347):

(347) a. È morto Mario.
died Mario
'Mario died.'
[=Calabrese 1992, ex. 9]

b. Era salita tua sorella sull'autobus.
boarded your sister on the bus
'Your sister got on (the bus).'
[adapted from Saccon 1993:169, ex. 104]

In each of these examples, the PVNP represents an entity with which the hearer is presumably familiar; what licenses the subject postposing is the fact that it is new to the discourse. When an NP representing a discourse-old entity is postposed, infelicity results. Consider Saccon's (1993:169) example in (348) (slightly modified):

---

discussion to postposing with unaccusatives, about which native speaker judgments are relatively clear.

(348) A: Mi sono addormentato, ma mi è sembrato di
(I) fell asleep, but to me seemed

averti sentito parlare con qualcuno.
to have you heard speak with someone

'I fell asleep, but I thought I heard you talk to someone.'

B: Sì, infatti sono saliti tua sorella e tuo fratello.
yes, in fact boarded your sister and your brother

'Yes, in fact your sister and brother got on [the bus].'

A: È dove sono andati ora?
and where are gone now

'And where have they gone now?'

a. B: *È scesa tua sorella a far spese in centro.
got off your sister to do shopping in center
'Your sister got off to go shopping downtown.'

b. B: Tua sorella è scesa a far spese in centro.
your sister got off to do shopping in center
'Your sister got off to go shopping downtown.'

In the subject postposing in B's initial utterance in (348), the PVNP *tua sorella e tuo fratello* ('your sister and brother') represents a hearer-old, discourse-new entity (consisting of a set of two individuals) and, as such, it is fully felicitous as a postverbal subject. The unacceptability of B's reply in (348a), on the other hand, can be attributed to the discourse-old status of the PVNP in context. Note that the corresponding canonical-word-order utterance in (348b) is felicitous in the same context.

However, it is not the case that all previously evoked information is infelicitous in postposed position. As Pinto (to appear) notes, a postposed subject may represent previously evoked information just in case it represents the 'contrastive focus' of an utterance. Consider the (constructed) example in (349):

(349) E alla fine chi è arrivato, il poeta o la ragazza?
So at the end who arrived, the poet or the girl?
'So, in the end who was it that arrived, the poet or the girl?'

È arrivato, il poeta.
Arrived, the poet.

'The poet arrived.'
[=Pinto to appear, ex. 2]

Here, the postposed subject *il poeta* represents previously evoked information; crucially, however, this entity stands in a contrastive relationship with another salient entity (*la ragazza*). What is new to the discourse, then, is not the entity itself, but rather its selection as the appropriate member from among an evoked set of alternatives. As Pinto observes, without an explicit contrast in the discourse, postposing of (in our terms) discourse-old information is infelicitous. We may conclude, then, that both *ci*-sentences and postposed subjects in Italian, like presentational *there*-sentences in English, are sensitive to the discourse-status of the postposed subject.

Italian inversion

Italian, like English and Farsi, also has an argument-reversing construction that involves the postposing of subjects with concomitant preposing. And as we would predict, Italian inversion, like inversion in English and Farsi, is sensitive to *relative* rather than *absolute* discourse-status. First, consider (350):

(350) a. C'è un nuovo albergo a Verona. In questo albergo lavora
there's a new hotel in Verona. in this hotel works

un greco.
a Greek man

'There's a new hotel in Verona. In this hotel, a Greek man works.'

b. C'è un nuovo albergo a Verona. In questo albergo lavora
there's a new hotel in Verona. in this hotel works

Chelsea Clinton.
Chelsea Clinton

'There's a new hotel in Verona. In this hotel, Chelsea Clinton works.'

In each of the inversions in (350), the preverbal position is occupied by information that is discourse-old (*this hotel*). The postverbal position may be felicitously occupied by information that is either hearer-new (*a Greek man*), as in (350a), or hearer-old (*Chelsea Clinton*), as in (350b), as long as it is discourse-new. On the other hand, when the preverbal constituent represents discourse-new information and the postverbal constituent represents discourse-old information, as in (351), infelicity results:

(351) A: Come va tuo amico Carlo?
how goes your friend Carlo?
'How's your friend Carlo?'

B: Bene, grazie. #In un albergo lavora Carlo adesso.
well, thanks. In a hotel works Carlo now.

'Good, thanks. Carlo now works in a hotel.'

Here, the postverbal *Carlo* represents discourse-old information while the preverbal constituent represents discourse-new information (a hotel), and the inversion is infelicitous. Thus, as with inversion in English and Farsi, the postposed constituent of an Italian inversion may not represent information that is more familiar than that represented by the preposed constituent.

However, that is not to say that the postposed constituent in an Italian inversion may never represent discourse-old information; on the contrary, postverbal position may be occupied by a discourse-old NP just in case there is another entity more recently evoked within the same discourse that is realized in preverbal position. Consider the following example of an inversion with a PVNP representing a discourse-old entity:

(352) Il presidente doveva fare un discorso alla Camera e aveva bisogno del supporto di tutto il governo. Dubitava peró dell'appoggio del vicepresidente, e fino all'ultimo minuto tutti i suoi collaboratori piú stretti avevano dubitato che il vicepresidente si sarebbe presentato. Quando la seduta cominció, i collaboratori del presidente tirarono un sospiro di sollievo. *Dietro di lui sorrideva, sornione, il vicepresidente.*

The President had to give a speech to the Parliament and needed the support of the entire government. However, he had doubts about the support of the Vice President, and up to the last minute all of his closest advisors doubted that the Vice President would show up. When the meeting began, the President's advisors breathed a collective sigh of relief. *Behind him was smiling, coyly, the Vice President.*

In (352), the postposed NP *il vicepresidente* represents a familiar entity, having been evoked in the prior discourse. However, the NP within the preposed PP — *lui* ('him') — represents an even more familiar entity (the President), in the sense of having been more recently evoked than the entity represented by the postposed constituent, and the inversion is felicitous.

In this way, Italian inversion patterns exactly like argument reversal in English and Farsi.[5] That is, the felicity of each of these argument-reversing constructions depends on the relative discourse-familiarity of the preposed and postposed constituents. In the case of Italian subject postposing, on the other hand, there is no reversal of arguments, and the constraint on postverbal position is absolute rather than relative; the same is true for *ci*-sentences. The postposed subjects of both *ci*-sentences and subject postposing, then, pattern just like those of English presentational *there*-sentences: They must be new to the discourse in absolute, rather than relative, terms.

[5]Indeed, Italian informants agree that the most natural English translation of the Italian inversion in (352) is an English inversion.

Table 6.1: *Comparison of Six Noncanonical-Word-Order Constructions in English and Italian*

	be/essere	Non-*be/essere*
Discourse-new PVNP	Italian *ci*-sentences	English presentational *there*-sentences Italian subject postposing
Hearer-new PVNP	English existential *there*-sentences	
Relatively new PVNP	English inversion Italian inversion	

We can summarize our comparison of English and Italian postposing and argument-reversing constructions as in Table 6.1. Here, we see that both English and Italian employ different sentence-types for postposing depending on the matrix verb. In Italian, use of *essere* ('be') requires presentational *ci*; use of verbs other than *essere* requires subject postposing. Both constructions, however, are sensitive to the same constraint on the PVNP. In English, on the other hand, expletive *there* is possible with both *be* and non-*be* verbs; however, the PVNPs in these two cases are sensitive to different discourse constraints.

Yiddish 'es'-sentences

Finally, we consider very briefly one additional postposing construction in which postverbal position is sensitive to the discourse-status of the PVNP. Prince (1988b) provides a discourse-functional account of Yiddish *es*-sentences, exemplified in (353):

(353) Es iz geshtorbn a raykher goy.
it is died a rich gentile
'A rich gentile died.'
[=Prince 1988b, ex. 1]

Like the other postposing constructions we have examined, Yiddish *es*-sentences serve to postpose new information; in (353), the gentile is being introduced to the hearer for the first time. In this case, the PVNP is both discourse-new and hearer-new; however, as Prince points out, postposed subjects are not restricted to those representing hearer-new information. Consider the examples in (354):

(354) a. Es klingt mit der meydl di velt.
it rings with the girl the world
'The whole world is fooling around with this girl.'
[=Prince 1988b, ex. 22]

b. Un es loyft arayn vite.
and it runs PRT Vite
'And Vitte runs in.'
[=Prince 1988b, ex. 23]

The postposed subjects of these naturally occurring Yiddish *es*-sentences represent information that would be familiar to the hearer/reader in context. In (354a), the PVNP *di velt* ('the world') can safely be assumed to be represent familiar information, while in (354b), the PVNP *vite* ('Vitte') is a proper name referring to the Czar's minister, who would be known to the hearer of the story from which this utterance is taken.

As these examples indicate, subject postposing in Yiddish, as in Italian, permits hearer-old information in postverbal position; what may not be postposed, according to Prince, are those subjects that "represent entities which have already been evoked in the discourse" (1988b:184). Thus, the PVNP in Yiddish *es*-sentences patterns very much like that in English presentational *there*-sentences, Italian *ci*-sentences, and Italian subject inversion in being constrained to represent discourse-new information.

Summary of Constraints on Noncanonical Word Order

A number of observations can be made at this point. First, we have seen that it is possible for two formally equivalent constructions in different languages — e.g., Italian *ci*-sentences and English existential *there*-sentences — to be subject to different pragmatic constraints. The PVNP in an English existential *there*-sentence must represent hearer-new information, while that of an Italian *ci*-sentence must represent discourse-new information. Second, two formally distinct constructions within a single language may be subject to precisely the same pragmatic constraint, as with Italian *ci*-sentences and subject postposing, and English inversion and *by*-phrase passives. Finally, formally distinct constructions in two different languages — e.g., presentational *there*-sentences in English and subject postposing in Italian — may share the same pragmatic constraint, in this case that the PVNP must represent discourse-new information. Thus, formally equivalent constructions in different languages can be subject to distinct discourse constraints, while distinct constructions both across and within languages can nonetheless share discourse constraints.

Nonetheless, certain broad generalizations can be made concerning the correlation of syntactic form and discourse function. For example, our findings on the information status of preposed constituents in three languages are summarized in Table 6.2. Of the five preposing constructions we have examined, only English preposing is a 'pure' preposing construction in that only a single constituent appears in noncanonical (i.e., preposed) position. Correspondingly, the discourse constraint on the preposed constituent is absolute: It must represent discourse-old information. The four other preposing constructions we have examined are argument-reversing constructions, and the constraint, in turn, is

Table 6.2: *Constraints on Information Status: Preposed Constituent*

CONSTRUCTION	INFORMATION STATUS OF PREPOSED CONSTITUENT
English inversion Farsi inversion Italian inversion English *by*-phrase passive	relatively familiar in the discourse
English topicalization English focus preposing	discourse-old discourse-old

a relative one: namely, that the preposed constituent must not represent information that is less familiar than that represented by the postposed constituent. Nonetheless, we have found that all preposing constructions — whether the constraint on the preposed constituent is absolute or relative — share a general discourse constraint, in that the preposed constituent represents information that is familiar within the discourse. On the other hand, this constraint does not apply to left-dislocation, in which a pronoun that is coreferential with the marked constituent appears in that constituent's canonical position. Thus, the formal distinction between left-dislocation and preposing constructions corresponds to a functional distinction, while the formal similarity within the class of preposing constructions corresponds to a functional similarity.

Moreover, we have found that preposing constructions in English constitute a functionally unified class in that the link within the preposed constituent consistently represents information standing in a contextually licensed partially ordered set relationship with information evoked in or inferrable from the prior context. In addition, preposing constructions can be classified on the basis of the type of link that holds between the preposed constituent and the prior discourse: locative vs. presuppositional. Preposings and inversions with a non-locative link form a natural class on pragmatic grounds in that they require a presupposed open proposition to be salient or inferrable within the discourse. When no such open proposition is readily available, the preposed constituent is consistently semantically locative, and even apparently non-locative links take on a locative sense.

Finally, the data reveal that there is an imperfect correspondence between intonation and the information status of an element. In particular, although explicitly evoked and implicit elements behave as a single class with respect to preposing and argument reversal, they do not behave similarly with respect to whether they may felicitously be deaccented. In order to be deaccentable, the link within the preposed constituent must not only represent discourse-old information, but must represent information that has been explicitly evoked in the prior discourse. Information that is merely implicit may not be felicitously deaccented.

With respect to postposing, we again find that broad crosslinguistic generalizations may be made. Our findings on the information status of postposed constituents in four languages are summarized in Table 6.3. Of these nine postposing constructions, five are 'pure' postposing constructions (English existential and presentational *there*-sentences, Italian *ci*-sentences and subject postposing, and Yiddish *es*-sentences), while four are argument-reversing constructions involving both preposing and postposing (inversion in English, Farsi and Italian and passivization in English). And as with preposing, the 'pure' postposing constructions are subject to an absolute constraint on the status of the information represented by the postposed constituent; the constraint in this case is that the postposed constituent represent information that is new in some sense. English presentational *there*-sentences, Italian *ci*-sentences and subject postposing, and Yiddish *es*-sentences were all found to be sensitive to discourse-familiarity,

Table 6.3: *Constraints on Information Status: Postposed Constituent*

CONSTRUCTION	INFORMATION STATUS OF POSTPOSED CONSTITUE
English inversion Farsi inversion Italian inversion English *by*-phrase passive	relatively unfamiliar in the discourse
English existential *there*	hearer-new
English presentational *there* Italian *ci*-sentences Italian subject postposing Yiddish *es*-sentences	discourse-new

requiring that the postposed subject represent discourse-new information; existential *there*-sentences in English, on the other hand, require that the PVNP represent information that is not only new to the discourse, but also (presumed to be) new to the hearer.

While all of these constructions share the property of postposing information which is new in some sense, this property is not shared by right-dislocation, a superficially similar construction. Unlike the postposed NPs in postposing constructions, the marked NP in a right-dislocation is constrained to represent information that is familiar within the discourse; concomitantly, a pronoun coreferential with the marked constituent appears in this constituent's canonical position. This syntactic difference accounts for the fact that right-dislocation does not serve to keep unfamiliar information out of subject position; the presence of the pronoun rules out such a function. Here we see that a formal difference reflects a functional difference, while a formal similarity reflects a functional similarity.

Thus, all of the 'pure' postposing constructions we have considered require the postposed constituent to represent information that is new in an absolute sense. For argument-reversing constructions, however, the constraint on the postposed constituent is merely that it represent information that is less familiar within the discourse than that represented by the preposed constituent; i.e., the constraint for such constructions is a relative rather than an absolute one. That is, as seen above for preposing, constructions involving a single noncanonically placed constituent place a constraint on the absolute status of that constituent, while those involving two noncanonically placed constituents place a constraint on the relative status of those two constituents. Nonetheless, an examination of nine postposing constructions in four languages demonstrates that in every case, the postposed constituent is constrained to represent new information, while particular constructions vary with regard to the type of newness required (discourse-new vs. hearer-new, and absolute vs. relative).

Argument reversal, on the other hand, is subject to identical discourse constraints in English, Farsi, and Italian. In each case, the postposed subject is required to represent information that is no more familiar in the discourse than that represented by the preposed constituent. Abstracting away from language-specific syntactic factors, we can say that all three constructions represent distinct realizations of a single inversion construction. This finding not only supports Prince's (1994) observation that a single construction may be realized differently in syntactically dissimilar languages, but also raises the likelihood that future research will uncover further crosslinguistic generalizations concerning the correlation of syntax and discourse function.

The constraint on argument-reversing constructions, however, does not hold for sentences combining PP preposing and *there*-insertion; instead, such sentences are subject to the constraints on each of these two constructions. Thus, while inversion is a single argument-reversing construction subject to a single functional constraint, PP preposing + *there* insertion combines two distinct constructions and is correspondingly subject to two distinct constraints simultaneously. Finally, *by*-phrase passives in English, which similarly reverse the canonical position of two arguments, were found to be subject to the same constraint as the other argument-reversing constructions, in that the information represented by the syntactic subject is required to be at least as familiar within the discourse as that represented by the *by*-phrase NP. Once again, then, we see that argument reversal places a constraint on the relative information status of the reversed constituents.

Theoretical Implications

In this book, we have considered three broadly defined classes of noncanonical word order: preposing, postposing, and argument reversal. We have argued that preposed position in general is reserved for information that is familiar in that it is related to the prior context by means of one of a small number of linking relations; postposed position is reserved for information that is new in some sense; and argument-reversing constructions require that the information represented by the preposed constituent be at least as familiar as that represented by the postposed constituent. Moreover, we have argued that both preposing and inversion can be further classified on the basis of whether or not a salient or inferrable open proposition is presupposed in discourse; in the absence of such an OP, the preposed constituent is necessarily locative.

Our investigation of the discourse functions of various constructions both within and across languages has shown that a single syntactic form may serve different functions in different languages, as in English topicalization and Farsi inversion, and similarly in Italian *ci*-sentences and English existential *there*-sentences (see also Prince 1988c, 1994). Indeed, even within a single language, a single form may serve more than one function, as in the case of English topicalization and focus preposing (Prince 1981b, Ward 1988). Likewise, a single function may be served by different forms in different languages, as with English and Farsi inversion, or Italian subject inversion and English presentational *there*-sentences. Finally, even within a single language, a single function may be served by different forms, as with Italian *ci*-sentences and subject postposing. That is, the data show that, both crosslinguistically and intralinguistically, a single form may serve multiple functions, while on the other hand a single function may map onto multiple forms. Thus, there is no necessary correlation between specific forms and specific functions, and we may conclude that discourse function is not bound to syntactic form in this sense (cf. Siewierska 1991).

That is not to say, however, that the relationship between form and function is entirely arbitrary. For example, we have seen that the syntactic form of a right-dislocation constrains its function; due to the presence of the pronoun in syntactic subject position, right-dislocation is unsuitable for the function of postposing a logical subject representing new information. Moreover, we have argued that English, Farsi, and Italian inversion all represent the same abstract construction (in the sense of Prince 1994) on the grounds that in all three languages, a reversal of the linear order of the subject and some other argument of the verb corresponds to a pragmatic constraint on the relative information status of these two constituents. That is, it is not accidental that the constituents whose order is reversed are precisely those whose information status determines the felicity of the construction, nor that the resulting word order places the relatively familiar information in preverbal position. If, as we have argued, inversion serves an information-packaging function, specifically that of presenting relatively familiar information before relatively unfamiliar information in order to facilitate its assimilation into the discourse model, then clearly the resulting word order is particularly well suited to this function. Obviously, not every construction is equally well suited to presenting information in this order.

It has long been recognized that there exists a general tendency in language for 'given' information to precede 'new' information in an utterance; in light of the results presented here, it appears that the use of these argument-reversing constructions serves to preserve this ordering of information in cases where canonical word order would result in discourse-new information preceding discourse-old information.

In fact, our examination of 10 constructions from four languages uncovers the striking pattern illustrated in Table 6.4. As shown in the table, in all cases

Table 6.4: *Information Status by Number and Location of Noncanonically Positioned Arguments*

		Number of Noncanonically Positioned Arguments:	
		One	Two
Status of:	Preposed Constituent	Absolutely Old	Relatively Old
	Postposed Constituent	Absolutely New	Relatively New

of marked word order involving a single noncanonically positioned argument, if that argument is preposed it must represent old information in an absolute sense, while if it is postposed it must represent new information in an absolute sense (either to the hearer or to the discourse). On the other hand, in all cases involving two noncanonically positioned arguments, the preposed constituent represents information that is relatively old, while the postposed constituent represents information that is relatively new.

It should be noted that, in all of the languages under consideration, the basic or unmarked word order is either SVO or SOV, and the basic distribution of information presents familiar before unfamiliar information (with noncanonical constructions working to preserve this ordering, as shown throughout this book). However, as Siewierska (1988), Tomlin & Rhodes (1979, 1992), Creider & Creider (1983), and others have observed, languages displaying a different basic word order may also display a different basic information structure. For example, Ojibwa, an Algonquian language, is generally described as canonically VOS, and is said to present 'thematic' information in sentence-final position (Tomlin & Rhodes 1979, 1992). Interestingly, according to Tomlin & Rhodes, preposing in Ojibwa appears to be restricted to indefinite NPs — that is, in our terms, those representing hearer-new information — in direct contrast to the other languages we have examined.[6] Thus, as Herring (1990) and Polinsky (1997) note, generalizations about the information structure of a given language must be relative to that language's canonical word order. A great deal more research is needed to identify the typological correlations that may exist between a language's canonical word order, its canonical information structure, and the information structure of noncanonical-word-order constructions in that language. This book is intended as a first step in the development of such correlations.

The matrix illustrated in Table 6.4 correctly predicts the range of possible constraints for each of the 10 constructions we have discussed, including all of the English constructions we have discussed in detail throughout this book as well as the various constructions in other languages that we have sketched more briefly in this chapter. Within these limits, constructions are free to vary (arbitrarily, we believe) with respect to whether the constraints in question are sensitive to

[6]None of the Ojibwa examples discussed by Tomlin & Rhodes (1979, 1992) or Siewierska (1988) correspond to the argument reversal constructions we discuss in Chapter 4; therefore, we are unable to make any direct comparisons along those lines.

hearer- or discourse-status. In addition, individual constructions may be subject to further constraints regarding open propositions, locativity, the status of the verb, etc. However, we have found no construction in any of the SVO or SOV languages we have examined for which the general pattern illustrated in Table 6.4 does not hold.

While more research is needed on a greater variety of languages and constructions (including, for example, languages exhibiting a wider variety of canonical word orders), the results presented here strongly suggest a broad correlation between construction type and function type. The facts summarized in Table 6.4 indicate that, although there is no necessary correspondence between particular constructions and specific functional constraints, discourse functions nonetheless correlate with syntactic constructions in a principled way. That is, these facts indicate that the range of discourse functions a given construction may serve is constrained by the form of the construction; within that range, however, there is room for arbitrary variation with respect to the sorts of constraints imposed on the construction. This approach reconciles both the strong correlations we have found among construction types and function types and the equally strong evidence of both crosslinguistic and intralinguistic variation in the correlation between form and function. In short, our research suggests that this variation may be restricted in its range for any given construction based on that construction's form.

The use of noncanonical word order constitutes a powerful organizational force in language, serving to facilitate the orderly presentation of information in discourse. Whether or not the pattern we have sketched here ultimately leads to the identification of a universal property of language, it nonetheless succeeds in providing for the first time a rigorous and predictive delimitation of the notions of given and new information and the role that these notions play in the structuring of natural discourse.

Appendix

The tokens used in this book come from a variety of oral and written sources. Where tokens are taken from books or articles within books, these are cited in the text by author and date only; full references are provided below.

Barwise, Jon and John Perry. 1983. *Situations and Attitudes*. Cambridge, MA: MIT Press.

Bowen, Elizabeth. 1968. *Eva Trout*. New York: Alfred A. Knopf. Penguin edition 1982.

Chomsky, Noam. 1980. *Rules and Representations*. New York: Columbia University Press.

Colwin, Laurie. 1990. *Goodbye Without Leaving*. New York: Poseidon.

Dahl, Roald. 1964. *Charlie and the Chocolate Factory*. New York: Knopf.

Dahl, Roald. 1978. *The Enormous Crocodlie*. Puffin Books: New York.

Donoghue, William E. 1981. *William E. Donoghue's Complete Money Market Guide*. New York: Harper and Row.

Golding, William. 1984. *The Paper Men*. New York: Farrar, Straus and Giroux.

Goldstein, Rebecca. 1989. *The Late-Summer Passion of a Woman of Mind*. New York: Farrar, Straus and Giroux.

Grant-Adamson, Lesley. 1986. *Guilty Knowledge*. Boston: Faber and Faber.

Grey, Zane. 1912. *Riders of the Purple Sage*. New York: Harper & Brothers.

Holtby, Winifred. 1936. *South Riding*. New York: Macmillan. Virago Press reprint, 1988.

Irving, John. 1985. *The Cider House Rules*. New York: William Morrow.

Jupp, T.C., Celia Roberts, and Jenny Cook-Gumperz. 1982. "Language and Disadvantage: The Hidden Process." In John Gumperz, ed., *Language and Social Identity*. Cambridge: Cambridge University Press.

Kaplan, Jeffrey. 1989. *English Grammar: Principles and Facts*. Englewood Cliffs, NJ: Prentice Hall.

Langendoen, D. Terence. 1973. "The Problem of Grammatical Relations in Surface Structure." In K.R. Jankowsky, ed., *Georgetown University Round Table on Languages and Linguistics: Language and International Studies*. Washington, D.C.: Georgetown University Press.

L'Engle, Madeleine. 1962. *A Wrinkle in Time*. New York: Farrar, Straus and Giroux.

L'Engle, Madeleine. 1978. *A Swiftly Tilting Planet*. New York: Farrar, Straus and Giroux.

Lewis, Clive S. 1952. *The Voyage of the "Dawn Treader"*. London: Collins. Collier Books reprint, 1970.

Lewis, Clive S. 1954. *The Horse and His Boy*. London: Collins. Collier Books reprint, 1970.

Munthe, Axel. 1929. *The Story of San Michele*. London: John Murray.

Nixon, Richard. 1962. *Six Crises*. Garden City, NY: Doubleday.

Nixon, Richard. 1974. *The Presidential Transcripts*. New York: Delacorte Press.

Reinhart, Tanya. 1982. *Pragmatics and Linguistics: An Analysis of Sentence Topics*. Bloomington, IN: Indiana University Linguistics Club.

Roth, Philip. 1959. *Goodbye, Columbus*. Boston: Houghton Mifflin.

Roth, Philip. 1969. *Portnoy's Complaint*. New York: Random House.

Steinbeck, John. 1939. *The Grapes of Wrath.* New York: Viking. Penguin Books reprint, 1969.

Terkel, Studs. 1974. *Working.* New York: Avon.

Thane, Elswyth. 1943. *Dawn's Early Light.* New York: Duell, Sloan and Pearce.

Updike, John. 1981. *Rabbit is Rich.* New York: Knopf.

Upfield, Arthur W. 1931. *The Sands of Windee.* London: London House and Maxwell reprint, 1968.

Upfield, Arthur W. 1937. *Winds of Evil.* Sydney: Angus and Robertson. Collier Books reprint, 1987.

Upfield, Arthur W. 1940. *No Footprints in the Bush.* New York: Collier Books reprint, 1986.

Upfield, Arthur W. 1946. *The Devil's Steps.* Sydney: Angus and Robertson. Collier Books reprint, 1987.

Upfield, Arthur W. 1950. *The Bachelors of Broken Hill.* New York: Collier Books reprint, 1984.

Upfield, Arthur W. 1953. *Murder Must Wait.* New York: Collier Books reprint, 1987.

Upfield, Arthur W. 1954. *Sinister Stones.* New York: Collier Books reprint, 1986.

Upfield, Arthur W. 1960. *Bony and the Kelly Gang.* London: Heinemann. Collier Books reprint, 1988.

Wakefield, Hannah. 1991. *A Woman's Own Mystery.* New York: St. Martin's Press.

Waugh, Evelyn. 1945. *Brideshead Revisited.* Boston: Little, Brown and Co.

Wilder, Laura I. 1933. *Farmer Boy.* Eau Claire, WI: E.M. Hale. Harper reprint, 1953.

References

Abbott, Barbara. 1992. "Definiteness, Existentials, and the 'List' Interpretation." *Proceedings of Semantics and Linguistic Theory II*, 1-16.

Abbott, Barbara. 1993. "A Pragmatic Account of the Definiteness Effect in Existential Sentences." *Journal of Pragmatics* 19: 39-55.

Aissen, Judith. 1975. "Presentational-*There* Insertion: A Cyclic Root Transformation." Chicago Linguistic Society 11: 1-14.

Aissen, Judith and Jorge Hankamer. 1972. "Shifty Subjects: A Conspiracy in Syntax?" *Linguistic Inquiry* 3: 501-4.

Arnold, Jennifer, Tony Losongco, Ryan Ginstrom, Amy Brynolfson, and Thomas Wasow. 1997. "Save the Worst for Last: The Effects of Syntactic Complexity and Information Structure on Constituent Ordering." Paper presented at the Annual Meeting of the Linguistic Society of America, Chicago.

Babby, Leonard H. 1980. *Existential Sentences and Negation in Russian*. Ann Arbor: Karoma.

Ball, Catherine. 1991. *The Historical Development of the* It-*Cleft*. Ph.D. dissertation, University of Pennsylvania.

Beedham, Christopher. 1982. *The Passive Aspect in English, German, and Russian*. Tübingen: Narr.

Belletti, Adriana. 1988. "The Case of Unaccusatives." *Linguistic Inquiry* 19: 1-34.

Bernardo, Robert. 1980. "Subjecthood and Consciousness." In Wallace Chafe, (ed.), *The Pear Stories: Cognitive, Cultural, and Linguistic Aspects of Narrative Production*. Norwood, NJ: Ablex, 275-99.

Berruto, Gaetano. 1986. "Un Tratto Sintattico dell'Italiano Parlato: Il *C'è* Presentativo." In Klaus Lichem, Edith Mara, and Susanne Knaller, (eds.), *Parallela 2: Aspetti della Sintassi dell'Italiano Contemporaneo.* Tübingen: Narr, 61-73.

Biber, Douglas. 1986. "Spoken and Written Textual Dimensions in English." *Language* 62: 384-414.

Biber, Douglas. 1988. *Variation Across Speech and Writing.* Cambridge: Cambridge University Press.

Birner, Betty J. 1994. "Information Status and Word Order: An Analysis of English Inversion." *Language* 70: 233-59.

Birner, Betty J. 1995a. "Pragmatic Constraints on the Verb in English Inversion." *Lingua* 97: 233-56.

Birner, Betty J. 1995b. "Inference and Intonation in English Inversion." *Proceedings of LP '94: Item Order in (Natural) Languages.* Prague: Charles University Press, 245-64.

Birner, Betty J. 1996a. "Form and Function in English *By*-Phrase Passives." Chicago Linguistic Society 32: 23-31.

Birner, Betty J. 1996b. "Review of *From Discourse Process to Grammatical Construction: On Left-Dislocation in English* (1992) by Ronald Geluykens." *Studies in Language* 20: 455-65.

Birner, Betty J. 1996c. *The Discourse Function of Inversion in English.* New York: Garland.

Birner, Betty J. 1998. "Recency Effects in English Inversion." In Marilyn A. Walker, Aravind K. Joshi, and Ellen F. Prince, (eds.), *Centering Theory in Discourse.* Oxford: Oxford University Press, 309-26.

Birner, Betty J. In prep. "Functional Constraints on Argument Reversal."

Birner, Betty J. and Shahrzad Mahootian. 1996. "Functional Constraints on Inversion in English and Farsi." *Language Sciences* 18: 127-38.

Birner, Betty J. and Gregory Ward. 1989. "A Semantico-Pragmatic Taxonomy of English Inversion." Paper presented at the Annual Meeting of the Linguistic Society of America, Washington, D.C.

Birner, Betty J. and Gregory Ward. 1992. "On the Interpretation of VP Inversion in American English." *Journal of Linguistics* 28: 1-12.

Birner, Betty J. and Gregory Ward. 1993. "*There*-Sentences and Inversion as Distinct Constructions: A Functional Account." Berkeley Linguistics Society 19: 27-39.

Birner, Betty J. and Gregory Ward. 1994. "Uniqueness, Familiarity, and the Definite Article in English." Berkeley Linguistics Society 20: 93-102.

Birner, Betty J. and Gregory Ward. 1996. "A Crosslinguistic Study of Postposing in Discourse." *Language and Speech: Special Issue on Discourse, Syntax, and Information* 39: 111-40.

Bolinger, Dwight. 1972. "Accent is Predictable (If You're a Mindreader)." *Language* 48: 633-44.

Bolinger, Dwight. 1977. *Meaning and Form.* London: Longman.

Bolinger, Dwight. 1989. *Intonation and its Uses: Melody in Grammar and Discourse.* London: Edward Arnold.

Breivik, Leiv Egil. 1981. "On the Interpretation of Existential *There.*" *Language* 57: 1-25.

Breivik, Leiv Egil. 1990. *Existential There: A Synchronic and Diachronic Study.* Oslo: Novus Press.

Bresnan, Joan. 1994. "Locative Inversion and the Architecture of Universal Grammar." *Language* 70: 72-131.

Bresnan, Joan and Jonni Kanerva. 1989. "Locative Inversion in Chicheŵa: A Case Study of Factorization in Grammar." *Linguistic Inquiry* 20: 1-50.

Burzio, Luigi. 1986. *Italian Syntax: A Government-Binding Approach.* Dordrecht: Reidel.

Calabrese, Andrea. 1992. "Some Remarks on Focus and Logical Structures in Italian." *Harvard University Working Papers in Linguistics* 1: 91-127.

Chafe, Wallace. 1976. "Givenness, Contrastiveness, Definiteness, Subjects, Topics, and Point of View." In Charles Li, (ed.), *Subject and Topic*. New York: Academic Press, 25-55.

Chafe, Wallace. 1980. "The Deployment of Consciousness in the Production of a Narrative." In Wallace Chafe, (ed.), *The Pear Stories: Cognitive, Cultural, and Linguistic Aspects of Narrative Production*. Norwood, NJ: Ablex, 9-50.

Chafe, Wallace. 1994. *Discourse, Consciousness, and Time: The Flow and Displacement of Conscious Experience in Speaking and Writing*. Chicago: University of Chicago Press.

Chafe, Wallace and Deborah Tannen. 1987. "Relation Between Written and Spoken Language." *Annual Review of Anthropology* 16: 383-407.

Chomsky, Noam. 1971. "Deep Structure, Surface Structure, and Semantic Interpretation." In Danny Steinberg and Leon Jakobovits, (eds.), *Semantics: An Interdisciplinary Reader in Philosophy, Linguistics, and Psychology*. Cambridge: Cambridge University Press, 183-216.

Christophersen, Paul. 1939. *The Articles: A Study of Their Theory and Use in English*. Munksgaard: Copenhagen.

Clark, Herbert H. 1977. "Bridging." In Philip Nicholas Johnson-Laird and Peter Cathcart Wason, (eds.), *Thinking: Readings in Cognitive Science*. Cambridge: Cambridge University Press, 411-20.

Clark, Herbert H. and Eve V. Clark. 1977. *Psychology and Language*. New York: Harcourt, Brace and Jovanovich.

Clark, Herbert H. and Catherine R. Marshall. 1981. "Definite Reference and Mutual Knowledge." In Aravind Joshi, Bonnie Webber, and Ivan Sag, (eds.), *Elements of Discourse Understanding*. Cambridge: Cambridge University Press, 10-63.

Coopmans, Peter. 1989. "Where Stylistic and Syntactic Processes Meet: Locative Inversion in English." *Language* 65: 728-51.

Creider, Chet. 1979. "On the Explanation of Transformations." In Talmy Givón, (ed.), *Syntax and Semantics 12: Discourse and Syntax.* New York: Academic Press, 3-22.

Creider, Chet A. and Jane T. Creider. 1983. "Topic-Comment Relations in a Verb-Initial Language." *Journal of African Languages and Linguistics* 5: 1-15.

Cumming, Susanna and Tsuyoshi Ono. 1996. "Ad Hoc Hierarchy: Lexical Structures for Reference in *Consumer Reports* Articles." In Barbara Fox, (ed.), *Studies in Anaphora.* Amsterdam and Philadelphia: John Benjamins, 69-94.

Davison, Alice. 1984. "Syntactic Markedness and the Definition of Sentence Topic." *Language* 60: 797-846.

Du Bois, John W. 1980. "Beyond Definiteness: The Trace of Identity in Discourse." In Wallace Chafe, (ed.), *The Pear Stories: Cognitive, Cultural, and Linguistic Aspects of Narrative Production.* Norwood, NJ: Ablex, 203-74.

Emonds, Joseph. 1976. *A Transformational Approach to English Syntax: Root, Structure-Preserving, and Local Transformations.* New York: Academic Press.

Erdmann, Peter. 1976. *There Sentences in English.* Munich: Tuduv.

Ertel, Suitbert. 1977. "Where Do the Subjects of Sentences Come From?" In Sheldon Rosenberg, (ed.), *Sentence Production: Developments in Research and Theory.* Hillsdale, NJ: Erlbaum, 141-68.

Feinstein, Michael. 1980. "Ethnicity and Topicalization in New York City English." *International Journal of the Sociology of Language* 26: 15-24.

Fillmore, Charles. 1968. "The Case for Case." In Emmon Bach and Robert T. Harms, (eds.), *Universals in Linguistic Theory.* New York: Holt, Rinehart and Winston, 1-88.

Fillmore, Charles. 1988. "The Mechanisms of 'Construction Grammar'." Berkeley Linguistics Society 14: 35-55.

Firbas, Jan. 1964. "On Defining the Theme in Functional Sentence Analysis." *Travaux Linguistiques de Prague* 1: 267-80.

Firbas, Jan. 1966. "Non-Thematic Subjects in Contemporary English." *Travaux Linguistiques de Prague* 2: 239-56.

Fox, Barbara. 1987. *Discourse Structure and Anaphora: Written and Conversational English.* Cambridge: Cambridge University Press.

Fraurud, Kari. 1990. "Definiteness and the Processing of Noun Phrases in Natural Discourse." *Journal of Semantics* 7: 395-433.

Freeze, Ray. 1992. "Existentials and Other Locatives." *Language* 68: 553-95.

Garrod, Simon C. and Anthony J. Sanford. 1994. "Resolving Sentences in a Discourse Context: How Discourse Representation Affects Language Understanding." In Morton Ann Gernsbacher, (ed.), *Handbook of Psycholinguistics.* New York: Academic Press, 675-98.

Gary, Norman. 1976. *A Discourse Analysis of Certain Root Transformations in English.* Indiana University Linguistics Club.

Geluykens, Ronald. 1987. "Tails (Right Dislocations) as a Repair Mechanism in English Conversations." In Jan Nuyts and G. de Schutter, (eds.), *Getting One's Words into Line: On Word Order and Functional Grammar.* Dordrecht: Foris, 119-30.

Geluykens, Ronald. 1992. *From Discourse Process to Grammatical Construction: On Left-Dislocation in English.* Amsterdam and Philadelphia: John Benjamins.

Givón, Talmy. 1976. "Topic, Pronoun, and Grammatical Agreement." In Charles Li, (ed.), *Subject and Topic.* New York: Academic Press, 149-58.

Givón, Talmy. 1984. *Syntax: A Functional-Typological Introduction. Vol. 1.* Amsterdam and Philadelphia: John Benjamins.

Givón, Talmy. 1993. *English Grammar: A Function-Based Introduction. Vol. II.* Amsterdam and Philadelphia: John Benjamins.

Givón, Talmy and Lynne Yang. 1994. "The Rise of the English GET-Passive." In Barbara Fox and Paul J. Hopper, (eds.), *Voice: Form and Function.* Amsterdam and Philadelphia: John Benjamins, 119-50.

Goldberg, Adele. 1995. *Constructions: A Construction Grammar Approach to Argument Structure*. Chicago: The University of Chicago Press.

Green, Georgia. 1980. "Some Wherefores of English Inversions." *Language* 56: 582-601.

Green, Georgia. 1982. "Colloquial and Literary Uses of Inversions." In Deborah Tannen, (ed.), *Spoken and Written Language: Exploring Orality and Literacy*. Norwood, NJ: Ablex, 119-53.

Green, Georgia. 1985. "The Description of Inversions in Generalized Phrase Structure Grammar." Berkeley Linguistics Society 11: 117-46.

Grice, H. Paul. 1975. "Logic and Conversation." In Peter Cole and Jerry Morgan, (eds.), *Syntax and Semantics 3: Speech Acts*. New York: Academic Press, 41-58.

Grice, H. Paul. 1978. "Further Notes on Logic and Conversation." In Peter Cole, (ed.), *Syntax and Semantics 9: Pragmatics*. New York: Academic Press, 113-28.

Grosz, Barbara, Aravind Joshi, and Scott Weinstein. 1983. "Providing a Unified Account of Definite Noun Phrases in Discourse." *Proceedings of the 21st Annual Meeting of the Association for Computational Linguistics*. San Francisco: Morgan Kaufman Publishers, 44-50.

Guéron, Jacqueline. 1980. "On the Syntax and Semantics of PP Extraposition." *Linguistic Inquiry* 11: 637-78.

Gundel, Jeanette. 1974. *The Role of Topic and Comment in Linguistic Theory*. Ph.D. dissertation, University of Texas.

Gundel, Jeanette. 1985. "'Shared Knowledge' and Topicality." *Journal of Pragmatics* 9: 83-107.

Gundel, Jeanette, Nancy Hedberg, and Ron Zacharski. 1990. "Givenness, Implicature, and the Form of Referring Expressions in Discourse." Berkeley Linguistics Society 16: 442-53.

Gundel, Jeanette, Nancy Hedberg, and Ron Zacharski. 1993. "Cognitive Status and the Form of Referring Expressions in Discourse." *Language* 69: 274-307.

Halliday, Michael A.K. 1967. "Notes on Transitivity and Theme in English, Part 2." *Journal of Linguistics* 3: 199-244.

Halliday, Michael A.K. and Ruqaiya Hasan. 1976. *Cohesion in English.* London: Longman.

Hankamer, Jorge. 1979. *Deletion in Coordinate Structure.* New York: Garland Press.

Hannay, Michael. 1985. *English Existentials in Functional Grammar.* Dordrecht: Foris

Hartvigson, Hans and Leif Jakobsen. 1974. *Inversion in Present-Day English.* Odense: Odense University Press.

Haviland, Susan and Herbert Clark. 1974. "What's New? Acquiring New Information as a Process in Comprehension." *Journal of Verbal Learning and Verbal Behavior* 13: 512-21.

Hawkins, John A. 1978. *Definiteness and Indefiniteness.* Atlantic Highlands, NJ: Humanities Press.

Hawkins, John A. 1991. "On (In)definite Articles: Implicatures and (Un)grammaticality Prediction." *Journal of Linguistics* 27: 405-42.

Hawkins, John A. 1994. *A Performance Theory of Order and Constituency.* Cambridge: Cambridge University Press.

Herring, Susan C. 1990. "Information Structure as a Consequence of Word Order Type." Berkeley Linguistics Society 16: 163-74.

Hetzron, Robert. 1971. "Presentative Function and Presentative Movement." *Studies in African Linguistics*, Supplement 2: 79-105.

Hirschberg, Julia. 1991. *A Theory of Scalar Implicature.* New York: Garland.

Hoekstra, Teun and Rene Mulder. 1990. "Unergatives as Copular Verbs: Locational and Existential Predication." *Linguistic Review* 7: 1-79.

Holmback, Heather. 1984. "An Interpretive Solution to the Definiteness Effect Problem." *Linguistic Analysis* 13: 195-215.

Hooper, Joan and Sandra Thompson. 1973. "On the Applicability of Root Transformations." *Linguistic Inquiry* 4: 465-97.

Horn, Laurence R. 1972. *On the Semantic Properties of Logical Operators in English.* Ph.D. dissertation, UCLA. [Reprinted in 1976, Bloomington, IN: Indiana University Linguistics Club.]

Horn, Laurence R. 1984. "Toward a New Taxonomy for Pragmatic Inference: Q-Based and R-Based Implicature." In Deborah Schiffrin, (ed.), *Meaning, Form, and Use in Context: Linguistic Applications.* Washington, DC: Georgetown University Press, 11-42.

Horn, Laurence R. 1986. "Presupposition, Theme and Variations." *Papers from the Parasession on Pragmatics and Grammatical Theory.* Chicago Linguistic Society 22: 168-92.

Horn, Laurence R. 1991. "Given as New: When Redundant Affirmation Isn't." *Journal of Pragmatics* 15: 305-28.

Huffman, Alan. 1993. "Full-Verb Inversion in English: A Functional Analysis." Unpublished ms., City University of New York.

Jackendoff, Ray. 1972. *Semantic Interpretation in Generative Grammar.* Cambridge, MA: MIT Press.

Jenkins, Lyle. 1975. *The English Existential.* Tübingen: Niemeyer.

Jespersen, Otto. 1969. *Analytic Syntax.* New York: Rineholt and Winston.

Karttunen, Lauri. 1973. "Presuppositions of Compound Sentences." *Linguistic Inquiry* 4: 169-93.

Kilby, David. 1984. *Descriptive Syntax and the English Verb.* London: Croom Helm.

Kirkwood, H. 1977. "Discontinuous Noun Phrases in Existential Sentences in English and German." *Journal of Linguistics* 13: 53-66.

Kirsner, Robert. 1979. *The Problem of Presentative Sentences in Modern Dutch.* Amsterdam: North-Holland.

Kroch, Anthony. 1981. "On the Role of Resumptive Pronouns in Amnestying Island Constraint Violations." Chicago Linguistic Society 17: 125-35.

Kroch, Anthony. 1982. "A Quantitative Study of the Syntax of Speech and Writing." National Institute of Education final report #G78-0169.

Kucera, Henry and W. Nelson Francis. 1967. *Computational Analysis of Present-Day American English.* Providence, RI: Brown University Press.

Kuno, Susumu. 1971. "The Position of Locatives in Existential Sentences." *Linguistic Inquiry* 2: 333-78.

Kuno, Susumu. 1972. Functional Sentence Perspective: A Case Study from Japanese and English. *Linguistic Inquiry* 3: 269-320.

Kuno, Susumu. 1975. "Conditions for Verb-Phrase Deletion." *Foundations of Language* 13: 161-75.

Labov, William. 1972. *Sociolinguistic Patterns.* Philadelphia: University of Pennsylvania Press.

Ladd, D. Robert. 1980. *The Structure of Intonational Meaning.* Bloomington, IN: Indiana University Press.

Lakoff, George. 1987. *Women, Fire, and Dangerous Things.* Chicago: University of Chicago Press.

Lakoff, George and Claudia Brugman. 1987. "The Semantics of Aux-Inversion and Anaphora Constraints." Paper presented at the Annual Meeting of the Linguistic Society of America, San Francisco.

Lambrecht, Knud. 1981. "Topic, Anti-Topic and Verb Agreement in Non-Standard French." *Pragmatics and Beyond* II,6. Amsterdam and Philadelphia: John Benjamins.

Lambrecht, Knud. 1994. *Information Structure and Sentence Form.* Cambridge: Cambridge University Press.

Langacker, Ronald. 1974. "Movement Rules in Functional Perspective." *Language* 50: 630-64.

Larson, Richard. 1988. "Light Predicate Raising." *Lexicon Project Working Papers* 27. MIT: Center for Cognitive Science.

Lasnik, Howard. 1992. "Case and Expletives: Notes Toward a Parametric Account." *Linguistic Inquiry* 23: 381-405.

Levin, Beth. 1993. *English Verb Classes and Alternations: A Preliminary Investigation*. Chicago: University of Chicago Press.

Levin, Beth and Malka Rappaport Hovav. 1995. *Unaccusativity: At the Syntax-Lexical Semantics Interface*. Cambridge, MA: MIT Press.

Levin, Lori. 1983. *Operations on Lexical Forms: Unaccusative Rules in Germanic Languages*. Ph.D. dissertation, MIT.

Levine, Robert. 1989. "On Focus Inversion: Syntactic Valence and the Role of a SUBCAT List." *Linguistics* 27: 1013-55.

Levine, Robert. In prep. *Linearization and the Syntax of Main Verb Inversion*. Stanford University: Center for the Study of Language and Information.

Levinson, Stephen C. 1983. *Pragmatics*. Cambridge: Cambridge University Press.

Ljung, Magnus. 1980. *Reflections on the English Progressive*. Göteborg, Sweden: Gotab.

Lumsden, Michael. 1988. *Existential Sentences: Their Structure and Meaning*. London: Croom Helm.

Lyons, John. 1977. *Semantics*. Cambridge: Cambridge University Press.

Mahootian, Shahrzad. 1993. *A Null Theory of Codeswitching*. Ph.D. dissertation, Northwestern University.

McCawley, Noriko A. 1977. "What is the 'Emphatic Root Transformation' Phenomenon?" Chicago Linguistic Society 13: 384-400.

McNally, Louise. 1992. *An Interpretation for the English Existential Construction*. Ph.D. dissertation, University of California at Santa Cruz.

McNally, Louise. To appear. "Existential Sentences Without Existential Quantification." *Linguistics and Philosophy*.

Milsark, Gary. 1974. *Existential Sentences in English*. Ph.D. dissertation, MIT.

Milsark, Gary. 1977. "Toward an Explanation of Certain Peculiarities of the Existential Construction in English." *Linguistic Analysis* 3: 1-30.

Nunberg, Geoffrey. 1979. "The Non-Uniqueness of Semantic Solutions: Polysemy." *Linguistics and Philosophy* 3: 143-84.

Ochs, Elinor. 1979. "Planned and Unplanned Discourse." In Talmy Givón, (ed.), *Syntax and Semantics 12: Discourse and Syntax.* New York: Academic Press.

Peirce, Charles S. 1931-58. In Charles Hartshorne and Paul Weiss, (eds.), *Collected papers of Charles Sanders Peirce.* Cambridge, MA: Harvard University Press.

Penhallurick, John. 1984. "Full-Verb Inversion in English." *Australian Journal of Linguistics* 4: 33-56.

Perlmutter, David. 1978. "Impersonal Passives and the Unaccusative Hypothesis." Berkeley Linguistics Society 4: 157-89.

Pettinari, Catherine. 1980. "The Function of *There*-Insertion in Surgical Reports." Unpublished ms., University of Oregon.

Pierrehumbert, Janet. 1980. *The Phonology and Phonetics of English Intonation.* Ph.D. dissertation, MIT.

Pierrehumbert, Janet and Julia Hirschberg. 1990. "The Meaning of Intonational Contours in the Interpretation of Discourse." In Philip R. Cohen, Jerry Morgan, and Martha E. Pollack, (eds.), *Intentions in Communication.* Cambridge, MA: MIT Press, 271-323.

Pinto, Manuela. 1994. "Subjects in Italian: Distribution and Interpretation." In Reineke Bok-Bennema and Crit Cremers, (eds.), *Linguistics in the Netherlands.* Amsterdam and Philadelphia: John Benjamins, 175-86.

Pinto, Manuela. To appear. "Definite Subjects and Inversion." *Proceedings of the Workshop 'Definieten Dag', UiL OTS Working Papers*, Utrecht University.

Polinsky, Maria. 1997. "SO/OS Languages: Interactions with Topic and Focus." Chicago Linguistic Society 33. In press.

Prince, Ellen F. 1981a. "Toward a Taxonomy of Given/New Information." In Peter Cole, (ed.), *Radical Pragmatics.* New York: Academic Press, 223-54.

Prince, Ellen F. 1981b. "Topicalization, Focus-Movement, and Yiddish-Movement: A Pragmatic Differentiation." Berkeley Linguistics Society 7: 249-64.

Prince, Ellen F. 1981c. "On the Inferencing of Indefinite-*This* NPs." In Aravind Joshi, Bonnie Webber, and Ivan Sag, (eds.), *Elements of Discourse Understanding*. Cambridge: Cambridge University Press, 231-50.

Prince, Ellen F. 1984. "Topicalization and Left-Dislocation: A Functional Analysis." In Sheila White and Virginia Teller, (eds.), *Discourses in Reading and Linguistics*. New York: Annals of the New York Academy of Sciences, 213-25.

Prince, Ellen F. 1986. "On the Syntactic Marking of Presupposed Open Propositions." *Papers from the Parasession on Pragmatics and Grammatical Theory*. Chicago Linguistic Society 22: 208-22.

Prince, Ellen F. 1988a. "Discourse Analysis: A Part of the Study of Linguistic Competence." In Frederick J. Newmeyer, (ed.) *Linguistics: The Cambridge Survey. Vol. 2. Linguistic Theory: Extensions and Implications*. Cambridge: Cambridge University Press, 164-82.

Prince, Ellen F. 1988b. "The Discourse Functions of Yiddish Expletive *Es* + Subject-Postposing." *Papers in Pragmatics* 2: 176-94.

Prince, Ellen F. 1988c. "Discourse and the Notion 'Construction'." Presented at the International Workshop on Discourse Processing and the Representation of Coherence. University of Brabant, Tilburg (The Netherlands).

Prince, Ellen F. 1988d. "On Pragmatic Change: The Borrowing of Discourse Functions." *Journal of Pragmatics* 12: 505-18.

Prince, Ellen F. 1992. "The ZPG Letter: Subjects, Definiteness, and Information-Status." In Sandra Thompson and William Mann, (eds.), *Discourse Description: Diverse Analyses of a Fundraising Text*. Amsterdam and Philadelphia: John Benjamins, 295-325.

Prince, Ellen F. 1994. "The Notion 'Construction' and the Syntax-Discourse Interface." Paper presented at the 25th Annual Meeting of the North East Linguistic Society, University of Pennsylvania.

Prince, Ellen F. 1997. "On the Functions of Left-Dislocation in English Discourse." In Akio Kamio, (ed.), *Directions in Functional Linguistics*. Amsterdam and Philadelphia: John Benjamins, 117-43.

Quakenbush, J. Stephen. 1992. "Word Order and Discourse Type: An Austronesian Example." In Doris L. Payne, (ed.), *Pragmatics of Word Order Flexibility*. Amsterdam and Philadelphia: John Benjamins, 279-304.

Rando, Emily N. and Donna Jo Napoli. 1978. "Definites in *There*-Sentences." *Language* 54: 300-13.

Reinhart, Tanya. 1981. "Pragmatics and Linguistics: An Analysis of Sentence Topics." *Philosophica* 27: 53-94.

Reuland, Eric and Alice ter Meulen. 1987. *The Representation of (In)definiteness*. Cambridge, MA: MIT Press.

Rochemont, Michael. 1978. *A Theory of Stylistic Rules in English*. Ph.D. dissertation, University of Massachusetts at Amherst.

Rochemont, Michael. 1986. *Focus in Generative Grammar*. Amsterdam and Philadelphia: John Benjamins.

Rochemont, Michael and Peter Culicover. 1990. *English Focus Constructions and the Theory of Grammar*. Cambridge: Cambridge University Press.

Rodman, Robert. 1974. "On Left Dislocation." *Papers in Linguistics* 7: 437-66.

Rooth, Mats. 1992. "A Theory of Focus Interpretation." *Natural Language Semantics* 1.1.

Rosten, Leo. 1982. *Hooray for Yiddish!* New York: Simon and Schuster.

Rubin, Ann. 1978. "A Theoretical Taxonomy of the Differences Between Oral and Written Language." Technical Report No. 35. Center for the Study of Reading. BBN. Cambridge, MA.

Saccon, Graziella. 1993. *Post-Verbal Subjects*. Ph.D. dissertation, Harvard University.

Safir, Kenneth. 1985. *Syntactic Chains*. Cambridge: Cambridge University Press.

Schiffrin, Deborah. 1987. *Discourse Markers.* Cambridge: Cambridge University Press.

Schmerling, Susan F. 1976. *Aspects of English Sentence Stress.* Austin: University of Texas Press.

Siewierska, Anna. 1984. *The Passive: A Comparative Linguistic Analysis.* London: Croom Helm.

Siewierska, Anna. 1988. *Word Order Rules.* London: Croom Helm.

Siewierska, Anna. 1991. *Functional Grammar.* London and New York: Routledge.

Sperber, Dan and Deirdre Wilson. 1981. "Irony and the Use-Mention Distinction." In Peter Cole, (ed.), *Radical Pragmatics.* New York: Academic Press, 295-318.

Sperber, Dan and Deirdre Wilson. 1986. *Relevance: Communication and Cognition.* Cambridge, MA: Harvard University Press.

Strand, Kjetil. 1996a. "Computing the Implicatures Carried by 'the Φ'." *Computational Implicature: Computational Approaches to Interpreting and Generating Conversational Implicature. Working notes.* American Association of Artificial Intelligence 1996 Spring Symposium Series, 103-9.

Strand, Kjetil. 1996b. "A Taxonomy of Linking Relations." Paper presented at the IndiAna Workshop on Indirect Anaphora, Lancaster, England.

Szabolcsi, Anna. 1986. "From the Definiteness Effect to Lexical Integrity." In Werner Abraham and Sjaak de Mey, (eds.), *Topic, Focus, and Configurationality.* Amsterdam and Philadelphia: John Benjamins, 321-48.

Takami, Ken-ichi. 1992. *Preposition Stranding: From Syntactic to Functional Analyses.* Berlin: Mouton de Gruyter.

Tannen, Deborah (ed.). 1982. *Spoken and Written Language: Exploring Orality and Literacy.* Norwood, NJ: Ablex.

Terken, Jacques and Julia Hirschberg. 1994. "Deaccentuation and Words Representing 'Given' Information: Effects of Persistence of Grammatical Function and Surface Position." *Language and Speech* 37(2): 125-45.

Thompson, Sandra. 1987. "The Passive in English: A Discourse Perspective." In Robert Channon and Linda Shockey, (eds.), *In Honor of Ilse Lehiste*. Dordrecht: Foris, 497-511.

Tomlin, Russell S. 1985. "Interaction of Subject, Theme, and Agent." In Jessica R. Wirth, (ed.), *Beyond the Sentence: Discourse and Sentential Form*. Ann Arbor: Karoma, 59-80.

Tomlin, Russell S. 1986. *Basic Word Order: Functional Principles*. London: Croom Helm.

Tomlin, Russell S. 1995. "Focal Attention, Voice, and Word Order: An Experimental, Cross-Linguistic Study." In Pamela Downing and Michael Noonan, (eds.), *Word Order in Discourse*. Amsterdam and Philadelphia: John Benjamins, 517-554.

Tomlin, Russell S. and Richard Rhodes. 1979. "The Distribution of Information in Ojibwa Texts." Chicago Linguistic Society 15: 307-20.

Tomlin, Russell S. and Richard Rhodes. 1992. "Information Distribution in Ojibwa." In Doris L. Payne, (ed.), *Pragmatics of Word Order Flexibility*. Amsterdam and Philadelphia: John Benjamins, 117-35.

Välimaa-Blum, Riitta. 1988. *Finnish Existential Clauses — Their Syntax, Pragmatics and Intonation*. Ph.D. dissertation, The Ohio State University.

Vallduví, Enric. 1992. *The Informational Component*. New York: Garland.

van Dijk, Teun A. 1977. "Connectives in Text Grammar and Text Logic." In Teun van Dijk and Janos Petofi, (eds.), *Grammars and Descriptions*. New York: de Gruyter, 11-63.

Wald, Benji. 1983. "Referents and Topic Within and Across Discourse Units: Observations from Current Vernacular English." In Flora Klein-Andreu, (ed.), *Discourse Perspectives of Syntax*. New York: Academic Press, 91-116.

Ward, Gregory. 1983. "A Pragmatic Analysis of Epitomization: Topicalization It's Not." *Papers in Linguistics* 17: 145-61.

Ward, Gregory. 1988. *The Semantics and Pragmatics of Preposing*. New York: Garland.

Ward, Gregory. 1990. "The Discourse Functions of VP Preposing." *Language* 66: 742-63.

Ward, Gregory. 1995. "Review of *From Discourse Process to Grammatical Construction: On Left-Dislocation in English* (1992) by Ronald Geluykens." *Language* 71: 366-69.

Ward, Gregory. 1998. "A Comparison of Postposed Subjects in English and Italian." In Akio Kamio and John Whitman, (eds.), *A Festschrift for Susumu Kuno*. Amsterdam and Philadelphia: John Benjamins. In press.

Ward, Gregory and Betty J. Birner. 1994a. "A Unified Account of English Fronting Constructions." *Penn Working Papers in Linguistics* 1: 159-65. University of Pennsylvania Department of Linguistics.

Ward, Gregory and Betty J. Birner. 1994b. "English *There*-Sentences and Information Status." *Proceedings of the Ninth Annual Conference and of the Workshop on Discourse*. The Israeli Association for Theoretical Linguistics, 165-83.

Ward, Gregory and Betty J. Birner. 1995. "Definiteness and the English Existential." *Language* 71: 722-42.

Ward, Gregory and Betty J. Birner. 1996. "On the Discourse Function of Rightward Movement in English." In Adele Goldberg, (ed.), *Conceptual Structure, Discourse and Language*. Stanford University: Center for the Study of Language and Information, 463-479.

Ward, Gregory and Julia Hirschberg. 1985. "Implicating Uncertainty: The Pragmatics of Fall-Rise Intonation." *Language* 61: 747-76.

Ward, Gregory and Julia Hirschberg. 1988. "Intonation and Propositional Attitude: The Pragmatics of L*+H L H%." *Proceedings of the Fifth Eastern States Conference on Linguistics*, 512-22.

Ward, Gregory and Ellen F. Prince. 1991. "On the Topicalization of Indefinite NPs." *Journal of Pragmatics* 16: 167-77.

Warner, Richard G. 1985. *Discourse Connectives in English*. New York: Garland.

Wasow, Thomas. 1997. "Remarks on Grammatical Weight." *Language Variation and Change* 9: 81-106.

Watanabe, Akira. 1994. "Locative Inversion: Where Unaccusativity Meets Minimality." Paper presented at the Annual Meeting of the Linguistic Society of America, Boston.

Wilson, Deirdre and Dan Sperber. 1979. "Ordered Entailments: An Alternative to Presuppositional Theories." In Choon-Kyu Oh and David Dinneen, (eds.), *Syntax and Semantics 11: Presupposition.* New York: Academic Press, 299-323.

Woisetschlaeger, Erich. 1983. "On the Question of Definiteness in 'An Old Man's Book'." *Linguistic Inquiry* 14: 137-54.

Zacharski, Ronald. 1993. *A Discourse Pragmatics Model of Pitch Accent in English.* Ph.D. dissertation, University of Minnesota.

Ziv, Yael. 1982a. "Getting More Mileage Out of Existentials in English." *Linguistics* 20: 747-62.

Ziv, Yael. 1982b. "Another Look at Definites in Existentials." *Journal of Linguistics* 18: 73-88.

Ziv, Yael and Barbara Grosz. 1994. "Right Dislocation and Attentional State." *Proceedings of the Ninth Annual Conference and of the Workshop on Discourse.* The Israeli Association for Theoretical Linguistics, 184-99.

Index

In the STUDIES IN LANGUAGE COMPANION SERIES (SLCS) the following volumes have been published thus far or are scheduled for publication:

1. ABRAHAM, Werner (ed.): *Valence, Semantic Case, and Grammatical Relations. Workshop studies prepared for the 12th Conference of Linguistics, Vienna, August 29th to September 3rd, 1977.* Amsterdam, 1978.
2. ANWAR, Mohamed Sami: *BE and Equational Sentences in Egyptian Colloquial Arabic.* Amsterdam, 1979.
3. MALKIEL, Yakov: *From Particular to General Linguistics. Selected Essays 1965-1978. With an introd. by the author + indices.* Amsterdam, 1983.
4. LLOYD, Albert L.: *Anatomy of the Verb: The Gothic Verb as a Model for a Unified Theory of Aspect, Actional Types, and Verbal Velocity.* Amsterdam, 1979.
5. HAIMAN, John: *Hua: A Papuan Language of the Eastern Highlands of New Guinea.* Amsterdam, 1980.
6. VAGO, Robert (ed.): *Issues in Vowel Harmony. Proceedings of the CUNY Linguistics Conference on Vowel Harmony (May 14, 1977).* Amsterdam, 1980.
7. PARRET, H., J. VERSCHUEREN, M. SBISÀ (eds): *Possibilities and Limitations of Pragmatics. Proceedings of the Conference on Pragmatics, Urbino, July 8-14,* 1979. Amsterdam, 1981.
8. BARTH, E.M. & J.L. MARTENS (eds): *Argumentation: Approaches to Theory Formation. Containing the Contributions to the Groningen Conference on the Theory of Argumentation,* Groningen, October 1978. Amsterdam, 1982.
9. LANG, Ewald: *The Semantics of Coordination.* Amsterdam, 1984.(English transl. by John Pheby from the German orig. edition *"Semantik der koordinativen Verknüpfung"*, Berlin, 1977.)
10. DRESSLER, Wolfgang U., Willi MAYERTHALER, Oswald PANAGL & Wolfgang U. WURZEL: *Leitmotifs in Natural Morphology.* Amsterdam, 1987.
11. PANHUIS, Dirk G.J.: *The Communicative Perspective in the Sentence: A Study of Latin Word Order.* Amsterdam, 1982.
12. PINKSTER, Harm (ed.): *Latin Linguistics and Linguistic Theory. Proceedings of the 1st Intern. Coll. on Latin Linguistics, Amsterdam, April 1981.* Amsterdam, 1983.
13. REESINK, G.: *Structures and their Functions in Usan.* Amsterdam, 1987.
14. BENSON, Morton, Evelyn BENSON & Robert ILSON: *Lexicographic Description of English.* Amsterdam, 1986.
15. JUSTICE, David: *The Semantics of Form in Arabic, in the mirror of European languages.* Amsterdam, 1987.
16. CONTE, M.E., J.S. PETÖFI, and E. SÖZER (eds): *Text and Discourse Connectedness.* Amsterdam/Philadelphia, 1989.
17. CALBOLI, Gualtiero (ed.): *Subordination and other Topics in Latin. Proceedings of the Third Colloquium on Latin Linguistics, Bologna, 1-5 April 1985.* Amsterdam/Philadelphia, 1989.
18. WIERZBICKA, Anna: *The Semantics of Grammar.* Amsterdam/Philadelphia, 1988.
19. BLUST, Robert A.: *Austronesian Root Theory. An Essay on the Limits of Morphology.* Amsterdam/Philadelphia, 1988.
20. VERHAAR, John W.M. (ed.): *Melanesian Pidgin and Tok Pisin. Proceedings of the First International Conference on Pidgins and Creoles on Melanesia.* Amsterdam/Philadelphia, 1990.

21. COLEMAN, Robert (ed.): *New Studies in Latin Linguistics. Proceedings of the 4th International Colloquium on Latin Linguistics*, Cambridge, April 1987. Amsterdam/Philadelphia, 1991.
22. McGREGOR, William: *A Functional Grammar of Gooniyandi.* Amsterdam/Philadelphia, 1990.
23. COMRIE, Bernard and Maria POLINSKY (eds): *Causatives and Transitivity.* Amsterdam/Philadelphia, 1993.
24. BHAT, D.N.S. *The Adjectival Category. Criteria for differentiation and identification.* Amsterdam/Philadelphia, 1994.
25. GODDARD, Cliff and Anna WIERZBICKA (eds): *Semantics and Lexical Universals. Theory and empirical findings.* Amsterdam/Philadelphia, 1994.
26. LIMA, Susan D., Roberta L. CORRIGAN and Gregory K. IVERSON (eds): *The Reality of Linguistic Rules.* Amsterdam/Philadelphia, 1994.
27. ABRAHAM, Werner, T. GIVÓN and Sandra A. THOMPSON (eds): *Discourse Grammar and Typology.* Amsterdam/Philadelphia, 1995.
28. HERMAN, József: *Linguistic Studies on Latin: Selected papers from the 6th international colloquium on Latin linguistics, Budapest, 2-27 March, 1991.* Amsterdam/Philadelphia, 1994.
29. ENGBERG-PEDERSEN, Elisabeth et al. (eds): *Content, Expression and Structure. Studies in Danish functional grammar.* Amsterdam/Philadelphia, 1996.
30. HUFFMAN, Alan: *The Categories of Grammar. French lui and le.* Amsterdam/Philadelphia, 1997.
31. WANNER, Leo (ed.): *Lexical Functions in Lexicography and Natural Language Processing.* Amsterdam/Philadelphia, 1996.
32. FRAJZYNGIER, Zygmunt: *Grammaticalization of the Complex Sentence. A case study in Chadic.* Amsterdam/Philadelphia, 1996.
33. VELAZQUEZ-CASTILLO, Maura: *The Grammar of Possession. Inalienability, incorporation and possessor ascension in Guaraní.* Amsterdam/Philadelphia, 1996.
34. HATAV, Galia: *The Semantics of Aspect and Modality. Evidence from English and Biblical Hebrew.* Amsterdam/Philadelphia, 1997.
35. MATSUMOTO, Yoshiko: *Noun-Modifying Constructions in Japanese. A frame semantic approach.* Amsterdam/Philadelphia, 1997.
36. KAMIO, Akio (ed.): *Directions in Functional Linguistics.* Amsterdam/Philadelphia, 1997.
37. HARVEY, Mark and Nicholas REID (eds): *Nominal Classification in Aboriginal Australia.* Amsterdam/Philadelphia, 1997.
38. HACKING, Jane F.: *Coding the Hypothetical. A Comparative Typology of Conditionals in Russian and Macedonian.* Amsterdam/Philadelphia, 1998.
39. WANNER, Leo (ed.): *Recent Trends in Meaning-Text Theory.* Amsterdam/Philadelphia, 1997.
40. BIRNER, Betty and Gregory WARD: *Information Status and Noncanonical Word Order in English.* Amsterdam/Philadelphia, 1998.
41. DARNELL, Michael, Edith MORAVSCIK, Michael NOONAN, Frederick NEWMEYER and Kathleen WHEATLY (eds): *Functionalism and Formalism in Linguistics. Volume I: General papers.* Amsterdam/Philadelphia, n.y.p.

42. DARNELL, Michael, Edith MORAVSCIK, Michael NOONAN, Frederick NEWMEYER and Kathleen WHEATLY (eds): *Functionalism and Formalism in Linguistics. Volume II: Case studies.* Amsterdam/Philadelphia, n.y.p.
43. OLBERTZ, Hella, Kees HENGEVELD and Jesús Sánchez GARCÍA (eds): *The Structure of the Lexicon in Functional Grammar.* Amsterdam/Philadelphia, n.y.p.